Foreword from the Publisher

Wiley's publishing vision for the Microsoft Official Academic Course series is to provide students and instructors with the skills and knowledge they need to use Microsoft technology effectively in all aspects of their personal and professional lives. Quality instruction is required to help both educators and students get the most from Microsoft's software tools and to become more productive. Thus our mission is to make our instructional programs trusted educational companions for life.

To accomplish this mission, Wiley and Microsoft have partnered to develop the highest quality educational programs for information workers, IT professionals, and developers. Materials created by this partnership carry the brand name "Microsoft Official Academic Course," assuring instructors and students alike that the content of these textbooks is fully endorsed by Microsoft, and that they provide the highest quality information and instruction on Microsoft products. The Microsoft Official Academic Course textbooks are "Official" in still one more way—they are the officially sanctioned courseware for Microsoft IT Academy members.

The Microsoft Official Academic Course series focuses on *workforce development*. These programs are aimed at those students seeking to enter the workforce, change jobs, or embark on new careers as information workers, IT professionals, and developers. Microsoft Official Academic Course programs address their needs by emphasizing authentic workplace scenarios with an abundance of projects, exercises, cases, and assessments.

The Microsoft Official Academic Courses are mapped to Microsoft's extensive research and job-task analysis, the same research and analysis used to create the Microsoft Technology Associate (MTA) and Microsoft Certified Technology Specialist (MCTS) exams. The textbooks focus on real skills for real jobs. As students work through the projects and exercises in the textbooks, they enhance their level of knowledge and their ability to apply the latest Microsoft technology to everyday tasks. These students also gain resume-building credentials that can assist them in finding a job, keeping their current job, or furthering their education.

The concept of life-long learning is today an utmost necessity. Job roles, and even whole job categories, are changing so quickly that none of us can stay competitive and productive without continuously updating our skills and capabilities. The Microsoft Official Academic Course offerings, and their focus on Microsoft certification exam preparation, provide a means for people to acquire and effectively update their skills and knowledge. Wiley supports students in this endeavor through the development and distribution of these courses as Microsoft's official academic publisher.

Today educational publishing requires attention to providing quality print and robust electronic content. By integrating Microsoft Official Academic Course products, *WileyPLUS*, and Microsoft certifications, we are better able to deliver efficient learning solutions for students and teachers alike.

Bonnie Lieberman

General Manager and Senior Vice President

Preface

Welcome to the Microsoft Official Academic Course (MOAC) program for Web Development Fundamentals. MOAC represents the collaboration between Microsoft Learning and John Wiley & Sons, Inc. publishing company. Microsoft and Wiley teamed up to produce a series of textbooks that deliver compelling and innovative teaching solutions to instructors and superior learning experiences for students. Infused and informed by in-depth knowledge from the creators of Microsoft products, and crafted by a publisher known worldwide for the pedagogical quality of its products, these textbooks maximize skills transfer in minimum time. Students are challenged to reach their potential by using their new technical skills as highly productive members of the workforce.

Because this knowledge base comes directly from Microsoft, creator of the Microsoft Certified Technology Specialist (MCTS), Microsoft Certified Professional (MCP), and Microsoft Technology Associate (MTA) exams (www.microsoft.com/learning/certification), you are sure to receive the topical coverage that is most relevant to your personal and professional success. Microsoft's direct participation not only assures you that MOAC textbook content is accurate and current—it also means that you will receive the best instruction possible to enable your success on certification exams and in the workplace.

■ The Microsoft Official Academic Course Program

The *Microsoft Official Academic Course* series is a complete program for instructors and institutions to prepare and deliver great courses on Microsoft software technologies. With MOAC, we recognize that, because of the rapid pace of change in the technology and curriculum developed by Microsoft, there is an ongoing set of needs beyond classroom instruction tools for an instructor to be ready to teach the course. The MOAC program endeavors to provide solutions for all these needs in a systematic manner in order to ensure a successful and rewarding course experience for both instructor and student—technical and curriculum training for instructor readiness with new software releases; the software itself for student use at home for building hands-on skills, assessment, and validation of skill development; and a great set of tools for delivering instruction in the classroom and lab. All are important to the smooth delivery of an interesting course on Microsoft software, and all are provided with the MOAC program. We think about the model below as a gauge for ensuring that we completely support you in your goal of teaching a great course. As you evaluate your instructional materials options, you may wish to use this model for comparison purposes with other available products:

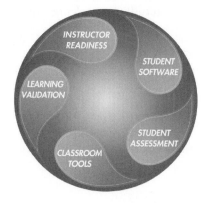

■ Pedagogical Features

The MOAC textbook for Web Development Fundamentals is designed to cover all the learning objectives for the MTA exam 98-363, which is referred to as its "exam objective." The Microsoft Technology Associate (MTA) exam objectives are highlighted throughout the textbook. Many pedagogical features have been developed specifically for the *Microsoft Official Academic Course* program.

Presenting the extensive procedural information and technical concepts woven throughout the textbook raises challenges for the student and instructor alike. The Illustrated Book Tour that follows provides a guide to the rich features contributing to the *Microsoft Official Academic Course* program's pedagogical plan. The following is a list of key features in each lesson designed to prepare students for success as they continue in their IT education, on the certification exams, and in the workplace:

- Each lesson begins with a **Lesson Skill Matrix**. More than a standard list of learning objectives, the Lesson Skill Matrix correlates each software skill covered in the lesson to the specific exam objective.

- Concise and frequent **step-by-step** Exercises teach students new features and provide an opportunity for hands-on practice. Numbered steps give detailed, step-by-step instructions to help students learn software skills.

- **Illustrations**—in particular, screen images—provide visual feedback as students work through the exercises. These images reinforce key concepts, provide visual clues about the steps, and allow students to check their progress.

- Lists of **Key Terms** at the beginning of each lesson introduce students to important technical vocabulary. When these terms are used later in the lesson, they appear in bold, italic type where they are defined.

- Engaging point-of-use **Reader Aids**, located throughout the lessons, tell students why a topic is relevant (*The Bottom Line*) or provide students with helpful hints (*Take Note*). Reader Aids also provide additional relevant or background information that adds value to the lesson.

- **Certification Ready** features throughout the text signal students where a specific certification objective is covered. They provide students with a chance to check their understanding of that particular MTA objective and, if necessary, review the section of the lesson where it is covered. MOAC offers complete preparation for MTA certification.

- **End-of-Lesson Questions:** The Knowledge Assessment section provides a variety of multiple-choice, true-false, matching, and fill-in-the-blank questions.

- **End-of-Lesson Exercises:** Competency Assessment case scenarios, Proficiency Assessment case scenarios, and Workplace Ready exercises are projects that test students' ability to apply what they've learned in the lesson.

■ Lesson Features

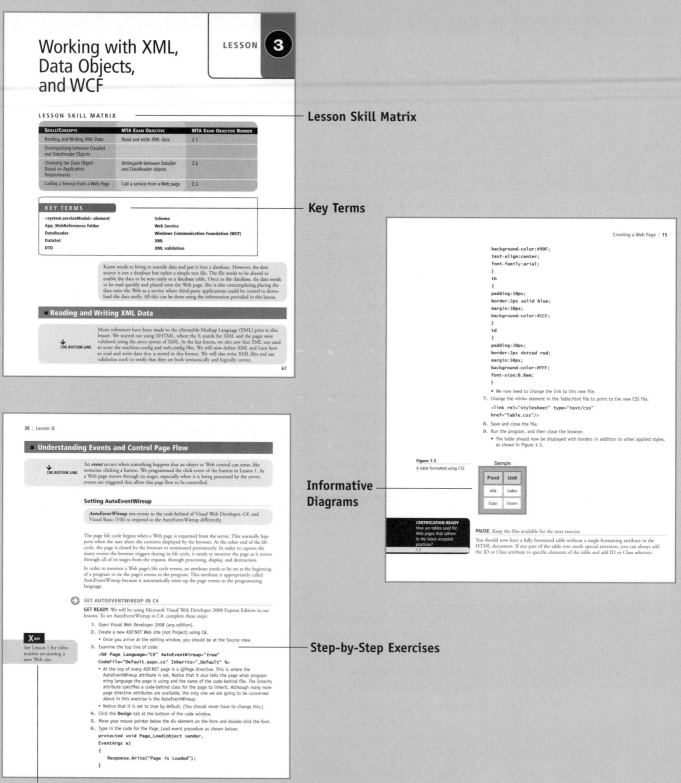

Lesson Skill Matrix

Key Terms

Informative Diagrams

Step-by-Step Exercises

X Ref Reader Aid

The Bottom Line Reader Aid

136 | Lesson 5

■ Understanding Client-Side Scripting

THE BOTTOM LINE

So far, we had the server run our programs and recreate the Web pages, had the pages posted back to the browser for display. An alternative to postbacks is having the browser process programs rather than the server. This is called *client-side scripting*. It allows the page to respond immediately to user activities rather than waiting on the server to build a new page and send it to the browser.

One would assume that having your computer run programs from the Internet is dangerous. This, of course, is true for desktop applications, but not as much for browser-run scripts. Since the browser is in charge of the application, it has much more control over malware attacks than if the local operating system was running it as a desktop application. However, since the browser is acting as a virtual operating system for client-side scripts, malware attacks are becoming more focused on this platform because the popularity of client-side scripting is on the rise. This does not mean we should abandon client-side scripting any more than we should abandon the Internet. The benefits of using client-side scripting far outweigh the dangers of threats like JavaScript malware.

Do not confuse JavaScript with Java. *JavaScript* is embedded into HTML for the browser to run when Java applets are downloaded along with HTML as separate files. These files are run on the locally installed Java Virtual Machine. JavaScript is text-based commands while a Java applet is compiled code generated from a complex high-level language that only a computer can read. Java is a full-fledged object-oriented programming language that can also create stand-alone applications. Although both are relatively secure because neither is allowed to write to local storage devices, the Java Virtual Machine has exhibited better control over malware attacks using Java than browsers attempting to control these attacks via JavaScript.

Since we are working with client-side scripting, the following two exercises do not need to connect to a Web server. This means that postbacks do not need to be addressed. We also do not need to be concerned about the Java Virtual Machine because we will not be doing exercises using Java. All the code will be run on a browser where the code may be interpreted differently depending on the browser used. Even though the sample code uses IE (Internet Explorer), you may want to try different browsers to see how they handle the code differently.

 WRITE JAVASCRIPT

GET READY. We will be using a simple text editor for this exercise.

1. Open your Web browser and make sure JavaScript is enabled.
   - JavaScript needs to be enabled for JavaScript-enabled pages to display properly.
   - To enable scripting: Open a browser window and go to the Tools menu item. Choose **Internet Options**, choose **Custom Level**, go to **Active Scripting**, and click the **Enable** option. Click the **OK** button, click the **OK** button on the next window, close the browser window, and reopen it.
2. Using Windows Explorer, create a text file and rename it **hi.html**.
   - Remember to have Windows show file extensions so you do not create a hi.html.txt file.

ANOTHER WAY

You can also create the text file in the Notepad Accessory. When saving the file put the file name in quotes—"hi.html". The quotes will cause the file to be saved with the html extension and will avoid the .txt extension being added to the file name.

Another Way Reader Aid

Certification Ready Alert

Working with Data | 117

There are many data-aware controls listed in the Toolbox. All of these controls are very complex and most are designed to be used with their provided dialog boxes and to be data bound.

Standard Category
- DropDownList
- ListBox
- CheckBoxList
- RadioButtonList
- BulletedList
- AdRotator

Data Category
- GridView
- DataList
- DetailsView
- FormView
- Repeater
- ListView

Navigation Category
- Menu
- TreeView

CERTIFICATION READY
How do you turn a control into a data-bound control in ASP.NET?
2.5

It would take an entire chapter to cover each of these dialog boxes because each has a specific purpose. As you start working with ASP.NET, you should make a point to become familiar with these controls. They can save you hours of unnecessary work.

■ Managing Data Connections and Databases

THE BOTTOM LINE

There is an abundance of continually changing data that Web sites are able to access. This data comes in many forms, from text files to very large and complex databases. Managing the connections of the hundreds of users who could be simultaneously reading and writing this data on a single Web site is no small feat. This lesson will introduce various data sources, the options available to the Web developer for connecting the Web pages to the data sources, and a technology used for Web sites that enables them to handle the overhead of hundreds of connections opening and closing without bringing down the site. We will also introduce an object that allows the execution of multiple SQL statements as a single unit to ensure that each one completes successfully.

ASP.NET uses ADO.NET to handle all of its *database connections*. The compiled code that ASP.NET generates from your .NET programs and objects is called *managed code*. Managed code is created to run on Microsoft's Common Language Runtime (CLR) rather than creating an executable that is limited to a particular hardware platform. However, this does not mean that the older unmanaged COM objects, such as OleDB and ODBC, cannot be used for .NET programs.

126 | Lesson 4

CERTIFICATION READY
What do connection pools do to help the performance of the database when it is connected to a Web page?
2.6

A *connection pool* is a collection of open data connections that Web applications presumed were closed. Behind the scenes, however, ADO.NET has taken the "closed" connections and kept them open. By default, there are 100 such connections in the pool. If the same connection is needed again, an unused and still-open connection is assigned to the application.

All .NET data providers support connection pooling. This includes SQL Server, OleDB, ODBC, and Oracle. Although there are many settings available for us to use to fine-tune the service, most applications work fine with the defaults. If changes are made, third-party applications are available to monitor the changes in performance or you can write your own simulations.

Understanding Transaction Objects

A *transaction object* allows multiple SQL statements to be processed as a group. If any of the statements in the group fail, all the statements in the group that have been processed will be rolled back and the whole transaction is aborted. ASP.NET includes the transaction object that allows us to do this in code.

Before looking at transaction objects, we must understand the concept of the transaction. For a simple financial transaction such as buying a cup of coffee, you pay an employee and expect coffee in return. An example of a failed transaction would be if you paid for the cup of coffee just before the shop closed and the employee went home before returning with your coffee. Transactions are all-or-nothing propositions. Any location that sells coffee will guarantee that you receive your purchase or you get your money back. Moving this into the world of databases, getting your money back is equivalent to having a SQL transaction rolled back.

The official definition of a database transaction uses the term "Properties." Do not confuse this with the properties of the transaction object. The properties that define the goals of a perfect transaction via the ACID test are shown in Table 4-3.

Table 4-3

Properties of the ACID test for transactions

Atomic	There is no such thing as a partial transaction. Every step of the transaction must be completed.
Consistent	A transaction will not be considered successful if it produces any errors in the database.
Isolated	During a transaction process, changed data cannot be seen by other transactions. Other transactions only see the data before it is changed.
Durable	Upon successful completion, the results are permanent. Any undo's are turned over to the backup system.

As much as developers would like to achieve perfect transactions, the definition is simply a goal. It is unreasonable to achieve them on a busy system because so many locks would have to be in place that the database would slow to a crawl. A trade-off must be made between speed and the increased risk of data corruption. Since we are the only users of the sample database, we will not be addressing this issue.

A simple demonstration of the syntax needed for a database transaction will now be created. We will use our ShoppingList table in a scenario that requires two SQL statements to be executed as a single transaction.

Easy-to-Read Tables

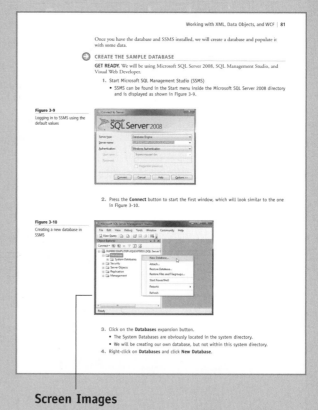

12. Rename your jpg file to **SampleX.jpg**.
   - This will prevent the browser from finding your file, which simulates the real-life problem of files that cannot be found.
13. Run your program to make sure the description of the image is displayed. Then close the browser.
   - The browser should have presented the text instead of the image.
14. Rename your jpg file back to its original name and make sure your browser once again displays the image.

PAUSE. You can now close the browser.

CERTIFICATION READY
How are images embedded into XHTML documents that adhere to the latest accepted practices?
1.1

When Web developers use the strict declaration in their Web pages, it forces them to drop many sloppy habits that are commonplace in the industry today. For example, leaving out the alternate attribute is acceptable for HTML but is required for XHTML. Although more coding is involved in meeting the XHTML requirements, it is well worth the effort.

✚ MORE INFORMATION

If you are not already familiar with the basics of HTML, you may want to seek out other resources before moving on to the next section.

Applying Cascading Style Sheets to a Web Page

HTML coding was never intended to format a document. Rather, it was developed primarily to define the content and layout of a Web document.

HTML elements define *what* content is to be displayed. ***Cascading Style Sheets (CSS)*** define *how* to display these HTML elements, including such characteristics as fonts, borders, color, size, etc. Although many HTML elements and attributes are already capable of doing this, they have fallen out of favor and certainly out of the XHTML standards; they have been replaced by CSS. The Web developer only needs to know the assigned names of the CSS formatting elements to apply them. Virtually all Web browsers now support CSS.

CSS can be located in three areas: embedded within the HTML code, included in the Web page but not embedded, and on a separate page. These locations are called inline, internal, and external, respectively.

- **Inline Style Sheet**
  - Embedded within HTML
  - Overrides all other style sheet settings
- **Internal Style Sheet**
  - Is within the page but separate from HTML
  - Overrides External style sheet settings
  - Does not override inline style sheet settings
- **External Style Sheet**
  - Resides in its own page
  - Has no overriding power

The simplest way to apply CSS to a Web page is to use inline styles. An inline style is created within a particular tag as an attribute and is applied only to that one tag set.

**More Information
Reader Aid**

**Take Note
Reader Aid**

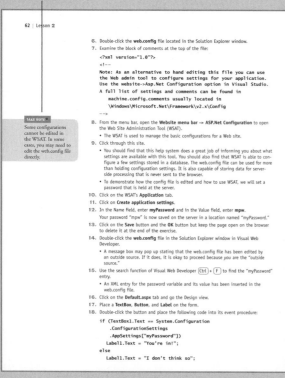

62 | Lesson 2

6. Double-click the **web.config** file located in the Solution Explorer window.
7. Examine the block of comments at the top of the file:

```
<?xml version="1.0"?>
<!--
Note: As an alternative to hand editing this file you can use
the Web admin tool to configure settings for your application.
Use the website->Asp.Net Configuration option in Visual Studio.
A full list of settings and comments can be found in
    machine.config.comments usually located in
    \Windows\Microsoft.Net\Framework\v2.x\Config
-->
```

8. From the menu bar, open the **Website menu bar -> ASP.Net Configuration** to open the Web Site Administration Tool (WSAT).
   - The WSAT is used to manage the basic configurations for a Web site.
9. Click through this site.
   - You should find that this help system does a great job of informing you about what settings are available with this tool. You should also find that WSAT is able to configure a few settings stored in a database. The web.config file can be used for more than holding configuration settings. It is also capable of storing data for server-side processing that is never sent to the browser.
   - To demonstrate how the config file is edited and how to use WSAT, we will set a password that is held at the server.
10. Click on the WSAT's **Application** tab.
11. Click on **Create application settings**.
12. In the Name field, enter **myPassword** and in the Value field, enter **mpw**.
   Your password "mpw" is now saved on the server in a location named "myPassword."
13. Click on the **Save** button and the **OK** button but keep the page open on the browser to delete it at the end of the exercise.
14. Double-click **web.config** file in the Solution Explorer window in Visual Web Developer.
   - A message box may pop up stating that the web.config file has been edited by an outside source. If it does, it is okay to proceed because you are the "outside source."
15. Use the search function of Visual Web Developer (Ctrl) + (F) to find the "myPassword" entry.
   - An XML entry for the password variable and its value has been inserted into the web.config file.
16. Click on the **Default.aspx** tab and go the Design view.
17. Place a **TextBox**, **Button**, and **Label** on the form.
18. Double-click the button and place the following code into its event procedure:

```
if (TextBox1.Text == System.Configuration
    .ConfigurationSettings
    .AppSettings["myPassword"])
    Label1.Text = "You're in!";
else
    Label1.Text = "I don't think so";
```

TAKE NOTE
Some configurations cannot be edited in the WSAT. In some cases, you may need to edit the web.config file directly.

Screen Images

Once you have the database and SSMS installed, we will create a database and populate it with some data.

CREATE THE SAMPLE DATABASE

GET READY. We will be using Microsoft SQL Server 2008, SQL Management Studio, and Visual Web Developer.
1. Start Microsoft SQL Management Studio (SSMS)
   - SSMS can be found in the Start menu inside the Microsoft SQL Server 2008 directory and is displayed as shown in Figure 3-9.

Figure 3-9
Logging in to SSMS using the default values

2. Press the **Connect** button to start the first window, which will look similar to the one in Figure 3-10.

Figure 3-10
Creating a new database in SSMS

3. Click on the **Databases** expansion button.
   - The System Databases are obviously located in the system directory.
   - We will be creating our own database, but not within this system directory.
4. Right-click on **Databases** and click **New Database**.

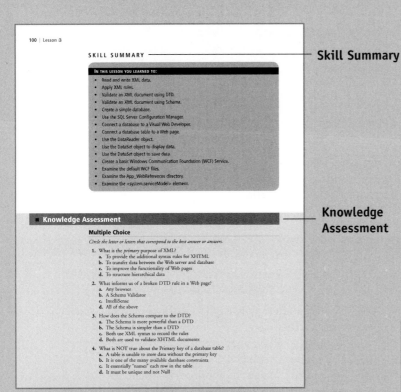

Skill Summary

100 | Lesson 3

SKILL SUMMARY

IN THIS LESSON YOU LEARNED TO:

- Read and write XML data.
- Apply XML rules.
- Validate an XML document using DTD.
- Validate an XML document using Schema.
- Create a simple database.
- Use the SQL Server Configuration Manager.
- Connect a database to a Visual Web Developer.
- Connect a database table to a Web page.
- Use the DataReader object.
- Use the DataSet object to display data.
- Use the DataSet object to save data.
- Create a basic Windows Communication Foundation (WCF) Service.
- Examine the default WCF files.
- Examine the App_WebReferences directory.
- Examine the <system.serviceModel> elements.

Knowledge Assessment

Multiple Choice

Circle the letter or letters that correspond to the best answer or answers.

1. What is the *primary* purpose of XML?
   a. To provide the additional syntax rules for XHTML
   b. To transfer data between the Web server and database
   c. To improve the functionality of Web pages
   d. To structure hierarchical data

2. What informs us of a broken DTD rule in a Web page?
   a. Any browser
   b. A Schema Validator
   c. IntelliSense
   d. All of the above

3. How does the Schema compare to the DTD?
   a. The Schema is more powerful than a DTD
   b. The Schema is simpler than a DTD
   c. Both use XML syntax to record the rules
   d. Both are used to validate XHTML documents

4. What is NOT true about the Primary key of a database table?
   a. A table is unable to store data without the primary key
   b. It is one of the many available database constraints
   c. It essentially "names" each row in the table
   d. It must be unique and not Null

Knowledge Assessment

Case Scenarios

176 | Lesson 6

7. Only users of the _____ _____ are privy to trace information.

8. The _____ attribute of the <trace> element, found in the web.config file controls the maximum number of requests for information on the server.

9. _____ is the name of the Web page that is automatically generated when the enabled attribute of the <trace> element is set to true.

10. There are _____ classes of HTTP Status Codes identified by their first digit.

Competency Assessment

Scenario 6-1: Watching State Values

The owner of Verbeck's Trucking Co. assigned you the task of creating a Web page that collects the number of loads and the cubic feet of gravel hauled at the end of each day. The data will be used in another page by another Web developer. All you need to do is ensure that the data are stored as state variables somewhere in your page. To prove that the data are actually saved, the owner insists on a printout of the portion of a tracing Web page containing the type of state used, variable names, and the data they contain.

Simulate this task by creating two Web pages. The first page will collect the number of loads and cubic feet. The second page will echo this information. When completed, enter the data into the first page and create a printout of a tracing page containing the type of state you used to send the data. Also, include the variable names and the data they hold.

Scenario 6-2: Displaying Error Information to the User

As you are developing your Web site, you want to have as much detailed information as possible for your errors. Now that you are about to deploy your site, what changes will you make to the web.config file to keep this information from the user?

Proficiency Assessment

Scenario 6-3: Displaying Trace Information to the User

As you are developing your Web site, you want to have as much tracing information as possible for your debugging activities. Now that you are about to deploy your site, what changes will you make to the web.config file to keep your debugging information from the user?

Scenario 6-4: Handling Web Application Errors Using HTTP Status Codes

After deploying your Web site, you discover that you have been confusing your users with generic error messages. You now want to provide them with custom Web pages that will improve your communication with your users without revealing sensitive site information. What changes will you make to the web.config file to make this possible?

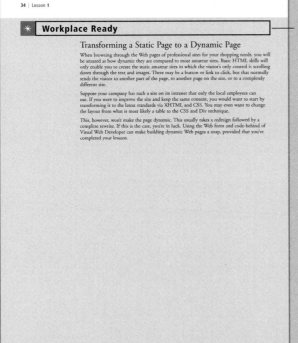

34 | Lesson 1

Workplace Ready

Transforming a Static Page to a Dynamic Page

When browsing through the Web pages of professional sites for your shopping needs, you will be amazed at how dynamic they are compared to most amateur sites. Basic HTML skills will only enable you to create the static amateur sites in which the visitor's only control is scrolling down through the text and images. There may be a button or link to click, but that normally sends the visitor to another part of the page, to another page on the site, or to a completely different site.

Suppose your company has such a site on its intranet that only the local employees can use. If you were to improve the site and keep the same content, you would want to start by transforming it to the latest standards via XHTML and CSS. You may even want to change the layout from what is most likely a table to the CSS and Div technique.

This, however, won't make the page dynamic. This usually takes a redesign followed by a complete rewrite. If this is the case, you're in luck. Using the Web form and code-behind of Visual Web Developer can make building dynamic Web pages a snap, provided that you've completed your lessons.

Workplace Ready

Conventions and Features Used in This Book

This book uses particular fonts, symbols, and heading conventions to highlight important information and call attention to special steps. For more information about the features in each lesson, refer to the Illustrated Book Tour section.

CONVENTION	MEANING
↓ THE BOTTOM LINE	This feature provides a brief summary of the material to be covered in the section that follows.
CERTIFICATION READY	This feature signals a point in the text where a specific certification objective is covered. It provides you with a chance to check your understanding of that particular MTA objective and, if necessary, review the section of the lesson where the objective is covered.
TAKE NOTE*	Reader Aids appear in shaded boxes found in your text. *Take Note* provides helpful hints related to particular tasks or topics.
ANOTHER WAY	*Another Way* provides an alternative procedure for accomplishing a particular task.
X REF	These notes provide pointers to information discussed elsewhere in the textbook or describe interesting features that are not directly addressed in the current topic or exercise.
Alt + Tab	A plus sign (+) between two key names means that you must press both keys at the same time. Keys that you are instructed to press in an exercise will appear in the font shown here.
Example	Key terms appear in bold, italic font when they are defined.

The *Microsoft Official Academic Course* programs are accompanied by a rich array of resources that incorporate the extensive textbook visuals to form a pedagogically cohesive package. These resources provide all the materials instructors need to deploy and deliver their courses. Resources available online for download include:

- The **MSDN Academic Alliance** is designed to provide the easiest and most inexpensive developer tools, products, and technologies available to faculty and students in labs, classrooms, and on student PCs. A free three-year membership is available to qualified MOAC adopters.

  Note: Microsoft Windows Server 2008, Microsoft Windows 7, and Microsoft Visual Studio can be downloaded from MSDN AA for use by students in this course.

- The **Instructor's Guide** contains solutions to all the textbook exercises and syllabi for various term lengths. The Instructor's Guide also includes chapter summaries and lecture notes. The Instructor's Guide is available from the Book Companion site (http://www.wiley.com/college/microsoft).

- The **Test Bank** contains hundreds of questions in multiple-choice, true-false, short answer, and essay formats, and is available to download from the Instructor's Book Companion site (www.wiley.com/college/microsoft). A complete answer key is also provided.

- A complete set of **PowerPoint presentations and images** is available on the Instructor's Book Companion site (http://www.wiley.com/college/microsoft) to enhance classroom presentations. Approximately 50 PowerPoint slides are provided for each lesson. Tailored to the text's topical coverage and Skills Matrix, these presentations are designed to convey key concepts addressed in the text. All images from the text are on the Instructor's Book Companion site (http://www.wiley.com/college/microsoft). You can incorporate them into your PowerPoint presentations or use them to create your own overhead transparencies and handouts. By using these visuals in class discussions, you can help focus students' attention on key elements of technologies covered and help them understand how to use these technologies effectively in the workplace.

- When it comes to improving the classroom experience, there is no better source of ideas and inspiration than your fellow colleagues. The **Wiley Faculty Network** connects teachers with technology, facilitates the exchange of best practices, and helps enhance instructional efficiency and effectiveness. Faculty Network activities include technology training and tutorials, virtual seminars, peer-to-peer exchanges of experiences and ideas, personal consulting, and sharing of resources. For details, visit www.WhereFacultyConnect.com.

MSDN ACADEMIC ALLIANCE—FREE 3-YEAR MEMBERSHIP AVAILABLE TO QUALIFIED ADOPTERS!

The Microsoft Developer Network Academic Alliance (MSDN AA) is designed to provide the easiest and most inexpensive way for universities to make the latest Microsoft developer tools, products, and technologies available in labs, in classrooms, and on student PCs. MSDN AA is an annual membership program for departments teaching Science, Technology, Engineering, and Mathematics (STEM) courses. The membership provides a complete solution to keep academic labs, faculty, and students on the leading edge of technology.

Software available in the MSDN AA program is provided at no charge to adopting departments through the Wiley and Microsoft publishing partnership.

As a bonus to this free offer, faculty will be introduced to Microsoft's Faculty Connection and Academic Resource Center. It takes time and preparation to keep students engaged while giving them a fundamental understanding of theory, and Microsoft Faculty Connection is designed to help STEM professors with this preparation by providing articles, curriculum, and tools that professors can use to engage and inspire today's technology students.

Contact your Wiley representative for details.

For more information about the MSDN Academic Alliance program, go to:

http://msdn.microsoft.com/academic/

Note: Microsoft Windows Server 2008, Microsoft Windows 7, and Microsoft Visual Studio can be downloaded from MSDN AA for use by students in this course.

▪ Important Web Addresses and Phone Numbers

To locate the Wiley Higher Education Representative in your area, go to http://www.wiley.com/college and click on the "*Who's My Rep?*" link at the top of the page, or call the MOAC Toll-Free Number: 1 + (888) 764-7001 (U.S. & Canada only).

To learn more about becoming a Microsoft Certified Technology Specialist and about exam availability, visit www.microsoft.com/learning/mcp/mcp.

▪ Additional Resources

Book Companion Web Site (www.wiley.com/college/microsoft)

The students' book companion Web site for the MOAC series includes any resources, exercise files, and Web links that will be used in conjunction with this course.

Wiley Desktop Editions

Wiley MOAC Desktop Editions are innovative, electronic versions of printed textbooks. Students buy the desktop version for up to 50% off the U.S. price of the printed text, and they get the added value of permanence and portability. Wiley Desktop Editions also provide students with numerous additional benefits that are not available with other e-text solutions.

Wiley Desktop Editions are NOT subscriptions; students download the Wiley Desktop Edition to their computer desktops. Students own the content they buy to keep for as long as they want. Once a Wiley Desktop Edition is downloaded to the computer desktop, students have instant access to all of the content without being online. Students can print the sections they prefer to read in hard copy. Students also have access to fully integrated resources within their Wiley Desktop Edition. From highlighting their e-text to taking and sharing notes, students can easily personalize their Wiley Desktop Edition as they are reading or following along in class.

▪ About the Microsoft Technology Associate (MTA) Certification

Preparing Tomorrow's Technology Workforce

Technology plays a role in virtually every business around the world. Possessing the fundamental knowledge of how technology works and understanding its impact on today's academic and workplace environment is increasingly important—particularly for students interested in exploring professions involving technology. That's why Microsoft created the Microsoft Technology Associate (MTA) certification—a new entry-level credential that validates fundamental technology knowledge among students seeking to build a career in technology.

The Microsoft Technology Associate (MTA) certification is the ideal and preferred path to Microsoft's world-renowned technology certification programs, such as Microsoft Certified Technology Specialist (MCTS) and Microsoft Certified IT Professional (MCITP). MTA is positioned to become the premier credential for individuals seeking to explore and pursue a career in technology, or augment related pursuits such as business or any other field where technology is pervasive.

MTA Candidate Profile

The MTA certification program is designed specifically for secondary and post-secondary students interested in exploring academic and career options in a technology field. It offers students a certification in basic IT and development. As the new recommended entry point for Microsoft technology certifications, MTA is designed especially for students new to IT and software development. It is available exclusively in educational settings and easily integrates into the curricula of existing computer classes.

MTA Empowers Educators and Motivates Students

MTA provides a new standard for measuring and validating fundamental technology knowledge right in the classroom while keeping your budget and teaching resources intact. MTA helps institutions stand out as innovative providers of high-demand industry credentials and is easily deployed with a simple, convenient, and affordable suite of entry-level technology certification exams. MTA enables students to explore career paths in technology without requiring a big investment of time and resources, while providing a career foundation and the confidence to succeed in advanced studies and future vocational endeavors.

In addition to giving students an entry-level Microsoft certification, MTA is designed to be a stepping stone to other, more advanced Microsoft technology certifications, like the Microsoft Certified Technology Specialist (MCTS) certification.

Delivering MTA Exams: The MTA Campus License

Implementing a new certification program in your classroom has never been so easy with the MTA Campus License. Through the one-time purchase of the 12-month, 1,000-exam MTA Campus License, there's no more need for ad hoc budget requests and recurrent purchases of exam vouchers. Now you can budget for one low cost for the entire year, and then administer MTA exams to your students and other faculty across your entire campus where and when you want.

The MTA Campus License provides a convenient and affordable suite of entry-level technology certifications designed to empower educators and motivate students as they build a foundation for their careers.

The MTA Campus License is administered by Certiport, Microsoft's exclusive MTA exam provider.

To learn more about becoming a Microsoft Technology Associate and exam availability, visit www.microsoft.com/learning/mta.

▪ Activate Your FREE MTA Practice Test!

Your purchase of this book entitles you to a free MTA practice test from GMetrix (a $30 value). Please go to www.gmetrix.com/mtatests and use the following validation code to redeem your free test: **MTA98-363-F72A661F7C49.**

The **GMetrix Skills Management System** provides everything you need to practice for the Microsoft Technology Associate (MTA) Certification.

Overview of Test features:

- Practice tests map to the Microsoft Technology Associate (MTA) exam objectives
- GMetrix MTA practice tests simulate the actual MTA testing environment
- 50+ questions per test covering all objectives
- Progress at own pace, save test to resume later, return to skipped questions
- Detailed, printable score report highlighting areas requiring further review

To get the most from your MTA preparation, take advantage of your free GMetrix MTA Practice Test today!

For technical support issues on installation or code activation, please email support@gmetrix.com.

Acknowledgments

■ MOAC MTA Technology Fundamentals Reviewers

We'd like to thank the many reviewers who pored over the manuscript and provided invaluable feedback in the service of quality instructional materials:

Yuke Wang, University of Texas at Dallas
Palaniappan Vairavan, Bellevue College
Harold "Buz" Lamson, ITT Technical Institute
Colin Archibald, Valencia Community College
Catherine Bradfield, DeVry University Online
Robert Nelson, Blinn College
Kalpana Viswanathan, Bellevue College
Bob Becker, Vatterott College
Carol Torkko, Bellevue College
Bharat Kandel, Missouri Tech
Linda Cohen, Forsyth Technical Community College
Candice Lambert, Metro Technology Centers
Susan Mahon, Collin College
Mark Aruda, Hillsborough Community College
Claude Russo, Brevard Community College

David Koppy, Baker College
Sharon Moran, Hillsborough Community College
Keith Hoell, Briarcliffe College and Queens College—CUNY
Mark Hufnagel, Lee County School District
Rachelle Hall, Glendale Community College
Scott Elliott, Christie Digital Systems, Inc.
Gralan Gilliam, Kaplan
Steve Strom, Butler Community College
John Crowley, Bucks County Community College
Margaret Leary, Northern Virginia Community College
Sue Miner, Lehigh Carbon Community College
Gary Rollinson, Cabrillo College
Al Kelly, University of Advancing Technology
Katherine James, Seneca College

Brief Contents

Contents

Creating a Web Page

LESSON SKILL MATRIX

SKILLS/CONCEPTS	MTA EXAM OBJECTIVE	MTA EXAM OBJECTIVE NUMBER
Customizing the Layout and Appearance of a Web Page	Customize the layout and appearance of a Web page	1.1
Understanding ASP.NET Intrinsic Objects	Understand ASP.NET intrinsic objects	1.2
Understanding State Information in Web Applications	Understand state information in Web applications	1.3

KEY TERMS

<!DOCTYPE>	HttpContext object
Application object	intrinsic objects
application state	objects
attribute minimization	Request object
attributes	Response object
Cascading Style Sheets (CSS)	Server object
class	Session object
Class selector	session state
control state	state
DTD (Document Type Definition)	view state
element	W3C
HTML (HyperText Markup Language)	XHTML

Karen has a small business with a Web presence. She had just enough basic HTML skills to put the site together all by herself. However, the site has no interaction with the visitors. She would like to add this interaction using the latest HTML standards. This means that she needs to learn about XHTML, CSS, and the latest in page layouts. Her pages will also need to interact with the Web server. She decides to make the big move to Microsoft Visual Web Developer to accomplish these tasks.

■ Customizing the Layout and Appearance of a Web Page

 THE BOTTOM LINE There are many ways to write Web pages. Because browsers are so forgiving and backward compatible, many obsolete techniques are still in use today. However, it is important to make the move to the latest standards, including XHTML and Cascading Style Sheets.

Using the Latest Standards of HTML

HTML is slowly being replaced by XHTML. **XHTML** stands for Extensible Hypertext Markup Language and is the current W3C standard for writing HTML.

HyperText Markup Language (HTML) is based on the standards presented by the World Wide Web Consortium. *W3C* is an international community consisting of over 300 member organizations, a full-time staff, and the public working together to develop Web standards. Their mission, found at w3.org, is "to lead the World Wide Web to its full potential by developing protocols and guidelines that ensure the long-term growth of the Web."

Document Type Definition (DTD) is a tool used by the developer to ensure that Web pages follow a specified markup language. Web pages are tested against these standards during development. If the developer wants a page to follow all the XHTML standards, the word "Strict" is placed in a declaration statement in the Web page. If the XHTML page includes some older HTML, the word "Transitional" is used. Finally, "Frameset" is used in pages containing HTML frames, which are on the brink of extinction. "Transitional" is the most commonly used DTD today because of the slow transition from HTML to XHTML. For this lesson, however, we will use "Strict" to ensure the use of the latest markup language syntax.

<!DOCTYPE> is the declaration statement that uses the three words described above: strict, transitional, and frameset. Although it looks like a tag, it is not. In addition to the level of strictness, it includes other information such as whether the page is using HTML or XHTML, the version of the markup language being used, and the location of the W3.org Web site containing the Document Type Definition. The online DTD contains the rules that are used to test the page.

The <!DOCTYPE> statement is optional in HTML but required for XHTML. Although browsers are not obligated to recognize this declaration statement, the newer browsers know what it is and take advantage of the information it provides. The following is an example of a <!DOCTYPE> declaration that informs the browser that the page is using XHTML1.0 and is strictly following its DTD:

```
<!DOCTYPE html PUBLIC
"-//W3C//DTD XHTML 1.0 Strict//EN"
"http://www.w3.org/TR/xhtml1/DTD
/xhtml1-strict.dtd">
```

WRITING HTML

In order to write HTML, you must understand some common terms and the basic building blocks of the language.

An *element* is the name of an XHTML structure; **tags** are used to create them. XHTML requires that every element that has been started with a tag also ends with a tag. The symbol used to end, or close, an element is the slash. It can either be placed within a separate ending tag or included at the end of the content within the starting tag. With an empty element, such as a break, the element could be written as either `<br></br>` or `<br />`. The second version, `<br />`, is preferred because some browsers will mistakenly see the first version as two breaks. Not having the space between the r and the slash will also cause difficulty with some browsers. For elements that are not empty, a closing tag must be placed at the end of the content, as in: `<p>Some text</p>`.

Attributes define any properties that an element might want to include. They are placed inside the starting tag after the element name. The attribute name is followed by an equal sign and its value: `<img src='myImage.jpg' />`. The quotation marks around the attribute value may either be single, as shown, or double.

Attribute minimization is an HTML coding technique that allows the developer to use the attribute name without writing its value when the name of the attribute is the same as the value of the attribute. This practice is not allowed in XHTML.

The HTML language commonly uses the <html>, <head>, <title>, and <body> elements in Web pages, and all of these elements are required for XHTML. The <html> element is the required "root" element of an XHTML page. All nested elements within the <html> starting and ending tags are called **child elements** of the <html> element. Nesting a new element with one of the child elements makes the new element a child of that element and the grandchild of the <html> element.

The <html> element also has a required XHTML attribute called xmlns. This attribute specifies the namespace for the document, which ensures that elements having the same name are uniquely identified. Although not recommended, this attribute is not included in the Web pages of many Web developers because the following value of the xmlns attribute is used by default: `http://www.w3.org/1999/xhtml`.

The <head> element contains information about the document but is not part of the document content. Although not required, a <meta> element should be included as a child element of the <head> element. It holds data about the data in the Web page such as type of content, page refresh rate, the author of the page, character set, etc. Data placed in this element will not be displayed on the page but can be useful for browsers, search engines, and other Web services. The following is an example of a meta element:

```
<meta http-equiv="Content-type"
content="text/html;charset=UTF-8" />
```

The <title> element is also a child of the <head> element. Although much less complicated than the <meta> element, the <title> element is required for XHTML. It provides the browser with a title and is used for bookmarking.

Finally, the <body> element contains the content of the Web page that will be displayed by the browser. Text placed within the tags of this element is displayed in HTML but not XHTML. XHTML requires another element to display text, such as the paragraph element <p>.

VALIDATING HTML

XHTML has more strict syntax rules than HTML and should always be validated. We will be validating our HTML pages against the rules for XHTML. Since these syntax rules are the very same rules used for XML, we can use an XML validator to validate our XHTML pages. If the page passes the validation test, it is considered a "Well Formed" document.

TAKE NOTE＊

We will be covering XML in Lesson 3.

CREATE A PAGE AND HAVE IT VALIDATED

GET READY. Before you begin these steps, be sure you have a connection to the Internet available.

1. Create a new folder in Windows.
   - We will use this folder for all the files in this lesson.

2. Create a new text document and name it **ValidateXHTML.txt**.

3. Rename the file **ValidateXHTML.html**.

4. Double-click the new file to verify that the file has not remained a text file having the `.txt` file extension.

   - If the text editor opens instead of the browser, you still have a text document. The file name and extension will be "ValidateXHTML.html.txt". You will need to close the text editor, allow Windows to display the registered file extensions, and then rename the file **XHTML.html**.

   - Once the file name has been named properly, double-click it again to make sure the browser opens.

5. Close the browser.

6. Right-click the file and open it for editing.

   - It should open Notepad if the default has not been changed.

   - Make sure you do not use a word processor because the file will contain formatting text.

   - Using an HTML editor would also work, but at this point, it would do too much of the work for you. This is a learning environment, not a production environment.

7. Type the following HTML code into your document.

   - Make sure lowercase text is used for all your tags. XHTML does not allow capital letters. However, since DOCTYPE is not considered a tag, it can be, and nearly always is, written in uppercase letters.

   - The last two characters in "xhtml1" can be easily misread. If uppercase text could be used, it would look like "XHTML1."

   ```
   <!DOCTYPE html PUBLIC "-//W3C//DTD XHTML 1.0
   Strict//EN"
   "http://www.w3.org/TR/xhtml1/DTD
   /xhtml1-strict.dtd">
   <html xmlns="http://www.w3.org/1999/xhtml">
     <head>
       <meta http-equiv="Content-type"
   content="text/html;charset=UTF-8" />
       <title>This is a sample document.</title>
   </head>
   <body>
       <p>This is a paragraph of text.</p>
   </body>
   </html>
   ```

8. Save and close the text editor.

9. Double-click the **ValidateXHTML.html** file.

   - This should open your default browser and display the text you placed into the paragraph element.

   - If you are not using Internet Explorer, you may want to consider using it to be consistent with the lessons.

   - We will now go to the W3C Web site and validate the syntax of your Web document.

10. With the browser open, type the following address into the address bar at the top of the browser:

`http://validator.w3.org/#validate-by-upload`

- Your browser should be displaying the W3C Markup Validation Service, as shown in Figure 1-1.

Figure 1-1

Uploading an XHTML file to be validated

11. On the W3C Web page, click the **Browse** button to locate your file. Once found, click the dialog box's **Open** button.

- The name of your file should now be in the text box of the W3C page.

12. Click the **Check** button on the W3C page.

- You have just validated your XTHML document for proper syntax, as seen in Figure 1-2.

Figure 1-2

A successfully validated XHTML file

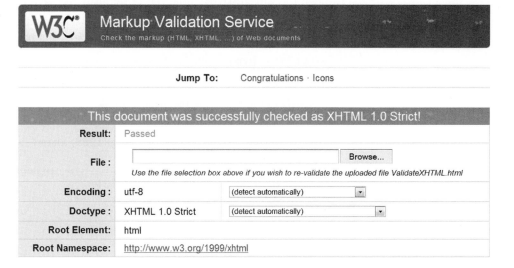

If your page fails to validate after verifying that your code has been typed correctly, read the fine print in the Web page to make sure your operating system is not the problem. For example, XP ServicePack 2 is known to have a bug that prevents validation.

PAUSE. Leave the browser open to the validator site for the next exercise.

As you have seen, an XHTML document can use the online W3C Markup Validation Service to make sure it is well formed.

WRITING HTML

The HTML used in this section focuses on the XHTML syntax rules. It can be a challenge to write strict XHTML for the simplest of Web pages.

Both XHTML and HTML use elements and attributes to create Web pages. This allows us to use the term "HTML" when writing XHTML pages. Unless syntax rules are involved, HTML will be used for most of our lessons.

Try to avoid using deprecated elements. Deprecated elements have either been replaced with new elements or have been dropped altogether in favor of Cascading Style Sheets (CSS), which are covered later in this lesson.

In an XHTML document, the <body> element often requires a container element for things such as displaying text. Text is not allowed to be placed directly within <body> tags. The paragraph (<p>) element is often used for this purpose.

Container elements are required for some elements placed within the <body> element. The break and anchor elements cannot stand alone in the <body> element but work well within the <p> tags. However, the heading tag cannot be placed within the paragraph tags but can be used in place of the paragraph element as a container to display text.

 WRITE A WELL-FORMED XHTML PAGE

GET READY. We will use the code from our ValidateXHTML.html file.

1. Open the ValidateXHTML.html file in Notepad and save it as **Paragraph.html**.
2. Edit your code to match the following HTML. Only the text within the <body> tags needs to be changed. Ignore any XHTML-specific syntax warnings you may notice.

```
<!DOCTYPE html PUBLIC "-//W3C//DTD XHTML 1.0
Strict//EN"
"http://www.w3.org/TR/xhtml1/DTD
/xhtml1-strict.dtd">
<html xmlns="http://www.w3.org/1999/xhtml">
  <head>
    <meta http-equiv="Content-type"
    content="text/html;charset=UTF-8" />
    <title>This is a sample document.</title>
  </head>
  <body>
    <p><h1>This is a </h1><h4>paragraph</h4>
    <h6>of text.</h6></p>
    <p>
```

```
<a href="#TheAnchor">From Source Anchor
to Destination Anchor</a>
<br /><br /><br /><br /><br /><br /><br />
<br /><br /><br /><br /><br /><br /><br />
<br /><br /><br /><br /><br /><br /><br />
These page breaks are used to create
a long page.
<br /><br /><br /><br /><br /><br /><br />
<br /><br /><br /><br /><br /><br /><br />
<br /><br /><br /><br /><br /><br /><br />
</p>
<p>
<a name="TheAnchor">Destination Anchor</a>
</p>
</body>
</html>
```

3. Save and close the text file.
4. Double-click the Paragraph.html file.
   - If the entire page is displayed, either reduce the size of the window or increase the text size in your browser.
   - You should see the three different heading sizes and a link that sends you to the bottom of the page.
5. Press the link to verify that the code is working directly.

   You should have been sent to the bottom of the page.
   - Most likely, the browser ignored the DOCTYPE declaration and interpreted the code as HTML. We will need to run it through the Markup Validation Service to see if this document is well formed.
6. If the browser is still at the Markup Validation Service Web site, click the Back button on the browser and do the same thing you did to validate your first html file. If you closed the browser, go back to http://validator.w3.org/#validate-by-upload and test your new html file.
   - The validator should have caught three errors showing that the heading tags are not properly placed with the document.
7. Edit the file and erase the pair of paragraph tags around the heading tags; they are located in the first line of code following the <body> tag.
8. Save the file and run the program through the validator again.
   - Your XHTML document is now well formed.
   - Notice that heading elements can be used in place of the paragraph tags but not within them.
9. Remove the paragraph tags surrounding the last paragraph element (TheAnchor).
10. Save the file and test it to see if it is still well formed.
    - This time it should fail, showing that the anchor element cannot be used alone.
11. Replace the paragraph elements and make sure your document is well formed before moving to the next exercise.

PAUSE. Leave the browser open to the validator site for the next exercise.

Even a very simple Web page can become very complex when verifying for XHTML syntax. However, these additional rules should provide increased consistency and stability when displayed with the newer browsers.

EMBEDDING IMAGES WITH HTML

The image element <img> is used in most Web pages along with the src attribute that points to the name of the image. However, many of these pages will not pass XHTML validation. We will begin by using the bare minimum to place an image on the page. Once we can see the image, we will try to validate the page.

 EMBED AN IMAGE INTO A WEB PAGE

GET READY. We will use the code from our Paragraph.html file.

1. Open the Paragraph.html file and save it as **Image.html**.
2. Right-click your new Image.html file and click **Edit**.
3. Replace the entire content of the <body> element with the following code.

```
<img src="sample.jpg" />
```

4. Save the file but leave it open for later editing.
   - Before you can run this program, there needs to be a sample.jpg file.
5. Find a jpg file, copy it to the same folder as your Image.html file, and rename it **sample.jpg**.
6. Run the program. Then close the browser.
   - The image should have been displayed by the browser. However, will it pass strict XHTML?
7. Validate the Image.html file.
   - The Web page should have failed the validation test. The first error should indicate that it is missing the alt attribute. The second error should indicate that it is missing a container element, such as the paragraph or header. The second error is easier to fix.
8. Place paragraph tags around the image element, save the file, and run the validation test again.
   - There should be one error, which will now be addressed.
   - Some browsers are unable to display images. Rather than show a blank image or produce an error when an image fails to load, text describing what you should see can be placed in the same location as the missing image.
   - Without providing the alternate attribute, the image element will not pass strict XHTML validation.
9. Add the alternate attribute to your image element describing your jpg file. Remember to save the file.

```
<p><img src="sample.jpg" alt="This is a sample
picture of something." /></p>
```

10. Validate the Image.html file.
    - Your page should have passed the strict validation test.
    - We now need to see if we can get your description of the image to display.
11. Run your program. Then close the browser.
    - The browser should have displayed the image again.
    - Under normal circumstances, the alt attribute value will not be displayed.

12. Rename your jpg file to **SampleX.jpg**.
    - This will prevent the browser from finding your file, which simulates the real-life problem of files that cannot be found.
13. Run your program to make sure the description of the image is displayed. Then close the browser.
    - The browser should have presented the text instead of the image.
14. Rename your jpg file back to its original name and make sure your browser once again displays the image.

PAUSE. You can now close the browser.

CERTIFICATION READY
How are images embedded into XHTML documents that adhere to the latest accepted practices?
1.1

When Web developers use the strict declaration in their Web pages, it forces them to drop many sloppy habits that are commonplace in the industry today. For example, leaving out the alternate attribute is acceptable for HTML but is required for XHTML. Although more coding is involved in meeting the XHTML requirements, it is well worth the effort.

➕ MORE INFORMATION

If you are not already familiar with the basics of HTML, you may want to seek out other resources before moving on to the next section.

Applying Cascading Style Sheets to a Web Page

HTML coding was never intended to format a document. Rather, it was developed primarily to define the content and layout of a Web document.

HTML elements define *what* content is to be displayed. *Cascading Style Sheets (CSS)* define *how* to display these HTML elements, including such characteristics as fonts, borders, color, size, etc. Although many HTML elements and attributes are already capable of doing this, they have fallen out of favor and certainly out of the XHTML standards; they have been replaced by CSS. The Web developer only needs to know the assigned names of the CSS formatting elements to apply them. Virtually all Web browsers now support CSS.

CSS can be located in three areas: embedded within the HTML code, included in the Web page but not embedded, and on a separate page. These locations are called inline, internal, and external, respectively.

- **Inline Style Sheet**
    - Embedded within HTML
    - Overrides all other style sheet settings
- **Internal Style Sheet**
    - Is within the page but separate from HTML
    - Overrides External style sheet settings
    - Does not override inline style sheet settings
- **External Style Sheet**
    - Resides in its own page
    - Has no overriding power

The simplest way to apply CSS to a Web page is to use inline styles. An inline style is created within a particular tag as an attribute and is applied only to that one tag set.

WRITE A WEB PAGE USING CSS

GET READY. We will use the code from our ValidateXHTML.html file.

1. Open the ValidateXHTML.html file with Notepad and save it as **CSS.html.**
2. Right-click your new CSS.html file and click **Edit.**
3. Change the paragraph element within the <body> tags to match the following:

```
<p style="font-family:Arial;font-size:8pt;">This
is a paragraph of text.</p>
```

4. Save the file and run the program. Then close the browser.
   - The browser should have displayed the message in very small 8-point font.
   - The style attribute consists of inline CSS declarations. Each declaration has a CSS property (font-family and font-size) that is assigned a value (Arial and 8pt) and terminated by a semicolon. Notice that a colon separates each property and its value.
   - The inline style sheet in our document only applies to the current element.
   - Next, we will convert our inline style sheet to an internal style sheet.
   - Unlike the inline style sheet, the internal style sheet allows us to apply the style information to every paragraph element in our HTML document.
   - Although the internal style sheet remains within the HTML document, it cannot reside within our paragraph element as an attribute. It must be placed in its own <style> element.
   - We will remove our inline style sheet from the paragraph element, <p>, and place it into the <style> element. To limit the style information to paragraph elements, the style sheet is preceded with a P.
   - An internal style sheet begins with a selector that identifies the HTML element the style will affect. A selector is followed by one or more style sheet value pairs, as shown below:

   ```
   selector {property:value;}
   ```

5. Insert the following <style> element and its internal style sheet within the <head> tags of the HTML document.

```
<style type="text/css">

P {font-family:Arial; font-size:24pt;}
</style>
```

   - The <style> element includes the type attribute value "text/css."
   - Because the P at the beginning of the style sheet represents a selector rather than an HTML element, you do not need to surround the paragraph with the < > symbols.
   - Because the internal style sheet does not use HTML attributes, quotation marks are not used for the style values.
   - Now that the internal style sheet is in place, we will remove the inline style sheet.

6. Change the body of the HTML document back to the original code by removing the style attribute (the inline style sheet). Then save the file.

```
<p>This is a paragraph of text.</p>
```

7. Run the program. Then close the browser.
   - The browser should display the larger text as defined by the internal style sheet.

- Now that we have two ways to define CSS within our document, what happens if both are used at the same time?

8. Replace the inline style sheet by inserting the style attribute and its value into the paragraph element.

   - You need to keep the internal style sheet in place.

   ```
   <p style="font-family:Arial;font-size:8pt;">
   This is a paragraph of text.
   </p>
   ```

9. Run the program. Then close the browser.

   - You should notice that the browser once again displays the smaller font.

   - Inline style sheets take precedence over internal style sheets. This allows you to make a change to all the designated elements within an HTML page and make exceptions when needed.

10. Remove the inline style sheet again; do not remove the internal style sheet.

    - If more than a single Web page is to use a style sheet, the style sheet must be in a location that is available to all the pages on the site. This is accomplished by using an external style sheet.

    - An external style sheet is a style sheet that is located in a separate file.

11. Create a new text file in the same folder as the CSS.html file and name it **External.css**.

    - Any file name may be used for external style sheets. However, it is highly recommended to use .css as the file name extension.

    - To create our external style sheet, we must move the internal style sheet from the CSS.html Web page to a separate file, the External.css file, and provide a reference to the new location of the style sheet.

12. Place the following style sheet into the External.css file and then delete the internal style sheet from the HTML document. (Leave the <style> tags.)

    - An easy way to do this is to cut it from the HTML document, paste it into the CSS file, and then change the font size to 48 point.

    ```
    P {font-family:Arial; font-size:48pt;}
    ```

13. Save and close the External.css file.

14. In the CSS.html file, replace the <style> tags with the following line of code:

    ```
    <link rel="stylesheet" type="text/css"
    href="External.css"/>
    ```

    - The <link> element is used as a reference to the style sheet so that it will be included in our HTML document.

    - Multiple link elements may be used for more style sheet documents if necessary.

    - The link element uses three attributes to reference an external CSS file. The relationship attribute ("rel") identifies the external file as a style sheet, the reference attribute ("href") provides the location of the style sheet, and the type attribute ("type") defines what Web standard it follows.

15. Save and close the CSS.html file.

16. Run the program. Then close the browser.

    - The browser should show very large text as defined in the external style sheet.

    - Our external style sheet can also be referenced from within other Web pages if desired. This allows us to set the exact same style for any page on the site.

- Just as the inline style sheet takes precedence over the internal style sheet, the internal sheet takes precedence over the external sheet. This allows us to make exceptions to the global changes made by the external style sheet.

PAUSE. Keep the files available for the next exercise.

In this exercise, we used CSS to allow HTML to do nothing but provide our content. We used CSS to describe this content. We also placed our CSS into three different areas and found that, although the browser produced the same output, each had its own advantages and disadvantages.

One of the most significant advantages of using the external style sheets is that a single sheet can be referenced from any of the pages on the site. This allows page consistency and more efficient site maintenance.

Finding Elements with CSS Selectors

Internal and external style sheets use selectors to direct the style information to designated elements. CSS selectors use complex pattern-matching techniques to locate these elements.

A selector is the first part of the internal and external style sheet. It can be used for matching more than element names, such as the paragraph in the previous exercise. The flexibility of the CSS selector allows the developer to locate any desired set of elements within a document.

There are various types of selectors, which are named and classified by their complexity and usage. In the previous exercise, we used one of the "simple" selectors called the "type" selector. Two other simple selectors, the ID selector and the Class selector, will be demonstrated in the next exercise.

The ID selector is assigned a name with a "#" prefix. The number sign tells the browser that a name is an ID selector. Using an ID selector allows you to create multiple style definitions for a single element in the same CSS document. For example, you could define multiple-paragraph font-family declarations, each with a different font or font size.

To use the ID selector, the ID attribute must be used in the Web page. The ID attribute is used to uniquely identify each element. There can be no duplicate ID values within a page.

 WRITE A WEB PAGE USING CSS ID AND CLASS SELECTORS

GET READY. We will use the `External.css` and code from our CSS.html file.

1. Replace the content of the External.css file with the following. Save the file but keep it open for more changes.

   ```
   #headers4 {font-family:arial;}
   #anotherp {font-family: comic sans ms;}
   #bodytext {font-family:script;}
   ```

   - The # characters in front of the selectors direct the browser to search for the ID attribute names rather than the type of HTML element that will be using the styles.
   - We will now place new tags in the body of our Web page so the browser can find the names.
   - The ID attribute uniquely identifies elements in a document.

2. Replace the body of our page with the following code:

```
<h4 id="headers4">This is h4 text.</h4>
<p id="bodytext">This is a paragraph of text.</p>
<p id="anotherp">This is another paragraph of text.
</p>
```

- Notice that the ID names are used to locate the elements. Finding the elements using the ID attribute make the element names irrelevant. Since each element has a unique ID, each can be located individually.
- Another selector, the **Class selector**, also uses an attribute to locate elements. However, it uses the Class attribute so that multiple elements using the same class name can be located. This allows groups of elements to be uniquely identified.
- The Class selector is prefixed by a period rather than the # symbol so the browser will look for Class names rather than ID or element names.
- We will now use the Class selector in place of the ID selector.

3. Save the file but keep it open for more changes.

4. Run the program.
- Each line of text should be displayed in a different font.
- Since the header and two paragraph elements in our HTML page were uniquely identified with the ID attribute, the style sheet was able to find them and style the output for each element.

5. Make the following change to the CSS.html file by adding the **Class** attributes to each of our three elements. Then save and close the file.

```
<h4 id="headers1" class="top">This is h4 text.</h4>
<p id="bodytext" class="top">This is a paragraph of text.</p>
<p id="anotherp" class="bot">This is another paragraph of
text.</p>
```

6. Change the External.css file by replacing the existing code with the following. Then save and close the file.

```
.top {font-family:arial;}
.bot {font-family:script;}
```

7. Run the program.
- The top two lines of text should both be Arial, although of different sizes, as defined by the style sheet. The last line should be script.
- Identifying the elements by class rather than by ID allows the Class selector to apply the same style to multiple elements.

8. Close the browser.

PAUSE. Keep the files available for the next exercise.

Other selectors use a special syntax for pattern matching to find elements. They can find an element using many techniques, such as using parts of element names. For example, you may want to find all elements starting with the letter A. This syntax can be very complex and is beyond the scope of this lesson.

Creating HTML Tables

Tables are very common elements in Web pages. They are constructed with a set of easy-to-remember element names. The table itself uses the <table> tag, while its components are <tr> for table row and <td> for table data. Some of the more specialized elements are <caption> to display the name and <th> for the headers.

 CREATE A TABLE ON A WEB PAGE

GET READY. We will use the code from our CSS.html file.

1. Open the CSS.html file and save it as **Table.html.**
   - If this file is unavailable, use the first document we created in this lesson, XHTML.html, and add the <link> element that was used to reference an external style sheet. We will be creating a new external CSS file and changing the <link> href attribute to point to the new CSS file. We will also be replacing the body of the document.

2. Replace the content of the body of the Table.html file with the following HTML code:

```
<table>
<caption>Sample </caption>
  <tr>
    <th>Food</th>
      <th>Unit</th>
  </tr>
<tr>
  <td>Milk</td>
  <td>Gallon</td>
</tr>
<tr>
  <td>Eggs</td>
  <td>Dozen</td>
</tr>
</table>
```

3. Save the file, but leave it open for additional editing.
4. Run the program. Then close the browser.
   - Notice that there were no borders. Although this practice is not recommended, these are often placed directly into the HTML code by either using attributes or inline style sheets. We will insert our borders properly by using an external style sheet.
5. Create a file named **Table.css** in the same folder as the Table.html file.
6. Place the following CSS into the new file. Then save and close the file.

```
table
{
padding:10px;
border:5px solid gray;
margin:50px;
```

```
background-color:#99F;
text-align:center;
font-family:arial;
}
th
{
padding:10px;
border:2px solid blue;
margin:50px;
background-color:#CCF;
}
td
{
padding:10px;
border:2px dotted red;
margin:50px;
background-color:#FFF;
font-size:0.8em;
}
```

   • We now need to change the link to this new file.

7. Change the <link> element in the Table.html file to point to the new CSS file.

```
<link rel="stylesheet" type="text/css"
href="Table.css"/>
```

8. Save and close the file.

9. Run the program, and then close the browser.

   • The table should now be displayed with borders in addition to other applied styles, as shown in Figure 1-3.

Figure 1-3

A table formatted using CSS

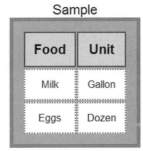

CERTIFICATION READY
How are tables used for
Web pages that adhere
to the latest accepted
practices?
1.1

PAUSE. Keep the files available for the next exercise.

You should now have a fully formatted table without a single formatting attribute in the HTML document. If any part of the table ever needs special attention, you can always add the ID or Class attribute to specific elements of the table and add ID or Class selectors.

LAYING OUT HTML ON A PAGE

Since people do not navigate a Web page in the same way they read a page from a book, Web pages are often divided into sections. CSS is now used to help create these sections.

Several elements are available for dividing Web pages into sections; however, most should no longer be considered. For example, even though the table element is used quite often for this purpose, it is gradually being replaced by CSS. In addition, using a table for page layout will prevent the page from complying with the XHTML standard.

The use of CSS is now the standard technique for laying out Web pages, and CSS is most often used jointly with the division element. Each division element is assigned a unique ID, which is then located using the CSS ID selector.

We will use two divisions on our Web page.

 LAY OUT A WEB PAGE FOR NAVIGATION

GET READY. We will use the code from our Table.html file.

1. Open the Table.html file and save it as **Div.html**.
   - If this file is unavailable, use the first document we created in this lesson, XHTML.html, and add the <link> element that was used to reference an external style sheet. We will be creating a new external CSS file and changing the <link> href attribute to point to the new CSS file. We will also be replacing the body of the document.

2. Replace the content between the <body> tags with the following HTML code.

```
<div id="formal">
  <h1>FORMAL</h1>
  <p>This is a paragraph of text.</p>
</div>
<div id="informal">
  <h1>INFORMAL</h1>
  <p>This is a paragraph of text.</p>
</div>
```

3. Save the file, but leave it open for additional editing.
4. Run the program. Then close the browser.
   - The browser should have displayed two pairs of lines in which the first of each pair is much larger than the second.
5. Create a new file named **Div.css**.
6. Place the following CSS into the new file:

```
#formal
{
font-family:arial;
border:2px solid gray;
background-color:silver;
color:purple;
width:250px;
}
#informal
```

```
{
font-family:lucida handwriting;
border:10px solid red;
background-color:blue;
color:yellow;
width:300px;
text-align:center;
```

- We now need to change the link to this new file.

7. Change the <link> element in the Table.html file to point to the new CSS file.

```
<link rel="stylesheet" type="text/css" href="Div.css"/>
```

8. Save and close the file.

9. Run the program, and then close the browser.

- The text within the <Div> elements should now be displayed with borders in addition to other applied styles, as shown in Figure 1-4.

Figure 1-4

Using the Div element with CSS for Web page layout

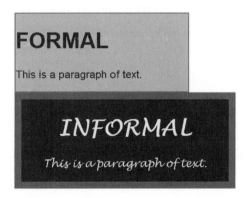

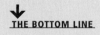

CERTIFICATION READY
What tools should be used to lay out a Web page and adhere to the latest accepted practices?
1.1

PAUSE. Although we will no longer be using our text files, keep them available because some of the code will be reused later.

Rather than using tables for layout, the latest standards call for CSS. Using CSS and the division element, we have total control over the page layout.

■ Understanding ASP.NET Intrinsic Objects

THE BOTTOM LINE

There are many ***intrinsic objects*** in ASP.NET. However, several intrinsic objects are considered *the* intrinsic objects because of their importance in Web development. These are HttpContext, Response, Request, Server, Application, and Session objects.

Creating Web Pages Using the Properties, Methods, and Events of ASP.NET Intrinsic Objects

Since ASP.NET is object-oriented, we need to begin this session with some of the terms used to describe the objects in this environment.

The .NET platform uses classes and *objects*. In the *class* structure, the programming code is written specifically for the objects rather than for the program itself. The class contains sets of programming code bundled with data meant to complete a specific task. Hundreds of pre-defined classes are available in the ASP.NET foundation for use in a Web site. If a pre-defined class cannot address a particular need, developers are free to create their own.

It is important to know that classes cannot be applied directly within the program. The class is similar to a cookie cutter. Cookies are stamped out for consumption but no one consumes the cookie cutter. From any given class, uniquely named objects can be created as needed. They are used as programming tools within the program to reduce the size of the application, reduce the errors, and reduce coding time.

An object has a number of assigned attributes called **properties** that describe the characteristics of the object. Some objects have behaviors called **methods** that can be called upon when needed. Some objects also respond to external stimuli; these activities are called **events**. We will take a closer look at properties, methods, and events by examining intrinsic objects.

Before we can step through the exercises to learn more about these objects, we will have to make sure the ASP.NET development environment is available. We will be using this environment for all the remaining lessons.

WRITING WEB PAGES IN MICROSOFT VISUAL WEB DEVELOPER 2008 EXPRESS

Visual Studio has one of the most comprehensive integrated development environments (IDEs) available today. It includes Visual Web Developer, which enables visual objects, such as labels and buttons, to be directly placed on Web pages. These objects can then be programmed in familiar programming languages such as C# or Visual Basic (VB). Even though this IDE uses HTML and ASP code in the background, the Web page looks and feels like a desktop environment.

Microsoft offers an Express edition of Visual Web Developer that is designed for non-professionals, hobbyists, students, and beginning Web developers who want to learn how to build ASP.NET Web applications. All the samples will also work using the Full edition if you have access to it. Otherwise, download and install the Express edition from Microsoft free of charge.

The first step, after installing Visual Web Developer, is to run through one or more tutorials that come with the product to get familiar with the environment. Since our lessons contain an overview of Web development, the details of the Integrated Development Environment (IDE) along with how to write programs are kept to a minimum. Our focus is on the fundamentals of developing Web sites.

When a Web site is deployed, Internet Information Services (IIS) is used for client-server communication. For training purposes, IIS is not needed. The Web Developer will simulate this connection using files located on the development computer. All that needs to be installed for our lessons is the Web Developer and the .NET 3.5 platform, which is installed automatically along with Visual Web Developer.

WRITING WEB PAGES IN ASP.NET

Although there are many languages used for creating and manipulating Web pages on the server, languages that use the .NET platform have many advantages over those that work alone.

The .NET framework is a programming platform containing thousands of objects and libraries. Of the dozens of programming languages that support this platform, the most common are C# and Visual Basic.

Although we can use the .NET platform and a .NET-supported language for either desktop applications or Web sites, additional support is needed to create Web pages. ASP.NET is Microsoft's solution to programming the pages and the IIS is Microsoft's solution to moving these pages to and from the browser.

The pages are created using C#, Visual Basic, or some other .NET language. This code is located on the server. The server then uses IIS to move these pages to the browser. From there, the browser can use a scripting language to manipulate the pages without having to request an updated page from the server.

VBScript can also be used as a scripting language run by the browser. This can be a problem for some users because only Internet Explorer is capable of processing programs written in VBScript. So to be browser neutral and Web safe, one of the more generic programming languages is normally used, such as JavaScript. We will address both of these client-side scripting languages in Lesson 5.

For our server-side programming, we will be using C# rather than Visual Basic for most of our lessons. However, there are times when using Visual Basic works better for demonstrating specific objectives. The best choice for development is strictly up to your language preferences; they are both used extensively by professional Web developers.

At any time during the lessons, you may want to consider walking through some of the Web Developer's tutorials that come free with Visual Web Developer.

 WRITE AN ASP.NET WEB PAGE USING VISUAL WEB DEVELOPER

GET READY. We will be using Microsoft Visual Web Developer 2008 Express Edition in our lessons.

1. Open Visual Web Developer 2008.
2. Create a new Web site from the Recent Projects window.

 **ANOTHER WAY** You can also create a new Web site by using File -> New Web Site . . . menu item (Shift + Alt + N).

3. From the **New Web Site** dialog box, make sure **ASP.NET Web Site** is highlighted, the **Location:** is **File System,** and **C#** is selected as the **Language:**. The path and file name can be changed if desired.
   • See Figure 1-5.

Figure 1-5

Using Microsoft Visual Web Developer 2008 Express to start a new ASP.NET Web site

4. Click the **OK** button.

- The **Source** view window should now be open. It is also referred to as the Inline Code view. The code that is displayed in the Source view window is ASP-embedded HTML. The ASP tags start and end with the <% . . . %> characters.

- Because we are creating a new Web form, the <form> . . . </form> tag contains a "runat" attribute indicating that any code within the form tags is to be processed on the server as directed.

- Notice that the default DOCTYPE validation for our ASP.NET Web page is Transitional rather than Strict. We will relax our standard in all our lessons when working with ASP.NET.

- We will not be using the Source view for writing code because directly coding in this window is becoming obsolete.

5. Click the **Design** tab at the bottom of the editing window.

- The **Design** view window should now be open. This view provides a what-you-see-is-what-you-get (WYSIWYG) display of the Web form. Any changes made in the Design view are also reflected in the other views, such as the Source view where the editor writes the code.

- Notice that there is a **Split** view tab located between the Design and Source views. This allows you to see both views at the same time. When you make a change to one view, you will immediately see the change in the other view.

- Although this is what you see in the browser when testing your Web application, the work area is not a Web page. The server only creates the Web page at runtime. The work area is referred to as the Web form. However, it is referred to as a page when looking at it from an outcome perspective.

- Notice the **ToolBox** to the left of the window. These are visual representations of the classes that define the objects. They are not objects until they are placed on the form. Since they are neither classes nor objects, they are given a special name, controls. However, most developers still call them controls after they are placed on the form.

- To place a control on the form, you have the choice of double-clicking or drag-and-drop.

6. Place a **Button** control on the form. The button is located in the Standard category of the Toolbox window to the left of the screen.

7. With the Button object highlighted, note the Properties window to the right of the screen. Change the Text property from **Button** to **Push Me**. Then click the button again.

- The button should immediately show the change you made to its Text property.

8. Click the play button at the top of the window to see your form turn into a Web page.

 **ANOTHER WAY**   You can also test your page by using Debug -> Start Debugging menu item (F5).

- Since this is the first time your Web site has been launched, a warning should pop up about modifying the web.config file to enable debugging. This is not a problem in a development environment. However, when a Web site is deployed, publicizing your debugging information creates a serious security risk.

9. If this is the first launch, leave the default setting in the dialog box to enable debugging and click the **OK** button. Override any security issues the browser may have with your Web page.

10. Click the button and close the browser.
    - Obviously nothing happened when you clicked the button. This can easily be fixed.

11. Double-click the button on the form.
    - You have now arrived at our last view in the IDE, the **code-behind** view. This is where you will be writing your C# or Visual Basic code. Writing your code in this view is preferred over writing explicit ASP or HTML in the Source view window.
    - Your code will execute only when an event occurs. When an object senses an external event, it can act on it. Common events are button clicks, text box changes, page loading, etc. We will write code that will execute when the visitor clicks our button.
    - If you have not clicked the mouse since double-clicking the button, the cursor should be blinking in the code-behind view. This is where you type the code for the button's click event. If you clicked the mouse, click it again between the curly braces under the Button1_Click procedure.

12. Type **but** for the first three letters of your code.
    - A list box should pop up giving you many choices for the first word of your code, as shown in Figure 1-6.
    - The drop-down list automatically highlights the first word matching your typed characters. "Button" is the name of the class that defines the Button1 object on the form, as shown in Figure 1-6. "Button1" is the name of the object you placed on the form.

Figure 1-6

IntelliSense helping with the syntax while coding

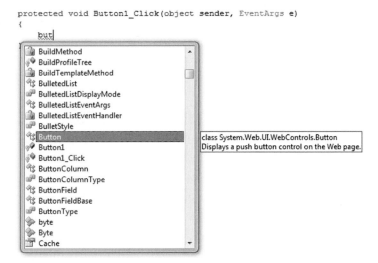

13. Double-click **Button1** and finish the code as shown below:

    Button1.Text = "Thank you";

    - Notice that you had help from IntelliSense in finding the Text property.
    - Remember that C# is case sensitive.
    - You can also press the Tab or Space key when the correct name is selected from the list. This helps in both speed and accuracy.

14. Run the program and click the button.
    - If you are unable to start the program, make sure the browser is not still running the previous program. You may have to click the **Stop Debugging** icon in the tool bar.

15. Close the browser.

PAUSE. Leave Visual Studio open to use in the next exercise.

You now have an interactive Web site. This program will be used for our next exercise where we begin using the intrinsic objects.

EXPLORING INTRINSIC OBJECTS

ASP.NET's intrinsic objects are objects that are built into the language. This section examines the intrinsic objects in ASP.NET used to control the data flow between the Web server and the client's browser.

TAKE NOTE*

Although there are technical differences between the terms *class* and *object*, most references use the terms interchangeably when the differences are not relevant to the discussion. These lessons will primarily use the term *object* to simplify the discussions and focus on the functionality of the objects.

Most of the objects available to ASP.NET will not be displayed in Web pages and are found under the namespace hierarchy. Namespaces are abstract containers used to identify groups of names that represent everything that ASP.NET needs to create Web pages. This includes classes, objects, properties, methods, and even other namespaces. The primary purpose of namespaces is to reduce ambiguity among all the names used in the .NET platform.

The System namespace contains the classes and interfaces that facilitate client server communication. The System.Web namespace includes the HttpContext, HttpRequest, HttpResponse, and HttpServerUtility classes that carry information about the contents of a page, a request for a page, the transmission of the page, and the access to server-side utilities to process the content of the page and user requests. The System.Web namespace also includes other classes for managing cookies, file transfers, and output control.

 USE INTELLISENSE TO VISUALIZE NAMESPACES

GET READY. We will continue with the same Web page created in the last exercise. You will see many of these namespaces and how they are related to each other by using IntelliSense.

1. Erase the one line of code located within your button's click-event procedure.
2. Type the letters **Sys** where the code was just removed.
   - Notice the **{} System** namespace, which is highlighted in the pop-up list box.
   - Everything in the .NET platform starts with the System namespace.
3. Press the **Tab** key followed by the **period** key, the letters **w-e-b**, and the **period** again.
   - Notice the **{} System.web** namespace, which is highlighted in the pop-up list box.
   - Everything in ASP.NET falls under the System.web namespace.
4. Continue typing **System.web.HttpContext.Current.U** and observe the names as they are displayed in the IntelliSense list box.
   - Notice that **HttpContext** is displayed in a different color from the other namespace names. This shows that HttpContext is a top-level ASP.NET object and can be used without typing the previous namespaces.
5. Clear the line and start over by typing **HttpCon** and observe the names.
   - HttpContext is so important that it can be used without the fully qualified namespace.
   - *HttpContext* provides us with information such as the current user.

6. Continue by typing **HttpContext.Current.** and observe the names.
   - A list box should pop up showing the list of the intrinsic objects.
7. Erase the line you just typed and start again with **User.** and observe the names.
   - "User" is also a top-level namespace along with HttpContext. Only a few of the many objects have this top-level status.
   - Before moving to the specific intrinsic objects, we will examine the "User" namespace.
8. Type the following code into the click event for the button:

   Button1.Text = User.Identity.Name;

9. Run the program and click the button. Then close the browser.
   - Although using the button for our output has been working, it is not designed for this purpose.
10. Place a **Label** object on the form and change the event procedure code:

    Label1.Text = User.Identity.Name;

    - The output is now written to a control made for displaying output.

PAUSE. Leave Visual Studio open to use in the next exercise.

HttpContext contains several methods but only one object, the Current object. The Current object is tied to all HTTP-specific information regarding page requests and facilitates getting or setting all HTTP requests. The HttpContext.Current object provides the other five intrinsic objects: Response, Request, Server, Application, and Session. Because HttpContext is a top-level object, these objects do not require a fully qualified namespace and can be accessed directly.

As you also learned in this exercise, IntelliSense can be used for more than code completions. You can use it to see the hierarchical structure of the namespaces used in the .NET platform.

USING HTTPCONTEXT OBJECTS

The HttpContext object is automatically constructed for every request given to an ASP.NET application and destroyed when the request has been completed. While it exists, detailed information can be retrieved and sometimes changed relating to the request.

The HttpContext objects commonly called the intrinsic objects are:
- Response
- Request
- Server
- Application
- Session

 WRITE A PAGE USING THE RESPONSE OBJECT

GET READY. This is a continuation of the previous exercise.

1. Replace the button's event procedure with the following code:

   Response.Write("Thank you");

2. Run the program and click the button. Then close the browser.
   - Notice that the text was printed directly to the page and not to the label.
   - You can also write HTML in ASP.NET Web pages.

3. Replace the button's event procedure with the following code:

```
Response.Write("<a href='http://www.msn.com'>Click Here</a>");
```

4. Run the program and click the button.
   • You should now have a working link on your Web page.

5. Click the link. Then close the browser.
   • Another commonly used method in the Response object is the action of redirect, which is actually a version of the Response.Write method.

6. Replace the button's event procedure with the following code:

```
Response.Redirect("http://www.msn.com");
```

7. Run the program and click the button. Then close the browser.
   • You should have been redirected to a third-party Web site.

PAUSE. Leave Visual Studio open to use in the next exercise.

The **Response object** is a top-level object in the HttpContext.Current object. It contains properties and methods relating to browser output. The two most popular uses of this object are to write text directly to the Web page using its Response.Write method and to redirect the browser to another page using its Response.Redirect method.

 WRITE A PAGE USING THE REQUEST OBJECT

GET READY. This is a continuation of the last exercise.

1. Replace the button's event procedure with the following code:

```
Response.Write(Request.UserHostAddress);
Response.Write("<br \\>");
Response.Write(Request.Browser.Browser);
Response.Write("<br \\>");
Response.Write(Request.FilePath);
Response.Write("<br \\>");
Response.Write(Request.HttpMethod);
```

2. Run the program and click the button. Then close the browser.
   • When the Request is used as the argument of the Write method, the Request is executed first so the Write has something to write.

PAUSE. Leave Visual Studio open to use in the next exercise.

The **Request object** is a top-level object from the HttpContext.Current object. It contains properties and methods related to the browser. This includes retrieving information about the browser, reading cookies, and passing values directly from the Web page. The Request object can also be used with the Response object to display browser information on the Web page.

 WRITE A PAGE USING THE SERVER OBJECT

GET READY. This is a continuation of the last exercise.

1. Replace the button's event procedure with the following code:

```
Response.Write("Machine Name is: "
+ Server.MachineName + "<br //>");
```

```
Response.Write("Physical Path is: "
+ Server.MapPath("") + "<br //>");
Response.Write("Time out value is: "
+ Server.ScriptTimeout + "<br //>");
```

- The plus signs are used to concatenate literal strings to the data returned from the server.

2. Run the program and click the button. Then close the browser.
   - The server name, the physical path to the page, and the value of the timeout script are the types of data the Server object fetches.

PAUSE. Leave Visual Studio open to use in the next exercise.

The ***Server object*** is a top-level object from HttpContext.Current. It contains properties and methods related to the Web server. The primary focus of the Server object is to make changes to the server.

Although we will not be changing it here, one of the Server properties that is often adjusted is ScriptTimeout. The default value is very large when debugging is turned on. When debugging is turned off, the value is automatically changed to 90 seconds.

If we were to extend it by another 10 seconds, the code would be

```
Server.ScriptTimeout = 100;
```

The Server object also has two very important methods: execute and transfer. These objects are used to tie multiple pages together on a Web site. Execute runs another page and returns to the calling page. Transfer runs another page but does not return.

The ability to gather information from the server is critical for interactive Web sites, user authentication, and general security.

 WRITE A PAGE USING THE APPLICATION OBJECT

GET READY. This is a continuation of the last exercise.

1. Replace the button's event procedure with the following code:

```
Response.Write(Application.Contents.StaticObjects
.NeverAccessed);
Response.Write("<br //>");
Response.Write(Application.Contents.StaticObjects
.IsReadOnly);
Response.Write("<br //>");
Response.Write(Application.Contents.Contents);
Response.Write("<br //>");
```

2. Run the program and click the button. Then close the browser.
   - The results show how easy it is to retrieve information about our application.

PAUSE. Leave Visual Studio open to use in the next exercise.

The ***Application object*** is a top-level object of HttpContext.Current. It contains properties and methods related to the currently running application.

WRITE A PAGE USING THE SESSION OBJECT

GET READY. This is a continuation of the last exercise.

1. Replace the button's event procedure with the following code:

```
Response.Write(Session.SessionID);
Response.Write("<br //>");
Response.Write(Session.Timeout);
Response.Write("<br //>");
Response.Write(Session.Contents);
Response.Write("<br //>");
```

2. Run the program and click the button. Then close the browser.

   • The results show how easy it is to retrieve information about our application.

PAUSE. Leave Visual Studio open to use in the next exercise.

> **CERTIFICATION READY**
> How do the ASP.NET intrinsic objects enhance a Web site and why does the HttpContext intrinsic object stand above the others?
> 1.2

The **_Session object_** is a top-level object from the HttpContext.Current object. It contains properties and methods related to individual users or instances of a Web site.

■ Understanding State Information in Web Applications

THE BOTTOM LINE

Unlike desktop applications, Web pages are often completely recreated whenever there is interaction between the Web page and the user. Previous activities are lost unless the **_state_** of the page is preserved between these interactions.

Understanding How State Is Stored and the Different Types of State

There are several ways to preserve state. Some are obsolete while others are a hybrid between the old ways and the new. Some are completely new.

All communication requires an agreed upon protocol. Something as common as a telephone conversation uses a protocol such as saying "hello" and "goodbye." Communication begins by establishing a physical connection followed by "handshaking" on an agreed method for the communication. Once connected, two-way communication can commence. Conversations continue until the connection is terminated.

Using the Internet for communication follows these same rules except that the connection is automatically terminated after a single exchange of data.

The problem with managing Web page communication is that it is based on the Internet Protocol (IP), which uses individual packets to send and retrieve data. Once a connection between the browser and server has been completed and a single message exchanged, the connection is immediately terminated. If the browser wants to follow up one message with another, the server sees it as a completely separate conversation. This can be very frustrating when writing interactive Web-based applications.

Unlike desktop applications, this stateless protocol must be addressed to maintain an ongoing dialog between the browser and server. ASP.NET includes several methods for saving the **state** of the page between requests.

Changes to a Web page, called the current state of the page, are not saved when using a stateless protocol. The browser requests a new page from the server and the server creates the new page using the original Web page. This round-trip to the server is called postback. Because Web page changes are not saved in the HTTP environment, data about changed pages must be retained on the client, on the server, or on both sides of the communication.

Cookies are client-side states in which data are saved to the hard drive or memory of the client's computer. At one time, developers had to manage these cookies directly. Although some of the new state-management strategies use cookies, the need to manage them directly has all but vanished with ASP.NET.

The query string technique places data at the end of the page URL for the server to use when it creates new pages. Since the user can easily see this data in the browser's address bar, the query string will not be used in our lessons.

Hidden elements on a Web page, often called hidden fields, are also created to preserve data. It is very common to see the <div> element used for hiding data on the form. It has an attribute named type that can be set to "hidden" to prevent the browser from displaying any data placed between the <div> tags. Since the data becomes part of the form, the server can use it to help create new pages related to the current page.

Cookies, query strings, and hidden elements can all be managed directly. However, ASP.NET uses higher-level strategies that are more easily managed by the Web developer. One of these techniques is just to store an ID number of the page on the client side and store the data for this number on the server. This ties the page to the data and hides the data from the user. ASP.NET can also pass data between pages and even between applications without requiring the programmer to manipulate cookies, query strings, or hidden fields.

CHOOSING SESSION STATE

Session state is a data repository for the user. It is a server-side technique that uses a session ID number stored on the server and assigned to the browser in the form of a cookie.

The Session object is used for managing session state. This object allows the page to store and retrieve values as the user navigates through ASP.NET pages. Session state retains the identity of the browser during multiple requests, at least for a limited time.

Although cookies are considered a server-side technique, they are used to save the unique session ID of the browser. Unlike cookie management in the past, cookies used in session state are saved in the client's memory rather than on the hard drive. If the "do-not-use-cookies" setting in the browser is set, session state can use query strings in the place of cookies but the data will be exposed in the URL.

We can easily access the session ID number using our Visual Web Developer application.

 CREATE A WEB PAGE THAT USES SESSION STATE

GET READY. This is a continuation of the last exercise.

1. Replace the button's event procedure with the following code:

   ```
   Response.Write(Session.SessionID);
   ```

2. Run the program and click the button several times. Then close the browser.
   - Notice that the number changes on every click of the button. This means that a new session is created on every page request.

- The Session object allows us to capture a SessionID so that every button click will be processed within a single session. This will allow us to save any needed data between requests.
- We can observe session state by making up a session name and assigning it the data we want to preserve.

3. Replace the button's event procedure with the following code:

```
Response.Write(Session.SessionID);
Session["MadeUpName"] = "Some value";
Response.Write(Session["MadeUpName"]);
```

- The first line generates the session ID on the first click.
- The ID is then preserved by assigning it a name and a value.
- The third line shows us that the value "Some value" is preserved under the name "MadeUpName" on round trips to the server.

4. Run the program and click the button several times. Then close the browser.

- Notice that neither the SessionID nor the MadeUpName value changed during the round-trips. The data was saved as though it was a variable in a desktop application.
- Note that session state values are not shared with other users.
- There are a few other Session object properties and methods that can be used to control a Session, including:
  - **Session.Abandon()**
    - Forces an end to the session
  - **Session.Clear()**
    - Clears session information without ending the session
  - **Session.RemoveAll()**
    - Same action as the Clear method
  - **Session.Timeout**
    - Views or sets the number of minutes before a session times out when the browser goes idle
- Problems can arise if an attempt is made to use a session variable that has not been assigned a value. We will now address this with a solution.

5. Comment the button's event procedure with the following code and add the new line:

```
//Response.Write(Session.SessionID);
//Session["MadeUpName"] = "Some value";
//Response.Write(Session["MadeUpName"]);
Response.Write(Session["MadeUpName"] == null);
```

6. Run the program and click the button. Then close the browser.

- Testing the session variable against null verifies that the variable has not been assigned and should not be read.

7. Un-comment the three lines of code and re-run the program.

PAUSE. Leave Visual Studio open to use in the next exercise.

Session state is very common in Web pages to save the data for individual users. The Web developer only needs a few properties and methods to control the data for session variables along with the technique for detecting unused variables.

CHOOSING APPLICATION STATE

Application state is a data repository for the application. Application state is a server-side technique that uses the Web server to store data.

Unlike session state, where session data is saved for the user, application state saves data for everyone using the application. Where session state is temporary and can time out, application state is always available and never times out. Since multiple users have access to the same data, locks have to be placed on the data to keep two or more users from attempting to change the same data at the same time. The following code segment demonstrates how application state locks out other users, modifies the data, and then unlocks the data allowing access to other viewers.

We are unable to test this code because doing so would require another user to try to access the data at the same time we are making changes. Even with multiple users, the timing would make it very difficult to demonstrate.

```
Application.Lock();
Application["MadeUpName"] = "Some value";
Application.UnLock();
```

Like session state, this is considered a server-state technique where cookies or query strings are used to save the unique session ID of the browser.

CHOOSING VIEW STATE

View state is a data repository for Web form controls. View state is a client-side technique. Every control has a Boolean property that, when turned on, saves the state of the control on the Web page.

View state has a very different purpose from the session and application states. Rather than saving user-created values, view state is designed to save the state of the form and all its controls between postbacks automatically.

View state is a client-side technique because it uses hidden elements within the page to store state data rather than the server. The browser, of course, does not display the data placed into these elements.

If a user desires to view the data, a right-click on the browser will pop up a menu with a "View Source" option that opens a new window displaying the HTML. This is the server-generated code for displaying the page on the browser. This source code reveals the hidden elements along with all other data, which is typically unreadable because it is Base64 encoded.

Although this encoded data looks encrypted, it is not. It can easily be converted into its original form. A common mistake is to assume that the data is secure.

Every control placed on the form has the EnableViewState property. When EnableViewState is set True, it is turned on and when it is set to False, it is turned off. Since all data for all the controls are saved in the page, the page can get very large. It is wise to address the EnableViewSate property for all your controls so the ones not needing to save data can be turned off.

We will now use the EnableViewState property and observe the page when toggling it between True and False.

 ### CREATE A WEB PAGE THAT USES VIEW STATE

GET READY. This is a continuation of the last exercise.

1. Place a Label control on the form from the Toolbox.
2. Double-click the button and replace the button's event procedure with the following code:

```
Label1.Text = Label1.Text + " More";
```

3. Run the program and click the button several times. Then close the browser.

- With the assumption that the Label.Text property was set to **Label** when the page was initialized, each time the button control is clicked, the word "More" is appended to the existing string. If the EnableViewState for the Label control is set to True, the text in Label1.Text continues to grow. However, if EnableViewState is set to False, the Text property will be empty each time and will be set to just the phrase "More."

4. Go to **Design** view, single-click the **Label**, go to the Properties window, and change EnableViewState to **False**.

5. Run the program and click the button several times. Then close the browser. The data for the label is now lost between trips to the server.

6. Change the label's EnableViewState back to **True**. Since we do not need to save data for the button, view state will be turned off.

7. Change the button's EnableViewState to **False**.

8. Run the program and click the button several times. Then close the browser. The program runs as it did before, even when we chose not to save its data between postbacks.

PAUSE. You may now close Visual Studio.

Remember to always set EnableViewState to False for all controls on the form whose data need not be saved between postbacks. This prevents the pages from becoming unnecessarily large.

UNDERSTANDING CONTROL STATE

Control state is a data repository for Web form controls. Control state is a client-side technique. Every control automatically saves the state of the control on the Web page.

Control state is much like view state. However, unlike view state, control state cannot be disabled. Control state stores the essential data and properties of each control that must be available on postback so that the control is able to function.

Control state is a client-side technique because it uses hidden elements in the Web page. ASP.NET pages store control state data in the same hidden element used to store view state information. Whether view state is disabled or its state is managed with session state, the control state data moves with the page between the client and the server within the page.

> **CERTIFICATION READY**
> How does state enhance a Web site and how do the types of state differ?
> 1.3

SKILL SUMMARY

IN THIS LESSON, YOU LEARNED TO:

- Write a Web page using strict XHTML syntax.
- Validate your HTML for XHTML syntax.
- Embed an image using XHTML.
- Write inline, internal, and external CSS.
- Write CSS using Layout, ID, and Class selectors.
- Write HTML for a table that only uses CSS for its borders.
- Lay out a Web page using the division element and CSS.
- Use Microsoft Visual Web Developer to create a Web page.
- Use the Intrinsic objects of HttpContext.

- Use the Response object to write to the page.
- Use the Request object to retrieve browser information from the server.
- Use the Server object to retrieve server information from the server.
- Use the Application object to retrieve application information from the server.
- Use the Session object to retrieve session information from the server.
- Use session state to store values on the server for the user.
- Use application state to store values on the server for all users of the application.
- Use view state to optionally save the state of the controls on the client.
- Use control state to save essential values of the controls automatically.

■ Knowledge Assessment

Multiple Choice

Circle the letter or letters that correspond to the best answer or answers.

1. What is the markup language used exclusively to provide formatting and alter the appearance of Web page elements?
   a. ASP.NET
   b. CSS
   c. XHTML
   d. XML

2. What attribute that must be present for strict XHTML compliance is often missing when images are placed on a Web page?
   a. img
   b. src
   c. alt
   d. p

3. Which of the simple CSS selectors requires no special syntax?
   a. Class selector
   b. ID selector
   c. Internal style sheet
   d. Type selector

4. What is the generally accepted technique for page layout that also passes strict XHTML validation?
   a. CSS
   b. Tables
   c. Frames
   d. Partitions

5. What is the term used to describe an attribute of an object?
   a. Control
   b. Event
   c. Method
   d. Property

6. Which of the following is NOT a view in Visual Web Developer?
   a. Source
   b. Design
   c. Split
   d. Code-behind

7. Which of the following statements will redirect the current page to another URL?
   a. `Response("http://www.msn.com");`
   b. `Response.Write("http://www.msn.com");`
   c. `Response.Redirect("http://www.msn.com");`
   d. All of the above

8. Which of the following is NOT a top-level HttpContext.Current object?
   a. Client
   b. Server
   c. Response
   d. Application

9. What is the term used for the process of passing data from a Web page back to the server for processing and then back again to the browser?
   a. Passback
   b. Postback
   c. Request.Write
   d. Response.Write

10. What is the name of the client-side state where values and properties of the controls on the Web page are stored but should be turned off if not needed?
    a. Session
    b. Application
    c. View
    d. Control

Fill in the Blank

Complete the following sentences by writing the correct word or words in the blanks provided.

1. XHTML is the markup language created by forcing HTML to follow the syntax rules of the _____ markup language.

2. A validated XHTML document is considered _____ _____.

3. A validated XHTML document has been checked for proper _____.

4. The _____ attribute of the <img> tag is used to locate the file for embedding an image into a Web page.

5. A _____ Style Sheet is located within the same document as the HTML and uses the <style> tag rather than the style attribute.

6. The CSS Class selector uses the _____ symbol to locate the selected elements.

7. The _____ element should be limited to organizing data, not laying out Web pages.

8. The _____ object is one of the intrinsic objects and is used for supplying browser information to the program.

9. _____ state is commonly used to save data for individual users between postbacks.

10. _____ state can be set to save Web form data between postbacks.

■ Competency Assessment

Scenario 1-1: Creating a New Web Site

Your company wishes to create a new Web site for a new product it is planning to release in the near future. Although you don't have any of the design specifications for the Web site, you do know that it is company policy to develop all new Web sites using ASP.NET and C#. Using Visual Web Developer, create the new Web site as an empty site, add a Web form (new item), and save the project as "NewWidget01."

Scenario 1-2: Creating and Applying an External Cascading Style Sheet

You have been given the assignment to design and create a style standard for all company Web pages. On paper, develop a design standard, specifying the font, font size, appearance, and alignment for the top three levels of headers and the body text to be used by all sites. Enter the design standard into a CSS file named Standard.css for use by the company's Web developers.

■ Proficiency Assessment

Scenario 1-3: Displaying State Data

You have been asked to demonstrate the CSS styles you've developed (in Scenario 1-2) and apply them to a new Web page on which you are to add text boxes for a person's contact information, check boxes for the viewer's age group, and radio buttons indicating how long they have worked at the company. When the viewer clicks the submit button, the data is to be passed to a verification page for the viewer to approve. After the viewer clicks an approve button, the site is to return to the first page with all of the entries blanked out.

Scenario 1-4: Turning Off View State

You just finished the first of 36 ASP.NET Web pages for your company's new Web site. When you presented it to the IT department, it was immediately rejected because your pages will exceed the bandwidth available to the company. You are now instructed to prove that you can reduce the page size without changing any functionality.

Write an ASP.NET Web page that demonstrates the size reduction of your page when turning off unnecessary view state settings. Your demo page will use three input boxes for input and a submission button for each. A label for each input will echo the text placed into the associated text box.

You will report the percentage of the page size improvement after turning off unnecessary view state properties.

✳ Workplace Ready

Transforming a Static Page to a Dynamic Page

When browsing through the Web pages of professional sites for your shopping needs, you will be amazed at how dynamic they are compared to most amateur sites. Basic HTML skills will only enable you to create the static amateur sites in which the visitor's only control is scrolling down through the text and images. There may be a button or link to click, but that normally sends the visitor to another part of the page, to another page on the site, or to a completely different site.

Suppose your company has such a site on its intranet that only the local employees can use. If you were to improve the site and keep the same content, you would want to start by transforming it to the latest standards via XHTML and CSS. You may even want to change the layout from what is most likely a table to the CSS and Div technique.

This, however, won't make the page dynamic. This usually takes a redesign followed by a complete rewrite. If this is the case, you're in luck. Using the Web form and code-behind of Visual Web Developer can make building dynamic Web pages a snap, provided that you've completed your lessons.

Creating an Interactive Web Page

LESSON SKILL MATRIX

Skills/Concepts	MTA Exam Objective	MTA Exam Objective Number
Understanding Events and Control Page Flow	Understand events and control page flow	1.4
Understanding Controls	Understand controls	1.5
Understanding Configuration Files	Understand configuration files	1.6

KEY TERMS

AutoEventWireup

events

global.asax

HTML controls

IsPostBack property

page event

page life cycle

Page_Load

Postback property

PreviousPage

Response.Redirect

Server controls

Server.Transfer

User controls

Validation controls

ViewState object

web.config

Karen is now working with the XHTML standards, using CSS for presentation, and working with the intrinsic objects. Her Web pages are beginning to have the look and feel of a desktop application. However, she is finding it difficult to work with global variables because they are overwritten every time a page is changed, even by something as simple as a button press. She is also having trouble sending data to other pages on her site. After this lesson, she will know how to easily overcome all of these obstacles. She will also have a better understanding of what a page has to do whenever the user clicks a button.

■ Understanding Events and Control Page Flow

 THE BOTTOM LINE

An **event** occurs when something happens that an object or Web control can sense, like someone clicking a button. We programmed the click event of the button in Lesson 1. As a Web page moves through its stages, especially when it is being processed by the server, events are triggered that allow this page flow to be controlled.

Setting AutoEventWireup

AutoEventWireup ties events to the code-behind of Visual Web Developer, C#, and Visual Basic (VB) to respond to the AutoEventWireup differently.

The page life cycle begins when a Web page is requested from the server. This normally happens when the user alters the contents displayed by the browser. At the other end of the life cycle, the page is closed by the browser or terminated prematurely. In order to capture the many events the browser triggers during its life cycle, it needs to monitor the page as it moves through all of its stages from the request, through processing, display, and destruction.

In order to monitor a Web page's life cycle events, an attribute needs to be set at the beginning of a program to tie the page's events to the program. This attribute is appropriately called AutoEventWireup because it automatically wires up the page events to the programming language.

⊙ **SET AUTOEVENTWIREUP IN C#**

GET READY. We will be using Microsoft Visual Web Developer 2008 Express Edition in our lessons. To set AutoEventWireup in C#, complete these steps:

1. Open Visual Web Developer 2008 (any edition).
2. Create a new ASP.NET Web site (not Project) using C#.
   - Once you arrive at the editing window, you should be at the Source view.
3. Examine the top line of code:

   `<%@ Page Language="C#" AutoEventWireup="`*true*`"`

   `CodeFile="Default.aspx.cs" Inherits="_Default" %>`

   - At the top of every ASP.NET page is a @Page directive. This is where the AutoEventWireup attribute is set. Notice that it also tells the page what programming language the page is using and the name of the code-behind file. The Inherits attribute specifies a code-behind class for the page to inherit. Although many more page directive attributes are available, the only one we are going to be concerned about in this exercise is the AutoEventWireup.
   - Notice that it is set to true by default. (You should never have to change this.)
4. Click the **Design** tab at the bottom of the code window.
5. Move your mouse pointer below the div element on the form and double-click the form.
6. Type in the code for the Page_Load event procedure as shown below:

   ```
   protected void Page_Load(object sender,
   EventArgs e)
   {
       Response.Write("Page is Loaded");
   }
   ```

 REF

See Lesson 1 for information on starting a new Web site.

See Lesson 1 for information on starting the debugger.

The *Page_Load* event procedure executes every time the page is loaded into the browser.

7. Run your program.
   - Remember to allow debugging when the dialog box appears the first time you run a program.
   - Your browser should display the "Page is Loaded" message.
8. Close the browser.
9. Click the **Default.aspx** tab at the top of the code window.
10. Click the **Source** tab at the bottom of the Design window.
11. Turn off AutoEventWireup by setting it to false.

    ```
    <%@ Page Language="C#" AutoEventWireup="false"
    CodeFile="Default.aspx.cs" Inherits="_Default" %>
    ```

12. Run your program.
    - Notice that you no longer have the text displayed on the Web page.
    - Without AutoEventWireup, the page events are not fired because the events are no longer wired to the code-behind event procedures.
13. Close the browser.

PAUSE. Close Visual Web Developer, but keep it available for the next exercise.

As you have seen, AutoEventWireup should always be on when working with C#. Otherwise, none of your event procedures will run.

 SET AUTOEVENTWIREUP IN VISUAL BASIC

See Lesson 1 for information on starting a new Web site.

GET READY. We will be using Microsoft Visual Web Developer 2008 Express Edition in our lessons. To set AutoEventWireup in Visual Basic, complete these steps:

1. Open Visual Web Developer 2008 (any edition).
2. Create a new ASP.NET Web site, but this time select **Visual Basic** as your language.
   - Once you arrive at the editing window, you should be at the Source view.
3. Examine the top line of code.

   ```
   <%@ Page Language="VB" AutoEventWireup="false"
   CodeFile="Default.aspx.vb" Inherits="_Default" %>
   ```

   - Notice that this time it is set to false by default.
4. Click the **Design** tab at the bottom of the code window.
5. Move your mouse pointer below the div element on the form and double-click the form.
   - Notice that the syntax is a little different from C#.
6. Type in the following code for the Page_Load event procedure:

   ```
   Protected Sub Page_Load(ByVal sender As Object,
   ByVal e As System.EventArgs) Handles Me.Load
       Response.Write("Page is Loaded")
   End Sub
   ```

   - The "Me" part of the handle is the alias used for the current form where "Load" is the method of the form that triggers the event procedure.
7. Run your program.
   Remember to allow debugging when the dialog box appears the first time you run a program.
   - Your browser should display the "Page is Loaded" message.

See Lesson 1 for information on starting the debugger.

8. Close the browser.

9. Click the **Default.aspx** tab at the top of the code window.

10. Click the **Source** tab at the bottom of the Design window.

11. Turn off AutoEventWireup by setting it to **true**.

    ```
    <%@ Page Language="VB" AutoEventWireup="true"
    CodeFile="Default.aspx.vb" Inherits="_Default" %>
    ```

12. Run your program.
    - Notice that you still have "Page is Loaded" on the Web page.
    - With or without AutoEventWireup in Visual Basic, the page events still fired because the events are not wired to the code-behind event procedures as they are in C#.

PAUSE. Keep your application open for the next exercise.

As you have seen, AutoEventWireup can be turned on or off with Visual Basic.

UNDERSTANDING VISUAL BASIC'S ALTERNATIVE TO AUTOEVENTWIREUP

Visual Basic is unable to use all the benefits of AutoEventWireup, so this feature should be turned off. In its place, Visual Basic uses an event handler to "wire up" the events.

Visual Basic's event handler does more than handle events. It works with IntelliSense to help Visual Basic developers write code by giving them a list of events to choose from rather than forcing them to recall their names. Remember, the event handler does not work with C#.

 USE VISUAL BASIC'S ALTERNATIVE TO AUTOEVENTWIREUP

GET READY. Let's continue with our Visual Basic program in Microsoft Visual Web Developer by performing these actions:

1. Go back to the program from the previous exercise.
   - This program should be using Visual Basic for the code-behind language.
   - It should currently have the AutoEventWireup set to true in the Source view.
   - The Page_Load event procedure should write a message to the Web page.

2. Press the **Default.aspx.vb** tab to go to the code-behind window and place your cursor on the only line of code in the event procedure.
   - You should see two lightning bolts at the top of the window, as shown in Figure 2-1. This is the Class Name drop-down list box, which can be seen by holding the mouse over it long enough for the tooltips pop-up to appear.

Figure 2-1

Visual Basic shows "wired-up" events to IntelliSense

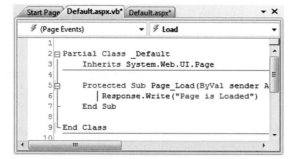

3. Open the **Method Name** drop-down list box located to the right of the Class Name drop-down list box.

   • This list shows all the events related to the Web page, as shown in Figure 2-2.

Figure 2-2

IntelliSense lists all the available Page events

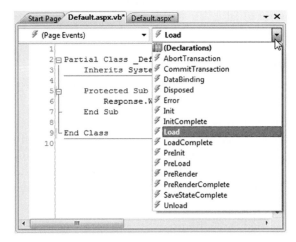

4. Go to **Source** view and change the AutoEventWireup to **false**.

   ```
   <%@ Page Language="VB" AutoEventWireup="false"
   CodeFile="Default.aspx.vb" Inherits="_Default" %>
   ```

   • This is the default setting for Visual Basic and will not be changed again.

5. Go back to the code-behind window and place the cursor on the event procedure code, as shown in Figure 2-1.

6. Click on the **Method Name** drop-down list box on the right, as shown in Figure 2-2.

   • Notice that AutoEventWireup is not responsible for providing this list of events.

7. Erase the event handler located at the end of the event procedure header:

   ```
   "Handles Me.Load"
   Protected Sub Page_Load(ByVal sender As Object,
   ByVal e As System.EventArgs)
       Response.Write("Page is Loaded")
   End Sub
   ```

8. Place the cursor on the event procedure code similar to what is shown in Figure 2-1.

   • Notice that in Figure 2-1 we had the lightning bolts, but now our Integrated Development Environment (IDE) shows something completely different.

9. Click on the **Method Name** drop-down list box that now says Page_Load.

   • Notice that the available events are no longer shown. See Figure 2-3.

Figure 2-3

Visual Basic's event handler is needed to show the available events

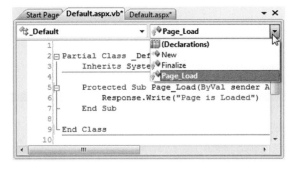

PAUSE. Keep your application open for the next exercise.

Because C# does not provide us with this event handler, the events must be typed manually. C# must also have AutoEventWireup set to true because this is the only way it can see events. Because Visual Basic uses event handlers instead of AutoEventWireup, the AutoEventWireup setting should be set to false.

UNDERSTANDING PAGE EVENTS

A *page event* is an alert that something is different about the Web page. We catch these events with our code-behind so we can write code for them.

A page life cycle is defined as the time the page request is given until the page is destroyed. Between these times, a page must go through an orderly series of stages. As the server processes HTML during the page-creation stages, it processes any additional code that may have been embedded into the HTML. ASP.NET sends this additional code in the form of a file containing our code-behind. After processing the HTML and code-behind, the Web page is sent back to the browser.

Events can be triggered throughout the life of a Web page, making it possible to write code at any of the triggered stages. This includes pages that have not yet been created. Code for these pages would be aimed at system and application needs rather than simply writing something to the page. Although most of the available events are seldom used in code, a few of them are used regularly to monitor and control the flow of Web pages.

We will be using Visual Basic to determine the firing order of the page events. Since we cannot write to the page at some stages, no code will be written within the body of the event procedures. However, we can place breakpoints at the top of each one to pause the program. By observing the sequence of the event procedures, we will see the ordered sequence of the page's life cycle.

 MONITOR PAGE EVENTS

GET READY. We will continue with our Visual Basic program in Microsoft Visual Web Developer.

1. Go back to the program from the previous exercise.
   - It should be using Visual Basic for the code-behind language.
   - It should have the AutoEventWireup set to false in the Source view.
   - The Page_Load event procedure should write a message to the Web page.
2. Place the **Handles Me.Load** back where it belongs at the end of the Page_Load header.
3. Set the breakpoint where the program will pause by clicking the gray area to the far left of the event procedure header, as shown in Figure 2-4.
   - This will create a large red dot telling the program to pause at the indicated line before executing the code.

Figure 2-4

A breakpoint is set using Visual Basics debugger

4. Run the program.

5. If the browser blocks your code-behind view, minimize it.

- Your program should be paused at the breakpoint. Notice that the line changed from red to yellow and a yellow arrow now appears over the red breakpoint button (Figure 2-5).

Figure 2-5

The breakpoint pauses the program before the event procedure has been executed

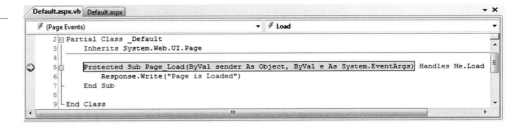

6. Move your mouse pointer over the triangular button in the toolbar that has been used to start your programs.

- Notice that it changed from "Start Debugging" to "Continue."

7. Click the triangular button to continue.

 **ANOTHER WAY**   You can also continue running your page by using the Debug -> Continue menu item (F5).

- The breakpoint should return to normal and the Web page should be up as normal.

8. Either close the browser or click the **Stop Debugging** button on the tool bar (square icon).

 **ANOTHER WAY**   You can also continue running your page by using the Debug -> Stop Debugging menu item (Shift + F5).

- We will be placing all the page events in our code and setting breakpoints. This will enable us to see which events are triggered and in what order.

9. Place the cursor within the body of the event procedure (in front of the only line of code).

10. Click on the **Method Name** drop-down list box arrow, to the right of "Load" at the top right corner of the code-behind editing window.

- You should now have the same list as we had in Figure 2-2.

11. Click the first event on the list, **Abort Transaction,** to create an event procedure for it.

12. Repeat, clicking on every item in the list.

- Each item in the drop-down list box that has been clicked will place the shell of an event procedure in your code-behind window and will be shown in bold text in the drop-down list box.

- If you click on a list item more than once (in bold text), the cursor will be moved to an existing procedure rather than creating duplicates.

13. Place breakpoints at each event procedure until all the items in the list box become bold.

14. Run the program and minimize the browser if necessary to see the code-behind window.
    - A breakpoint line should now be highlighted in yellow, **Page_PreInit**.

15. Press the **Continue** button repeatedly until all the events fire and the browser displays the message.
    - Notice the firing order.
    - You should have also noticed that not all the available events fired. This is normal because certain events did not take place in this particular page life cycle. For example, the Error event did not fire because we did not have an error.

16. Close the browser.

PAUSE. Keep your application open for the next exercise.

The events that fired should have done so in the order below.

- **PreInit:** This is where a test can be made to see if this is a postback page.
- **Init:** Buttons, labels, or the form itself, called controls, can have their properties read or initialized.
- **InitComplete:** Changes to the view state can be made here.
- **PreLoad:** Not a commonly used event.
- **Load:** This too can be used for setting control properties. It is also used for database connections.
- **LoadComplete:** Some controls need to be placed on the form before changes to their properties will take effect or before their methods can be run. This is where these changes should take place.
- **PreRender:** This is the last stage before ASP.NET starts converting everything into a Web page. Make any final changes here.
- **PreRenderComplete:** This is a special event for binding data to controls.
- **SaveStateComplete:** The view and control states have been saved at this stage. Placing code here will affect this page, but these changes will not be used for the next postback.
- **Unload:** This event fires for each control found on the page. Then, the unload event will fire for the page itself. This is commonly used for cleanup methods such as closing files and database connections. This is also where new pages can be called to pop up.

Understanding the order and the activities of these page events can be critical in choosing the right event for the right job.

CERTIFICATION READY
How can page events help make your Web pages more dynamic?
1.4

UNDERSTANDING APPLICATION EVENTS

An application has a life cycle similar to the page life cycle where a series of phases trigger events. These events are related to all the pages of the entire application rather than just the current page. Reading and writing values here can influence all users running the application.

The following is a list of application events related to handling requests. They are listed in the same order in which they trigger.

- **BeginRequest:** A request has been received.
- **AuthenticateRequest:** Identity of the user has been established.
- **DefaultAuthentication:** Ensures authentication has occurred.

- **AuthorizeRequest:** User authorization has been verified.
- **ResolveRequestCache**: Authorization has been verified to use the cache.
- **AcquireRequestState**: Current state has been acquired.
- **PreRequestHandlerExecute:** Event handling is about to start.
- **PostRequestHandlerExecute:** Event handling is finished.
- **ReleaseRequestState**: Requests for state have been saved.
- **UpdateRequestCache**: Cache is ready for subsequent requests.
- **EndRequest:** The request has been processed.

The most commonly programmed application events are listed below.

- **Application_Start:** This is triggered when the Web application is first launched. Since it is only fired once in the lifetime of the application, it is an ideal place to initialize variables that will be used throughout the life of the running site.
- **Application_End:** This is triggered just before the application is terminated. Typical coding in this event procedure is to free application-level resources or save logging information.
- **Application_Error:** This, of course, triggers when an error occurs on the site. This should not be triggered often because application code should be catching most errors and handling them in a manner that will keep the pages running smoothly. However, this is a catch-all event to handle those missed errors.
- **Application_LogRequest:** This is triggered only when a request has been made to the application; it is used for custom logging.

UNDERSTANDING SESSION EVENTS

A session has a life cycle similar to the page life cycle where a series of phases triggers events. These events are related to individual browser sessions rather than the entire application. Reading and writing values here only applies to each user individually.

The session life cycle only generates two events, OnStart and OnEnd. These events obviously trigger when a user starts a new session and when a user ends a session.

The OnStart event is triggered when a user, who currently does not have a session open already, opens a page on the site. Since this is user-centric, code can be placed here for the user, such as opening a shopping cart.

The OnEnd event is triggered when the session is terminated, which is usually on session timeout. This is where any saved user data is lost. Cleanup code is typically placed in this event procedure.

USING GLOBAL.ASAX WITH APPLICATION AND SESSION EVENTS

The events in the application and session stages of a Web page's life cycle occur only on the Web server. The coding for server-side events is programmed in a specific code file—global. asax.

Global.asax is an optional file on the server that, if present, contains program code for handling session and application events. These server-side events are only processed from the Global.aspx file and nothing from this file is ever passed to the client's browser.

The global.asax code snippet that follows uses both types of server-side events, Session and Application. It retrieves the number of user sessions currently using the Web application with inline script rather than code-behind.

The language attribute is set to "C#," but it could just as easily have been set to "VB" by changing the language attribute.

```
<script language="C#" runat="server">
public void Application_OnStart()
{
  Application["CurrentUsers"] = 0;
}
public void Session_OnStart()
{
  Application.Lock();
  Application["CurrentUsers "] =
  (int)Application["CurrentUsers "] + 1;
  Application.UnLock();
}
public void Session_OnEnd()
{
  Application.Lock();
  Application["CurrentUsers "] =
  (int)Application["CurrentUsers"] - 1;
  Application.UnLock();
}
</script>
```

In the above code, when the Application stage of a Web page begins, the variable "CurrentUsers" is initialized to zero. Then when the Session stage begins, the number of current users of the application is incremented by one. When the session is closed, the current user count for the application is decreased by one. Since the Application and Session stages occur at the server, these methods can only be invoked at the server.

Remember that the code for both the Application and Session events is not written in code-behind and that the events in the Session and Application stages of a Web page's lifecycle occur only on the Web server.

UNDERSTANDING CONTROL EVENTS

A control's life cycle is similar to the page life cycle where it is re-created along with the page. In addition to the events that can be triggered in this creation life cycle, the events for controls can also be triggered by user activities on the control.

 USE CONTROL EVENTS

GET READY. We will continue with our Visual Basic program in Visual Web Developer.

1. Go back to the program of the previous exercise.
   - It should be using Visual Basic for the code-behind language.
   - Creating a new Web site will also work with this exercise.
2. For the previous code, erase all your event procedures in the code-behind window.
   - You must leave the class structure along with the inherited namespace.

   ```
   Partial Class _Default
      Inherits System.Web.UI.Page
   End Class
   ```

TAKE NOTE*

You can go directly to the code-behind window by clicking the "View Code" icon in the Solution Explorer window.

3. Go to the Design view of the form by pressing the **Default** tab.

 **ANOTHER WAY** You can also click on the "View Designer" icon in the Solution Explorer window to go directly to the Design view of the form.

4. Single-click the **div** area found at the top of the form.
   - This should highlight the div tab.
   - The cursor should be blinking within the div area.
5. Double-click the **Label** control in the Standard category of the Toolbox.
   - You should now have a label control within the div area.
6. Single-click the area under the div area.
   - The cursor should now be blinking below the div area.
7. Double-click the **Button** control in the Standard category of the Toolbox.
   - This should have placed the button below the Label control.
8. Double-click the **Button** control on the form.
   - The cursor should be blinking within the body of the event procedure between "Protected Sub" and "End Sub."
   - Notice that the default event for the button is "Click," as shown in the Method Name drop-down list box with the lightning bolt at the top right corner of the editing window.
9. Click to the right of the Method Name drop-down list box with the lightning bolt to see the available events for the Button control.
   - Notice that it has many of the same events as the page events. In fact, the only ones that differ are Click and Command. The command event is slightly different because of the information it holds between the parentheses. Otherwise, they are the same; both will fire when the button is pressed. Coding both event procedures, Click and Command, will result in both firing when the button is clicked.
10. Go back to the form and double-click the Label control. You may have to click on the blank form area before the button appears on the form.
    - You should have arrived back at the code-behind window for the Button's click, not the Label control. This is because there are no unique events for the label in ASP.NET. The Label control is intended to be read only and not clicked.

CERTIFICATION READY
What are the similarities and differences among page, application, session, and control events?
1.4

PAUSE. Close Visual Web Developer.

Many controls have events that are designed to be used for that control. Others, like the Label control, are not designed to respond to events. However, this does not prevent event-enabled controls from changing the properties of other controls that have no events of their own. For example, the click event of a button has the ability to place text on the label by altering the label's Text property.

UNDERSTANDING POSTBACK

In a desktop application, the page only has to be loaded once for the user to work with it. A dynamic Web page is completely reloaded every time the server processes it. The *Postback* property of the Web page allows the developer to separate code that needs to be run only when the page is first loaded from the pages that have been re-created from user interaction since the page was first loaded.

Understanding the differences between how the load event works in Web-based applications and in desktop applications is critical. The load event for a desktop application, which is typically reserved for initialization code, fires just once when the desktop form is first used. In a Web page, the load event is triggered on every round-trip to the server. If not controlled, the Web page load event could cause the Web page to continually initialize each time data or content is requested from the server.

The *IsPostBack* property of the *ViewState object* is designed to solve this problem by sensing whether a page has had a previous round-trip to the server. It can then bypass the initialization of the Web page on all but the first page load event.

 USE THE ISPOSTBACK PAGE PROPERTY

GET READY. We will restart Microsoft Visual Web Developer but use C# instead of Visual Basic.

1. Open Visual Web Developer 2008 (any edition).
2. Create a new ASP.NET Web Site using C#.
3. Click the **Design** tab at the bottom of the page to go to the Web form.
4. Place a label and a button on the form as you did in the previous exercise with Visual Basic.
   - The label should be above the button.
5. Double-click on the form below the Button.
   - Make sure you do not accidentally double-click the Button or Label controls or you will enter the code-behind for these controls rather than the form's Page_Load event.
   - You should now be in the code-behind window and ready to write the Page_Load event procedure.
6. Write the following code for the Page_Load event.:

```
if (!IsPostBack)
{
    Label1.Text = "Initial page load.";
}
else
{
    Label1.Text = "The page is now a PostBack.";
}
```

   - Remember to stay within the inner set of curly braces.
7. Run the program.
   - Remember to agree to use the debugger when it asks about modifying the web.config file.
   - The first message should show on the label because IsPostBack is returned false. The ! is used for "not" in C#, so the condition of the "if" statement is "not False," which is equivalent to "True."
8. Click the button.
   - Since there was activity on the form (the button press), the page was sent to the browser to be re-created. This is called a postback. IsPostBack is not true, so the program's logic is read as "not True" and displays the second message.
9. Close the browser.

PAUSE. Keep Visual Web Developer open for the next exercise.

Having this programming area available in dynamic Web pages is critical in many applications. This prevents the page from processing the same code on every postback. Initialized properties and variables set in the "!IsPostBack" area will not be reinitialized on postbacks.

Navigating between Pages

In addition to the tools we have used so far, the primary tools available that allow a program to navigate and pass data between Web pages are Response.Redirect, Server.Transfer, and cross-page posting.

 USE RESPONSE.REDIRECT

GET READY. We will continue with our C# program in Visual Web Developer.

1. Go back to the program in the previous exercise.
   • If starting over, you will need to do the previous exercise before continuing.
2. Add another page to the site by using **File -> New File...** Ctrl + N from the menu.

 You can also add a new page by clicking the Add New Item icon on the toolbar or by right-clicking the drive/path in the Solution Explorer window and selecting Add New Item from the pop-up menu.

   • This will open the Add New Item dialog box.
3. Check the default template, name, and language (Web Form, Default2.aspx, and Visual C#), then press the **Add** button.
4. Place a label and a button on the new form as you have done previously.
   • Both forms should now have a Label and Button control.
5. Create a Page_Load event on the second form and insert the following code within it:

   Response.Write("This is the second page.");

6. Test the second page by running the debugger from the Design or code-behind window while still in the second page.
   • The Web page should have "This is the second page." written to it automatically when it loads.
7. Close the browser.
8. Insert the following code in the Button1_Click event method of the first page, Default.aspx:

   Response.Redirect("Default2.aspx");

   • This will call the second form when the button is clicked.
9. Run the debugger from the first form, Default.aspx, and click on the **Button** control.
   • You should have been directed to the second page where the message was written.
   • The controls on the two pages of our sample program have the same names and yet they are completely independent of each other. Because the pages are independent, variables with the same names are also allowed within each page. One way to share a common variable, however, is by using a session state variable.

- View state cannot be used for sharing variables between pages because data is saved on the current page (client side), whereas session state saves our data on the server (server side). This enables us to use the same data for any of the pages during our session.

10. Close the browser.

11. Insert the following line of code into the Button1_Click event procedure of the first page, Default.aspx. This code must be placed before the code that sends us to the second page:

```
Session["X"] = "Welcome from the first page!";
```

- If you do not place this line above the Response.Redirect, the session variable will never be assigned.
- Together, these two lines create a session variable called X and call the second page.

12. Insert the following line of code into the Button1_Click event procedure of the second page, Default2.aspx:

```
Label1.Text = Convert.ToString(Session["X"]);
```

- This statement assigns the Session variable X to the Label1.Text property when the button of the second form is clicked.
- The Session variable data had to be converted from Unicode (16-bit) to ASCII (7-bit) before being assigned to the text box.

13. Run the debugger from the Default.aspx form and press the button in the browser.

- This only takes you to the second form.

14. Press the button when the second page appears on the browser.

- Now you should see the Session variable data in the Label control.

15. Close the browser.

PAUSE. Keep your application open for the next exercise.

Response.Redirect is a common method for transferring to other Web pages and Web sites. When using it in combination with session state, variables can easily be shared among pages on a site for each user.

 USE SERVER.TRANSFER

GET READY. We will continue with our C# program in Visual Web Developer.

1. Go back to the program of the previous exercise.

- If starting over, do all the previous exercises since the Understanding Postback section.

2. Run the debugger from the Default.aspx form but do not press the button yet.

- You should be on the first page, Default.aspx.
- The top of the browser should show this name at the end of the URL (Universal Resource Locator), the address of the Web page. In this case, it is the ASP.NET file name.

3. Now press the button on the form.

- This should take you to the second form. The name of the page should be Default2.aspx.
- Pressing the button should bring the variable over to the second page, as before.

4. Close the browser.

5. On the first page, Default.aspx, replace the Response.Redirect code:

   From: Response.Redirect("Default2.aspx");

   To: Server.Transfer("Default2.aspx");

6. Run the debugger from the Default.aspx form but do not press the button yet.
   - Notice the URL of the first Web page. The name of the page should still be Default.aspx.

7. Press the button on the form.
   - This should take you to the second form.
   - The name of the page did not change to Default2.aspx as it did before; it remains Default.aspx.
   - This is the result of a server transfer in which the server sends a different page using the same URL.

8. Now press the button on the second form.
   - This time the URL changed to Default2.aspx.
   - Notice that the data was transferred using session state as before.

9. Close the browser.

PAUSE. Keep your application open for the next exercise.

The *Server.Transfer* method transfers the browser to another page on the Web site without changing the URL. As far as the browser is concerned, it is displaying the same page as before. The server, however, sends a different page than the one the browser requested.

 USE SERVER.TRANSFER TO SEND DATA

GET READY. We will continue with our C# program in Visual Web Developer.

1. Go back to the program of the previous exercise.
   - If starting over, do all the previous exercises since the Understanding Postback section.

2. Place the following code into the first page just under the curly brace following the class definition:

   ```
   public string MyFirstPageProperty
   {
     get { return "My Variable Data!"; }
   }
   ```

   - This code creates a "variable" that becomes a property of the page; page properties can be shared.
   - Server.Transfer only uses ViewState for the Page and its controls, not for ViewState variables. The workaround is to make the variable a property of the Page object for ViewState to use.

3. Go to the Source view of the second page and place the following directive just below the existing Page directive located at the top of the document:

   ```
   <%@ PreviousPageType VirtualPath="~/Default.aspx" %>
   ```

   - This directive allows the second page to see the Page object data (its public members) from the first page, also called the source page.

4. Place the following code within the Page_Load event procedure in the second page:

`Label1.Text = PreviousPage.MyFirstPageProperty;`

   • Because of the directive you placed in the second page, IntelliSense is aware of the property you created in the source page. However, you may need to press the Save All icon in the toolbar and wait a while for IntelliSense to find the relationship.

5. Run the debugger from the Default.aspx form and press the button.

   • The data from the property you created on the first page should now be in the label of the second page.

   • If you press the button on the second page, your program will crash because the data is only available before a postback.

6. Close the browser.

   • We will add to our code to prevent it from crashing.

7. Enclose your code, the Label1.Text assignment, with a conditional branch:

```
if (Page.PreviousPage != null)
{
    Label1.Text = PreviousPage
    .MyFirstPageProperty;
}
```

   • The *PreviousPage* property of the Page object identifies the page that transferred control to the current page.

8. Run the debugger from the Default.aspx form and press the button on the first page and the second page.

   • The program will no longer crash. The postback of the second page will not have previous page data and the code will be ignored. The label will display the session variable instead.

9. Close the browser.

   • We will now take advantage of ViewState's ability to share data from Web controls.

10. Change your conditional branch-processing code:

```
if (Page.PreviousPage != null)
{
    //Label1.Text = PreviousPage
    .MyFirstPageProperty;
    Label tempLabel =
    (Label)PreviousPage.FindControl("Label1");
    Label1.Text = tempLabel.Text;
}
```

   • The two slash marks comment out the Label assignment.

11. Run the debugger from the Default.aspx form and press the button.

   • The Label control now has the message "The page is now a PostBack."

PAUSE. Keep your application open for the next exercise.

Notice that the Label control gives us the message that this is a postback. Before explaining this, try to figure out where and why this message shows up.

The code we have been ignoring for quite some time is the old postback message of the first form. This has not been used because we have been posting to another page. The label got changed but we just never saw it. Now that we are viewing data from the previous page, this previously unseen message can be seen.

A summary of the differences between Response.Redirect and Server.Transfer is found in Table 2-1.

Table 2-1

Some differences between Response.Redirect and Server.Transfer

RESPONSE.REDIRECT	SERVER.TRANSFER
Redirects to any URL	Only transfers to the current server and only to aspx pages
Makes a complete round-trip to the server	Does only a partial round-trip to the server
User sees the actual URL	The previous page URL is displayed in the address bar
Does not preserve form data or the query string	Preserves form data

USE CROSS-PAGE POSTING

GET READY. We will continue with our C# program in Visual Web Developer.

1. Go back to the program of the previous exercise.
   - If starting over, do all the previous exercises since the Understanding Postback section.
2. Add a new Button control to the first form.
3. Single-click the new button.
4. Click on the **PostBackURL** property of the new button in the Properties Window.
   - A Select URL dialog box should pop up.
5. In the Contents of folder window, click the name of the second form, Default2.aspx, and click the **OK** button.
6. Run the debugger from the Default.aspx form and press the button on the first page.
   - You have just used cross-page posting!
   - Notice that you did not need to write code to call the second form. This was all done with the PostBackURL property of the button. You could call another page, if you had one, with another button by giving it the URL of the other page.
   - Notice that the PreviousPage method works as it did in the previous exercise. In fact, all the data transfer methods used above will work with cross-page posting as well.
   - Notice that the URL of the second page properly shows the second page.
7. Close the browser.

PAUSE. Close Visual Web Developer.

Both cross-page posting and Server.Transfer are able to use ViewState to transfer Web form data. However, neither is able to transfer data using ViewState variables. Our first exercise showed how you could send a "variable" by transforming it into a property of the Page object, which becomes the transferrable Web form data we need.

One of the major differences between Server.Transfer and cross-page posting (PostBackURL) is that the latter does a complete round-trip to the server, which properly displays the URL on the browser of the second page.

To use cross-page posting, the control that is used to call a page must have the PostBackURL property. This only comes with the set of controls from the IButtonControl Interface, `System.Web.UI.WebControls.IButtonControl` namespace, in ASP.NET 2.0 and above. No other controls will have this property.

Here is a brief summary of the three ways ASP.NET changes Web pages:

- Response.Redirect
  - Standard method
  - Can be redirected to any URL
  - ViewState not applicable
- Server.Transfer
  - The browser is unaware that the Web page changed
  - URL doesn't change (incomplete page cycle)
  - Limited to pages on the current site
  - ViewState is supported but does not include ViewState variables
- Cross-page posting
  - Simpler form of Server.Transfer
  - Uses the PostBackURL method of a Web control to change pages
  - URL changes (complete page cycle)
  - Limited to pages on the current site
  - ViewState is supported but does not include ViewState variables

All three can use session state variables.

CERTIFICATION READY
What are some of the advantages and disadvantages of using the three techniques of Web page navigation discussed in this section?
1.4

Understanding Controls

 THE BOTTOM LINE

Visual Web Developer provides a wide variety of controls that can be added to a Web form to provide viewer interaction. Each of these controls is designed to serve a specific purpose. By carefully choosing one or more of the controls, you can have your pages perform just about any action you desire.

Differentiating the Various Types of Controls

Not all controls are alike. Visual Web Developer differentiates the functions of its controls by grouping them into categories in its Toolbox window. The controls are grouped into the nine categories listed in Table 2-2.

Table 2-2

Visual Studio and Visual Web Developer Control Categories

Category	Description
AJAX Extensions	Client-side scripting support
Data	Anything having to do with databases
General	The developer manages this category
HTML	Creates true HTML elements as opposed to Server controls
Login	Focuses on establishing and tracking user authentication
Navigation	Has only three controls: SiteMapPath, Menu, and TreeView
Standard	General purpose and commonly used
Validation	Significantly reduces coding for validating user input
WebParts	Enables users to personalize and manage pages from the browser

Of the categories listed in Table 2-2, this lesson discusses the HTML, Standard, and Validation categories. Following lessons will cover Data controls and AJAX Extensions. Another type of control we will discuss is the User control. The User control is not actually a control at all, which is why it is not included in the Toolbox. However, it is something a developer can make work like a control.

UNDERSTANDING HTML CONTROLS

HTML controls are client-side HTML elements and attributes that provide limited interaction with the user.

The following list of controls is located in the HTML category of the Visual Web Developer Toolbox.

- **Input (Button):** This control creates a Button control on the Web form.
- **Input (Reset):** This control also creates a button. It is used to clear a form of viewer data.
- **Input (Submit):** Like the Standard button control, the Submit button control is used to trigger a processing event. Typically, the action of this button is to initiate the submission of the form data to the server for processing.
- **Input (Text):** This control creates a textbox element on the Web form. Either text is displayed by the Web form or the user can type text into the control for processing.
- **Input (File):** This control creates an input textbox that receives from the local computer the full pathname of a file that is to be uploaded to the server.
- **Input (Password):** This control creates an input text box that masks any text entered into the box to protect its value. As its name implies, this control is most commonly used for passwords.
- **Input (Check box):** This control creates a check box element on a Web form that can be toggled on or off by the viewer.
- **Input (Radio):** This control creates a radio button element on a Web form that can be toggled on or off or included in a group of mutually exclusive radio button controls.
- **Input (Hidden):** This control creates a hidden label control that can be used to hold data without being displayed on the Web page.
- **Textarea:** This control creates a multiline text box. It can also include scroll bars and have the capability of being resized by the viewer.
- **Table:** This control creates a table declaration in a Web form with a single row containing a single cell.

- **Image:** This control creates an image element on a Web form that contains null values for the alternate tag and the location of the source-image file.
- **Select (Dropdown):** This control creates a bare-bones drop-down list box element on a Web form. The element must be edited to supply the list value and the default selection to be displayed at startup.
- **Horizontal Rule:** This control inserts a horizontal line on the Web form. There is no interaction available; this element is purely for design purposes.
- **Div:** To understand the function of this control, you need to understand the Flow Layout Panel control. The Div control in the HTML category creates an element that essentially creates a Flow Layout Panel control. This control can be used to arrange its contents either horizontally or vertically.

X REF

For more information on table elements in an HTML page, see Lesson 1.

Notice that the HTML version of the Button control is labeled as Input (Button). Input is an HTML element that is used for a variety of inputs depending on its type attribute. This attribute is given in parentheses after the element name. For example, the Input (Button) control is actually an input element with a type="button" attribute.

This exercise shows how to differentiate the Standard button from the HTML Input (Button) controls of Visual Web Developer.

USE HTML CONTROLS

GET READY. We will restart Microsoft Visual Web Developer.

1. Open Visual Web Developer 2008 (any edition).
2. Create a new ASP.NET Web Site using C#.
3. Place a **Button** control on the form from the Standard menu as we have done before.
4. Place the **Input (Button)** control on the form from the HTML category.
5. Without running the program, alternate single-clicking each button several times and watch the Properties window.
   - Notice that our Standard button is from the .NET platform and the other is from the <Input> element.
   - Notice that the HTML Input (Button) properties look a lot like HTML attributes. Also, notice that its Type property has the value of button, just like the type attribute of the HTML input element.
6. Single-click the HTML **Input (Button)**.
7. Click the **Style** property followed by the small box to the right.
   - Visual Web Developer provides a comprehensive dialog box for setting the values of the inline style sheet.
8. Change any style of your choosing for this button.
9. Click on the **Source** view tab to see how your change is automatically embedded into the element.
10. Go back to Design view and double-click the HTML **Input (Button)** control on the Web form to display the coding statements of the Web form.
    - Notice that you were not taken to an event procedure in the code-behind window. Instead, the cursor is located in an HTML document for a client-side scripting language. In this case, Java Script is ready to execute any code you may write for the Button1_onclick event.
11. Go back to **Design** view and delete the HTML **Input (Button)** control.
12. Return to the **Source** view.
    - Notice that only part of the HTML code is removed along with the control on the form.

- To minimize the size of your Web pages, it is often necessary to examine the Source view for unused code left behind by the IDE.

PAUSE. Close Visual Web Developer.

Coding Web pages with HTML elements is considered by some to be doing it the old way. However, if only one or a few simple controls are needed, using an HTML control avoids server-side processing and simplifies the page.

UNDERSTANDING SERVER AND VALIDATION CONTROLS

Essentially all of the other non-HTML controls in the Toolbox are *Server controls*. The Standard category lists all the Server controls that are not grouped for a common purpose. The *Validation controls* are special controls used for automatically validating user input.

Server controls are compiled from a programming language such as C# or Visual Basic and are then processed at the server. They are also considered server-side controls. HTML controls are client-side controls and are processed by the browser in a client-side programming language such as JavaScript or VB script.

The Standard controls do not fit into a special category like controls for databases or validation of user input. Table 2-3 contains a partial list of the Standard controls and provides a brief description of their purposes.

X REF

See Lesson 1 for more information on XHTML and CSS.

See Lesson 5 for more information on the AJAX Extensions.

Table 2-3

The Standard controls available in Visual Studio

CONTROL	DESCRIPTION
Label	Any raw text displayed on the form should use the Label control; this should be used in place of Response.Write
Button	The standard pushbutton used to present an obvious action
TextBox	For typed-in user input
LinkButton	The Button control that is displayed as a hyperlink
ImageButton	The Button control that is displayed as an image
HyperLink	A simple hyperlink using NavigateUrl without code-behind
DropDownList	A list of items in which the first one is displayed until the list is clicked to display all
ListBox	A list of items that are always displayed
CheckBox	A single checkable control
CheckBoxList	A list of checkable items in which any number of them can be checked
RadioButton	A single selectable control that is useless when used alone; it must be used in multiples and grouped with the GroupName property
RadioButtonList	A list of mutually exclusive radio button items; these radio buttons are grouped within the control
Image	The control that puts an image on the form; code-behind is not available for an Image control
Calendar	Just one of many very complex controls available to ASP.NET; calendars have code-behind that can make them very powerful controls
Table	This is designed to be used as a table of items, not to break up an entire page; tables have no code-behind to program

All Server controls have properties. These are similar to the attributes of elements. And like attributes, some of these properties are falling out of favor. The presentation properties, such as fonts and colors, create what is called the "skin" of a control. The downside of using skins directly is that they can create unnecessary classes that must be processed by the server. Microsoft is reducing its support for skins and increasing support for the use of CSS.

Themes are now included in Visual Studio 2008 and 2010 for presentation. Rather than using a single CSS file, a theme consists of a folder holding multiple CSS files and, if necessary, skin files. As with CSS, themes can be applied to a single control, a page, or the entire site.

Validation Web controls are special controls designed specifically for validating user input.

Table 2-4 lists the Validation Web controls and their purposes.

Table 2-4

Validation Web controls in the Visual Studio Toolbox

CONTROL	DESCRIPTION
CompareValidator	Simple comparison of two input controls to one another or a fixed value
CustomValidator	Allows you to write your own validation code to validate the control
DynamicValidator	Catches exceptions identified in the data model during validation and creates a validation event on the Web page
RangeValidator	Input must be within a range of values
RegularExpressionValidator	Input must match a pattern as defined with a regular expression
RequiredField Validator	Does not allow an empty field
ValidationSummary	Reports all validation errors

CERTIFICATION READY
What are some of the major differences between HTML controls and Server controls?
1.5

UNDERSTANDING USER CONTROLS

User controls, custom Server controls, components, Web parts, and third-party controls are various sources for creating additional controls that can enhance Web development.

When you find yourself copying and pasting the same code in multiple locations, you might want to consider writing a User control. User controls are relatively easy to create. Although they are similar to Web pages, they do not use some of the basic elements of HTML, such as html, head, and form. Whereas the built-in Server controls are System.Web.UI.WebControls objects and are saved with your .aspx Web pages, User controls are System.Web.UI.UserControl objects and saved separately with .ascx extensions.

User controls look just like the Web pages we have been creating. They include Server controls with event procedures written in the code-behind window. However, they cannot be run directly in the browser like a Web page.

CREATE A USER CONTROL

GET READY. We will restart Microsoft Visual Web Developer.

1. Open Visual Web Developer 2008 (any edition).
2. Create a new ASP.NET Web Site using C#.
3. Open the **Add New** Item dialog box from the Website menu, and select the **Web User Control** item.
4. Verify that the language is C# and press the **Add** button.
   - This will add a new form to the project having an .ascx extension.
5. Verify that the Solution Explorer window has the WebUserControl.ascx highlighted.
   - This is not the "Web Form" that we have been using in the past.
   - You should have the Default.aspx file in the Solution Explorer window as well.
6. Click the **Design** tab at the bottom of the window in order to put two controls on the form.
7. Place a Standard button and label control on the new WebUserControl form.
   - Since it does not have the div element, the controls are lined up horizontally.
8. Move the cursor between the controls without highlighting either control and press the **Enter** key.
   - The label should not be above the button.
9. Double-click the button and write the code for its event procedure:

   Label1.Text = "Welcome";

10. Run the program from the WebUserControl rather than the Default form.
    Close the browser.
    - Notice that the default form runs instead and does not have any controls on it.
    - User controls cannot be run directly.
    - We will now place the User control on the default page.
11. From the Solution Explorer window, double-click the **Default.aspx** page to open it and go to the **Design** view.
12. Click on the **div** tag so the small tab above it shows up.
13. Click on the **div element** tab and delete it.
    - If right-clicking the mouse to select delete does not work, you will have to use the delete key.
14. Click on the **form element** tab and delete it too.
    - If right-clicking the mouse to select delete does not work, you will have to use the delete key.
15. Place two Panel controls on the form. This control is located near the bottom of the Standard category list.
16. From the Solution Explorer, drag the WebUserControl.ascx into the first pane.
17. Do the same thing as in the previous step but drag it into the second pane.
    - The panels allow the User controls to keep their relative positions when more than one is placed onto the default page.
18. Click on **Split** view and notice the new directive on the second line:

    **<%@ Register src="WebUserControl.ascx"
    tagname="WebUserControl" tagprefix="uc1" %>**

- Your control was automatically registered.
- The first attribute (src) names the file containing the source code. However, the code-behind source code for the control is not listed in the declaration but is available in the Solution Explorer window as the WebUserControl.ascx.cs page under the WebUserControl.ascx file. The cs extension stands for "C Sharp." If we were to write the code-behind in Visual Basic, the extension would be vb.
- The tagname attribute is automatically named WebUserControl and will be used in any code-behind that references your control. If you decide to rename the control, make sure you replace every appearance of the original name in both the Source view and code-behind view of all pages using the control.
- Notice that the tagprefix attribute says we are using "ucl."

19. Examine the body of the <form> element:

```
<asp:Panel ID="Panel1" runat="server">
    <ucl:WebUserControl ID="WebUserControl1"
    runat="server" />
</asp:Panel>
<asp:Panel ID="Panel2" runat="server">
    <ucl:WebUserControl ID="WebUserControl2"
    runat="server" />
</asp:Panel>
```

- ASP.NET recognizes this as a "ucl" object rather than what we have been using so far, which are "asp" objects. The ID value should be changed in production to provide better readability in the code. The ID value can be changed here or in the Design view property window.

20. Run the program from either form and press the buttons on the Web page.
21. Close the browser.

PAUSE. Close Visual Web Developer.

User controls not only make it easy to reuse code, but an entire form can be created and used multiple times throughout a site. However, if a User control is needed for another project, the file must be placed into the Solution Explorer window of the other project because User controls are limited to the current project. Although one might consider adding a User control to the Toolbox, this type of control is not designed for this purpose and is not allowed in the Toolbox.

KNOWING WHICH TYPE OF CONTROL TO USE FOR A GIVEN SCENARIO

Visual Web Developer categorizes controls within the Toolbox as an aid to Web developers. However, these groupings do not necessarily reflect the technical differences among these controls. We will quickly examine our controls to form more general categories.

We have two main types of controls, HTML and Server. HTML is just one of the categories in the IDE. This means that other types of controls, like Validation and the Standard Web controls, are also Server controls. Then we have the most interesting type of control, User, which is not even a real control.

Even though placing ASP.NET into categories and/or types may currently be a source of confusion, we have enough background that we should be able to know which type of control to use in a given scenario. Although Visual Web Developer displays nine categories for controls, Table 2-5 shows an alternative grouping that describes the best control for a given scenario.

Table 2-5

Choosing a control from a scenario

Control Category	Usage Scenario
User	The site has multiple pages in which each page has many of the same controls. The designer will benefit from code reuse.
Server	The Web page is very interactive and requires security for data as well as for the source code.
HTML	The Web page only requires simple unsecure client-side scripting in a language such as JavaScript. It may also make calls to the server for server-side scripting in a language such as PHP.
Validation	The site needs a lot of user input, possibly for populating a database with accurate data.

Understanding Configuration Files

THE BOTTOM LINE

Web sites require the ability to stay online as they go through minor adjustments. For example, it would be unacceptable to bring down a site being used by stockbrokers during trading hours to make an adjustment, even if it were an important security setting. Fortunately, most configuration changes to a Web server entail nothing more than editing a text file on the server as applications on the site are running.

Understanding ASP.NET configuration files requires a fundamental understanding of the .NET Framework. The .NET Framework is designed to be a common platform for creating both Windows-based (desktop) and Web-based applications. The framework consists of the Common Language Runtime (CLR) and the Framework Class Library (FCL). The FCL is the library of all the objects used in .NET.

The CLR is what runs .NET applications. The source code can be C#, Visual Basic, or a host of other .NET languages. These languages are compiled into the Common Intermediate Language (CIL). The CLR then executes the CIL. Once a program has been compiled, it can be run on any computer having CLR installed.

As the CLR executes .NET applications, it needs access to various configuration settings involving user, security, application, and policy preferences. The CLR will use the FCL's default values unless otherwise instructed. Administrators and developers can use the ASP.NET configuration system to alter these default values.

The configuration system has a single file that contains all the required changes to the default settings for the entire .NET system on a given computer. This file is *machine.config*. It is recommended that you don't make changes to this file unless you are well aware of the consequences.

If the .NET defaults or machine.config settings are unacceptable, you have the option of overriding them with additional web.config files for Web-based applications or *app.config* files for Windows-based applications. There is a *web.config* file located in the same directory as the machine.config file that resets the defaults for all Web sites on the machine. There is also an app.config file for each of the programming languages used in Visual Studio as well as for each application. Developers typically focus their attention on the local configuration files.

Since Web sites have such a diverse set of users sharing the same server, having multiple web.config files for a Web site is common. If all your sites use the same settings, a single web.config file can be placed in a shared directory. If an individual site needs a few adjustments that differ from a shared file, another web.config file can be placed in the site's directory. The web.config files closest to the Web page override all the previous files. This rule applies to each web.config as we traverse the directory path all the way back to the machine.config file, which only overrides the .NET defaults.

We do not have to redefine any previously changed settings. The values of all unchanged settings are "inherited" from changes made earlier. Each level from the original .NET defaults carries inherited values up from the previous level. This allows you to focus on only what needs to be changed at a given level, making it safe to assume that the lower changes will remain in force.

The machine.config and web.config files are stored using the XML format exactly like XHTML. Where XHTML contains tags that browsers understand, the configuration files contain data that CLR understands. Both come complete with elements, attributes, and tags. Both have the same syntax rules, such as being case-sensitive, using camel-case names, and requiring every beginning tag to have an ending tag. This means that both XHTML and the configuration files are languages. The first is for markup and the other two are for configuration. Unfortunately, the configuration languages have not yet been assigned names.

- Using XML to hold configuration data has many advantages over any of the alternatives.
- Unlike the Windows registry, we are not tied to a specific operating system.
- We do not have to rely on a database management system.
- Files can be placed into multiple directories as needed.
- Changes can be made while the site is running.
- The same XML file can be used on other sites with a simple copy-paste.
- With appropriate network rights, the files can be changed remotely.
- Since the data is stored as text, no special program is required to interpret it.
- The hierarchical nature of the XML data structure helps to organize and group data in an outline format.

 EXAMINE THE MACHINE.CONFIG FILE

GET READY. We will not be opening Microsoft Visual Web Developer with this lesson. However, it will most likely open on its own.

1. The machine.config file is located in the Windows directory on your computer's hard disk drive. Use your operating system's file management system, Windows Explorer, to find the file manually. It should be in a directory similar to this:

   C:\Windows\Microsoft.NET\Framework
   \v2.0.50727\CONFI3

   - Notice that there are many more config files of type "XML Configuration File" than machine.config.

2. Double-click the **machine.config** file to open it into whatever editor the operating system uses to open files having the config extension.

   - The configuration files are normally opened with Visual Web Developer.

 You can open the machine.config file directly from Visual Web Developer by using Open File from the File menu and navigating to its location.

3. Examine the block of comments at the top of the file:

```
<?xml version="1.0" encoding="UTF-8"?>
<!--
Please refer to machine.config.comments for a description
and the default values of each configuration section.
For a full documentation of the schema, please refer to
    http://go.microsoft.com/fwlink/?LinkId=42127
To improve performance, machine.config should contain only those
settings that differ from their defaults.
-->
```

- The last sentence of the comment block suggests that you insert only those configuration settings that have different default values from those internally assigned to .NET.
- Remember that as this file gets larger, it takes more time to read and interpret, so do not place any more settings in here than necessary.

4. Scroll through the rest of the file to get an idea of the data it holds, but do not make any changes.

5. Close the file.

6. Go to the Web site referenced in the comment at the top of the page for full documentation of the machine.config file and its contents.

   http://go.microsoft.com/fwlink/?LinkId=42127

7. After scanning through the configuration help, close the browser.

8. The comments at the top of the machine.config file also refer you to another config file:

   machine.config.comments

9. Double-click the machine.config.comments file to see the kind of data it holds.
   - This file is a help file for the machine.config file. The settings here are not actually applied, they are just described.

10. Close the file without saving any changes you may have accidentally made.

PAUSE. Keep the directory open so we can examine another config file in the next exercise.

The machine.config file holds very low-level settings that we should never need to change. However, it does not hold all the settings available. It only holds the ones that are not set by default by the .NET system.

 EXAMINE THE WEB.CONFIG FILE

GET READY. Make sure the directory remains open from the previous exercise. We will also be creating another new site with Visual Web Developer.

1. Notice that there is a web.config file and a web.config.comments file located in the same directory as the machine.config file.
   - There can be many web.config files throughout a Web site.

2. Double-click these two configuration files to examine them. Get an idea of what they hold.

3. Close the config files.

4. Open Visual Web Developer 2008 (any edition).

5. Create a new ASP.NET Web site using C#.

6. Double-click the **web.config** file located in the Solution Explorer window.

7. Examine the block of comments at the top of the file:

```
<?xml version="1.0"?>
<!--

Note: As an alternative to hand editing this file you can use
the Web admin tool to configure settings for your application.
Use the website->Asp.Net Configuration option in Visual Studio.
A full list of settings and comments can be found in
    machine.config.comments usually located in
    \Windows\Microsoft.Net\Framework\v2.x\Config

-->
```

8. From the menu bar, open the **Website menu bar -> ASP.Net Configuration** to open the Web Site Administration Tool (WSAT).

   • The WSAT is used to manage the basic configurations for a Web site.

9. Click through this site.

   • You should find that this help system does a great job of informing you about what settings are available with this tool. You should also find that WSAT is able to configure a few settings stored in a database. The web.config file can be used for more than holding configuration settings. It is also capable of storing data for server-side processing that is never sent to the browser.

   • To demonstrate how the config file is edited and how to use WSAT, we will set a password that is held at the server.

10. Click on the WSAT's **Application** tab.

11. Click on **Create application settings**.

12. In the Name field, enter **myPassword** and in the Value field, enter **mpw**.

    Your password "mpw" is now saved on the server in a location named "myPassword."

13. Click on the **Save** button and the **OK** button but keep the page open on the browser to delete it at the end of the exercise.

14. Double-click the **web.config** file in the Solution Explorer window in Visual Web Developer.

    • A message box may pop up stating that the web.config file has been edited by an outside source. If it does, it is okay to proceed because *you* are the "outside source."

15. Use the search function of Visual Web Developer (Ctrl) + (F) to find the "myPassword" entry.

    • An XML entry for the password variable and its value has been inserted in the web.config file.

16. Click on the **Default.aspx** tab and go the Design view.

17. Place a **TextBox**, **Button**, and **Label** on the form.

18. Double-click the button and place the following code into its event procedure:

```
if (TextBox1.Text == System.Configuration
    .ConfigurationSettings
    .AppSettings["myPassword"])
  Label1.Text = "You're in!";
else
  Label1.Text = "I don't think so";
```

CERTIFICATION READY
What are the major uses for the web.config and machine.config files and which one most often has to be configured?
1.6

19. Run the program to test your password (mpw). Then close the browser.

PAUSE. Close Visual Web Developer.

The web.config file is used in many locations throughout a Web site. It is important to be aware of where in the path these files are located so inherited settings can be monitored.

SKILL SUMMARY

IN THIS LESSON YOU LEARNED TO:

- Use AutoEventWireup in both C# and Visual Basic with different results.

- Monitor and control stages in the page life cycle with events.

- Write event procedures to respond to form control events.

- Write event procedures to interact with the server through the IsPostBack property of the page.

- Redirect a Web page using Response.redirect, Server.transfer, and cross-page posting.

- Write a Web page using HTML controls.

- Write a Web page using Server controls.

- Choose the appropriate control for a given scenario.

- Configure a Web page using .NET configuration files.

■ Knowledge Assessment

Multiple Choice

Circle the letter or letters that correspond to the best answer or answers.

1. What attribute can be set to allow you to monitor the events of a Web page's life cycle?
   a. AutoEventWireup
   b. Page.Monitor
   c. Global.asax
   d. web.config

2. What feature of the Visual Studio IDE can be applied to observe the order in which the events of a Web page are triggered?
   a. Breakpoint
   b. Output panel
   c. Step-through
   d. Watch list

3. Which one of the following is NOT a standard server-side event?
   a. Application_Start
   b. OnEnd
   c. OnRunning
   d. OnStart

4. When a Web page's data is returned to the server for processing by the browser, this action is known as a
   a. Get
   b. Post
   c. Postback
   d. Repost

5. Which of the following allows the developer to transfer variables to other pages when using cross-page posting?
   a. control state
   b. session state
   c. view state
   d. all state

6. What method sends the browser to a new page without changing the URL in its address bar?
   a. PostBackURL
   b. Response.Redirect
   c. Server.Transfer
   d. Cross-page posting

7. What page property does cross-page posting use to navigate to a new page?
   a. Cross.Page
   b. Cross.Post
   c. Navigate
   d. PostBackUrl

8. Which of the following is NOT included as a category in the Visual Studio Toolbox?
   a. Standard
   b. User
   c. Validation
   d. HTML

9. What is NOT one of the parts of the .NET Framework?
   a. CIA
   b. CIL
   c. CLR
   d. FCL

10. Which of the following files is most often changed?
    a. machine.config
    b. machine.config.comments
    c. web.config
    d. web.config.comments

Fill in the Blank

Complete the following sentences by writing the correct word or words in the blanks provided.

1. Code can be written when a page triggers an event during its _____ _____.

2. Programmers can write code to execute as soon as the page is loaded or reloaded after a postback. This event is called _____.

3. The _____ property of the Web page returns a Boolean variable indicating whether or not the page is new or returning from a postback.

4. The _____ file holds code for handling session and application events.

5. The _____ page attribute must be set to "true" for C# to detect the page events in code-behind.

6. There are only two _____ events: OnStart and OnEnd.

7. _____ events start with the BeginRequest and end with Application_ LogRequest.

8. _____ controls are the only controls in the Visual Web Developer Toolbox that are client-side, not server-side.

9. _____ controls are special controls that are specifically designed to ensure that the user correctly enters data into Web form controls.

10. Web.config files are used to override the settings found in the _____ file.

● Competency Assessment

Scenario 2-1: Validating Input Data

The design of a Web site calls for a viewer data form that collects the viewer's name, address, zip code, phone, and hobbies (from a list of check box items). The name must be alphabetic, the phone number must have a valid area code, the zip code must be between 42200 and 42599 (inclusive), and no more than three hobbies can be selected. All of the processing is to be performed at the server. Use input, user, and data validation controls to create a Web page that includes these actions.

● Proficiency Assessment

Scenario 2-2: Trapping an Error to Keep the Application Running

Your Web site has an error that crashes the program. You don't feel you can spend the time to find the error before the deployment due date. Your fix is to trap the unknown error and show a generic error message. This should keep the application alive while you continue looking for the error without the deadline pressure.

Write a small application that demonstrates how you would trap an error, show an error message, and keep the application alive. Use the Application_Error event procedure and find a way to generate an error that will trigger the event.

Scenario 2-3: Writing a Pop-Up

Your boss underestimates your ability to write Web pages and has made the comment that you wouldn't be able to pop up a new Web page when the current page is closed. Write a Web page for your boss that pops up a new page when the current page is closed. Put an appropriate image on the new page so your boss will respect your abilities. You will need to find the appropriate page event that fires when the page is closed. You may also need to enable the pop-up blocker on the browser.

Scenario 2-4: Knowing Which Type of Control Is Appropriate

Your site now has a page with sensitive information that requires only a few people to view, which creates the need for a login page. You will need to validate the username and password followed by an appropriate error message for failed validations. A welcome message will be displayed on the form when the username and password are correct before the sensitive page appears. What controls would you use for your login page so the user will be able to enter a name and password and either receive an error message or get sent to a new page?

 Workplace Ready

Using the IsPostBack Property

One of the most important techniques covered in this lesson is how to use the IsPostBack property of the Page object. If your workplace is moving from desktop applications to Web-based applications, this can be one of the largest hurdles to jump. One of the first things you will miss is global variables. These variables do not exist in this environment. All your initializing routines will be reprocessed on every postback, even when your variables are at the top of your code. You may use session variables, but they too will be reinitialized on postback. Applying the IsPostBack property to the Page_Load event is the key!

Working with XML, Data Objects, and WCF

LESSON SKILL MATRIX

SKILLS/CONCEPTS	MTA EXAM OBJECTIVE	MTA EXAM OBJECTIVE NUMBER
Reading and Writing XML Data	Read and write XML data	2.1
Distinguishing between DataSet and Dataheader Objects		
Choosing the Data Object Based on Application Requirements	Distinguish between DataSet and DataReader objects	2.2
Calling a Service from a Web Page	Call a service from a Web page	2.3

KEY TERMS

<system.serviceModel> element   Schema

App_WebReferences folder   Web Service

DataReader   Windows Communication Foundation (WCF)

DataSet   XML

DTD   XML validation

Karen needs to bring in outside data and put it into a database. However, the data source is not a database but rather a simple text file. The file needs to be altered to enable the data to be sent easily to a database table. Once in the database, the data needs to be read quickly and placed onto the Web page. She is also contemplating placing the data onto the Web as a service where third-party applications could be created to download the data easily. All this can be done using the information provided in this lesson.

■ Reading and Writing XML Data

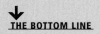
THE BOTTOM LINE

Many references have been made to the eXtensible Markup Language (XML) prior to this lesson. We started out using XHTML, where the X stands for XML and the pages were validated using the strict syntax of XML. In the last lesson, we also saw that XML was used to store the machine.config and web.config files. We will now define XML and learn how to read and write data that is stored in this format. We will also write XML files and use validation tools to verify that they are both syntactically and logically correct.

Understanding Applications and Origins of XML

XML is a very large part of the Web. It is used to simplify data storage, transport data between systems having incompatible formats, separate data from HTML, save configuration settings, define XHTML, etc.

Web pages would not be what they are today without data. Data can be packaged in many forms, from flat files to relational databases. A flat file is a text file that lists a simple sequence of data. A relational database is a complex structure requiring a database management system for support. XML lands between these in complexity. As with a flat file, data are stored in a text file. Unlike a database where data are normally organized in related tables, XML is organized in a simple hierarchical format similar to an outline.

As developers, we need to be able to read and write XML. This does not necessarily mean creating code to read from and write to these XML files. XML is not like HTML or XHTML, which we use to write code for browsers. XML is the framework used for creating new languages such as XHTML, not the language itself. We are now in control of the meaning of the elements; they are not pre-defined as in XHTML. Developers create their own language by defining the elements and tags needed to meet their requirements.

ASP.NET offers many programming objects to help create the applications to support XML data. For example, the XmlReader and XmlWriter objects can be programmed to read data into the application, process it and write it out to an XML file, and use it for display purposes or as transportation to another application. However, until you understand XML, these tools will do you no good. Our lesson will focus on XML itself, not how to write programs for it.

The first markup language was developed in the 1960s by IBM and was given the name Generalized Markup Language (GML). The International Organization for Standards (ISO) standardized GML by creating the Standardized Generalized Markup Language (SGML) in 1986. It was used for sharing large documents among major institutions such as the military, aerospace industry, and industrial publishing.

In 1993, HTML was created using a subset of this massive set of SGML rules. A year later, the first draft of XML was written to enable developers to create their own languages without having to use SGML directly. This is why the syntax rules for HTML and XML are very similar. XML simply received more rules from SGML than did HTML. In 1999 XHTML arrived, which brought Web documents a little closer to the SGML standards when HTML received the additional syntax rules of XML.

 READ AND WRITE XML DATA

GET READY. We will use a simple text editor such as Notepad for this exercise.

1. Create a new text document named ShoppingList.html.
   - Make sure your operating system shows file extensions so you can rename the default txt extension as html. Otherwise, the resulting file name will be ShoppingList.html.txt.
2. Edit the file by right-clicking the file name and selecting **Edit.**
3. Type in the HTML code:

```
<table>
  <caption>Sample</caption>
    <tr>
      <th>Food</th>
      <th>Unit</th>
```

```
      </tr>
      <tr>
        <td>Milk</td>
        <td>Gallon</td>
      </tr>
      <tr>
        <td>Eggs</td>
        <td>Dozen</td>
      </tr>
    </table>
```

4. Save and close the file.

5. Double-click the file to display it in the default browser.

   • A table is displayed because the browser knows the XML document is using the HTML language. This can be considered an XML document. When the browser reads the file with the html extension, it will interpret the tags and perform accordingly.

6. Close the browser, rename the ShoppingList.html document as **ShoppingList.xml**, and then double-click the file again to see how the browser interprets it.

   • This time the browser only sees the raw XML data and does not interpret it as HTML.

   • Our new XML file holds shopping list data, but does not describe it other than in rows and columns. We will now convert our HTML document into a new made-up language that describes the data it holds.

7. Edit the ShoppingList.xml document by right-clicking the file and selecting **Edit.**

8. Rewrite the contents with the following XML data:

```
<shopping_list>
  <title>Sample</title>
  <item>
    <food>Milk</food>
    <unit>Gallon</unit>
  </item>
  <item>
    <food>Eggs</food>
    <unit>Dozen</unit>
  </item>
</shopping_list>
```

   • This conversion turned the table into a document that is much easier to read. However, this created one small problem. No browser will understand the made-up tag names. Since we are only interested in the data and not in presenting the data in this document, it does not matter what we use for tag names.

9. Save and close the file.

10. Double-click the file to display it in a browser, and allow blocked content if a warning appears.

   • If you get errors, do not continue until the contents of the file are displayed.

   • As with HTML, browsers are not consistent in how they handle raw XML documents. Figures 3-1 through 3-4 show how different browsers handle our XML document.

Figure 3-1

Internet Explorer's display of
ShoppingList.xml

```
- <shopping_list>
    <title>Sample</title>
  - <item>
      <food>Milk</food>
      <unit>Gallon</unit>
    </item>
  - <item>
      <food>Eggs</food>
      <unit>Dozen</unit>
    </item>
  </shopping_list>
```

Figure 3-2

Opera's display of
ShoppingList.xml

```
<shopping_list>
  <title>
    Sample
  </title>
  <item>
    <food>
      Milk
    </food>
    <unit>
      Gallon
    </unit>
  </item>
  <item>
    <food>
      Eggs
    </food>
    <unit>
      Dozen
    </unit>
  </item>
</shopping_list>
```

Figure 3-3

Google Chrome's display of
ShoppingList.xml

```
Sample Milk Gallon Eggs Dozen
```

Figure 3-4

Firefox's display of
ShoppingList.xml

```
- <shopping_list>
    <title>Sample </title>
  - <item>
      <food>Milk</food>
      <unit>Gallon</unit>
    </item>
  + <item></item>
  - <shopping_list>
```

11. If your browser shows the minus symbols, click them to turn them into plus signs.
    - The plus and minus signs displayed in Internet Explorer and Firefox are used to collapse and expand elements containing child elements. For example, the last item displayed in Firefox shows a collapsed element as displayed in Figure 3-4.
    - Notice the inconsistency of displaying both the beginning and ending tags with the browsers.

12. Close the browser.

PAUSE. We will continue with a simple text editor and our ShoppingList.xml file for the next exercise.

If you made any mistakes in this exercise, you may have noticed that your browser was quick to point out the errors. Most modern browsers have XML parsers that detect errors in XML files. As we run through the XML syntax rules, it is expected that your browser has this feature.

APPLY XML RULES

GET READY. Make sure that ShoppingList.xml is available and contains valid XML data.

1. Double-click the **ShoppingList.xml** file to open it with the browser.
   - To speed up the following exercises, keep the browser open and use the refresh button to show any changes made to the XML file. You should also keep the XML file open between steps. Just press the **Save** button before testing your changes with the browser.
2. Right-click on the file name and select **Edit.**
3. Place the following comment at the top of the file:

   `<!-- This file contains at least one error -->`

   - This comment is placed at the top of the page as a warning that the page is not error free. This prevents you from accidentally using it as an example of a valid XML page.
4. Save the file but keep it open.
5. Refresh the browser.
   - The browser should now display the comment at the top of the page.
6. In the first tag, **<shopping_list>**, replace the underscore with a space, **<shopping list>**. Save the file and refresh the browser.
   - Internet Explorer will attempt to identify the error and point to the location where it believes there is a problem. In this case, it finds an invalid character at Line 2, Position 15, as shown in Figure 3-5.

Figure 3-5

Internet Explorer finds an XML error

The XML page cannot be displayed

Cannot view XML input using XSL style sheet. Please correct the error and then click the Refresh button, or try again later.

A name contained an invalid character. Error processing resource 'file:///C:/LABs/ShoppingList.xml'. Line 2, Position 15

`<shopping list>`

   - The broken rule is that names cannot contain spaces.
7. Remove the space from the top tag but do not replace the underscore as shown below:

   `<shoppinglist>`
8. Save and refresh.
   - Even though both the top and bottom tag names are legal, the browser registered the name of the first tag and failed to locate its matching ending tag.
   - The broken rule is that every starting tag name must have a matching ending tag name.
9. Rename the last tag from **</shopping_list>** to **</shoppingList>**, noting the capital L. Make sure the first tag remains `<shoppinglist>`. Save and refresh.
   - Again, the error message says that the tags do not match, even though they are the same except for the capital L.
   - The broken rule is that XML is case sensitive.
   - Even though it is syntactically legal to use upper- and lowercase characters in XML, it is standard practice to use lowercase only.
10. Replace the capital L in the ending tag with its lowercase equivalent. Save and refresh to make sure the browser runs it without errors.
11. Remove the content from the title element as shown below:

    `<title></title>`

12. Save and refresh.

- Internet Explorer will display the shortcut syntax for this element, **`<title />`**.
- A valid rule in XML is that it recognizes the shortcut syntax for empty elements.
- As in XHTML, it is valid to write **`<title />`** to represent **`<title></title>`**.

13. Create an empty tag for the shopping list element by moving the ending tag up to the starting tag as shown below:

`<shoppinglist></shoppinglist>`

14. Save and refresh.

- Notice that Internet Explorer lets you know that a rule was broken, as shown in Figure 3-6.

Figure 3-6

An important rule is that there can only be one top-level element

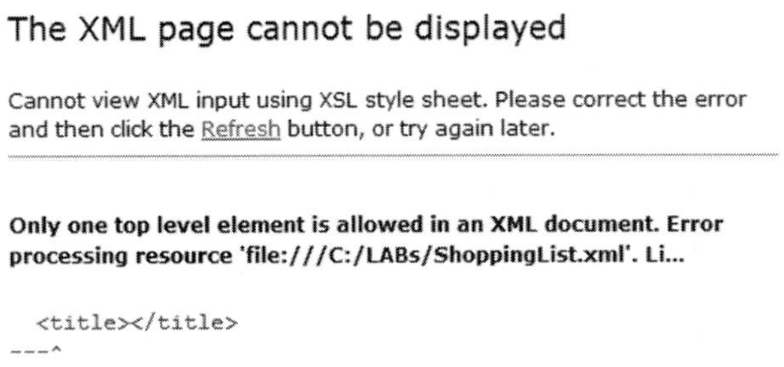

The XML page cannot be displayed

Cannot view XML input using XSL style sheet. Please correct the error and then click the Refresh button, or try again later.

Only one top level element is allowed in an XML document. Error processing resource 'file:///C:/LABs/ShoppingList.xml'. Li...

```
<title></title>
---^
```

- Every XML document must have only one top-level element. This is called the "root" element of an XML document. The last tag in the document must be the ending tag of the root element. No tags are allowed after the ending tag of the root element.
- Notice that the error was incorrectly located in line 3. This often occurs with debuggers. The error was not triggered until another tag was located after the ending root element. A syntactically valid way to repair this error would be to remove all the elements beyond the ending root element. Of course, removing all but the shopping list element from our XML file is not the correct approach to removing this error.

15. Move the ending root tag back where it belongs. Save and refresh to make sure the file is correct.

16. Replace the title element with the following:

`<title>lots  of  spaces</title>`

17. Save and refresh.

- Note that the spaces were removed, just as they are in HTML.
- The rule is that browsers strip white space from XML content.

18. Right-click the browser and click **View Source**.

- Notice that the spaces remain present in the HTML file.
- The rule is that white space is preserved when sent to the browser but removed when presented by the browser.
- Remember that, unlike HTML, XML is used for data, not presentation.
- We will now place spaces in various locations within tag names rather than content to test for valid syntax.

19. In the root tag, **`<shoppinglist>`**, place one space immediately before and one immediately after the tag name. In its ending tag, place one space immediately before the slash and one immediately after the slash. Save and refresh after making various changes to test the locations of these spaces to determine their valid locations. Develop an XML rule from your results.

- You should have found a rule similar to this: No white space is allowed anywhere before the name of an ending tag, but white space is allowed after the name.

20. Remove the content from the title element to get ready for the next step. Save and refresh to make sure the file is correct.

```
<title></title>
```

21. Place the ending tag of the title element just below the starting tag of the first item element, as shown below:

```
<!-- This file contains at least one error -->
<shoppinglist >
  <title>
  <item>
  </title>
    <food>Milk</food>
    <unit>Gallon</unit>
  </item>
  <item>
    <food>Eggs</food>
    <unit>Dozen</unit>
  </item>
</shoppinglist>
```

- Notice that XML has the same nesting rules as HTML.
- The rule is that XML requires proper nesting.

22. Put the ending title tag back where it belongs. Save and refresh to make sure the file is correct.

- So far, we have not addressed using attributes in our XML documents. We will add a "qty" attribute to our document, even though best practice would have us add a "qty" element rather than an attribute.
- Attributes should be avoided in favor of elements whenever possible. So although this is a poor design, it shows that XML caters to very creative developers.

23. Find the two **unit** elements and add an attribute named **qty** to each. Give the new attributes the values **"1"** and **"2"**, respectively:

```
<unit qty="1">Gallon</unit>
<unit qty="2">Dozen</unit>
```

24. Verify that there are no errors at this point by executing a save and refresh.

25. Remove the quotation marks from the attributes. Save and refresh.

- The rule is that XML attributes always require quotation marks, even for numeric values.

26. Place single quotes or apostrophes where the double quotes were previously removed. Save and refresh.

- Double or single quotes work equally well for attributes. The advantage of having both styles available is for situations where both are needed within the same attribute. For example, qty="Don't care."
- The rule is that XML attributes may use single or double quotes in matching pairs.
- Our next rule will not be tested here but needs to be included in our list of rules. It is important because XML allows you to use any word you want for element and attribute names.
- The rule is that, unlike programming languages, XML has no reserved or key words.
- A little caution is warranted in this last rule. It is best to avoid any reserved words or characters used for syntax of the programming and/or database environment where XML is used. For example, "no special characters other than the underscore" and "no names prefixed by a number" are common programming language rules. In

an object-oriented environment, it is best not to use periods or colons in the name because these are special characters in that environment.

27. Place the following directive at the top of the XML document, just to satisfy the prolog rule:

```
<?xml version="1.0" encoding="utf-8" ?>
```

- An optional rule for XML documents is to start the document with a prolog. This can include an XML declaration that gives the browser the XML version, encoding used for text characters, and other information.

28. Save and refresh to make sure there are no errors.

PAUSE. You can now close the browser.

CERTIFICATION READY
What is XML used for, and what are the rules you must follow to create an XML document?
2.1

Now that we can write an XML page following its rules, we need to make sure we did not make any mistakes. This can be done by using an *XML validation* program.

USING DTD VALIDATION

Verifying that an XML document is syntactically correct is only the beginning of the process of reading and writing an XML document. XML documents also include language rules as defined by the designer.

For example, you might want an XML rule stating that the document can only have one title element and any number of item elements. A Document Type Definition, or *DTD*, is one of several ways an XML document structure can be defined with rules. To "validate" a document is to make sure the elements in your XML document adhere to your rules.

You write your rules using DTD statements, which is a rule-making syntax. Using this syntax to create your rules defines the language of your XML document. Before an application is used to process your XML data, the DTD should first be verified against your XML document to ensure that the data are correctly formatted.

Far more DTD rules are available for us to use than we can cover in this lesson. Thus, we will limit the discussion to fit the scope of our XML document. The syntax for these rules need not be memorized. Our focus is on the concept of the DTD and how to make sure an XML document follows DTD rules.

Our DTD rules can be placed within our XML document or as a separate file. We will place the DTD rules within the XML file for simplicity and limit the rules to those listed in Table 3-1.

Table 3-1

The rules and syntax for our new language for our sample XML file

RULES	DTD SYNTAX
The title element can contain plain text.	`<!ELEMENT title (#PCDATA)>`
The food element can contain plain text.	`<!ELEMENT food (#PCDATA)>`
The unit element can contain plain text.	`<!ELEMENT unit (#PCDATA)>`
The only elements directly under the root are title and item, in that order. Title can only appear once but item can appear zero or more times.	`<!ELEMENT shoppinglist (title, item*)>`
The only elements allowed under the item element are food and unit, in that order. There can only be a single pair for each item element as well.	`<!ELEMENT item (food, unit)>`
The unit element contains a qty attribute with the default value of 1.	`<!ATTLIST unit qty CDATA "1">`

In Lesson 1, we used a Web site to validate our strict XHTML page. We were validating our pages against the DTD rules for HTML that were located on the Internet. We will be doing the same thing but with our own markup language where the DTD rules are located within our Web page.

 VALIDATE AN XML DOCUMENT USING DTD

GET READY. We will continue with our ShoppingList.xml file and a simple text editor.

1. Place the DTD at the top of our ShoppingList.xml file above the XML code.
   - The entire file should now contain the following code:
   ```
   <?xml version="1.0" encoding="utf-8" ?>
   <!DOCTYPE shoppinglist
   [
   <!ELEMENT title (#PCDATA)>
   <!ELEMENT food (#PCDATA)>
   <!ELEMENT unit (#PCDATA)>
   <!ELEMENT shoppinglist (title, item*)>
   <!ELEMENT item (food, unit)>
   <!ATTLIST unit qty CDATA "1">
   ]>
   <shoppinglist>
     <title>Sample</title>
     <item>
       <food>Milk</food>
       <unit qty="1">Gallon</unit>
     </item>
     <item>
       <food>Eggs</food>
       <unit qty="2">Dozen</unit>
     </item>
   </shoppinglist>
   ```

2. Save and refresh to make sure the file is free of errors.
3. Open your browser to the W3C's Markup Validation Service:
   http://validator.w3.org/#validate_by_upload
4. On the Web page, click the **Browse . . .** button to the right of the text box and locate your ShoppingList.xml file.
5. Give the file time to load, and then press the **Check** button.
   - If the result posted is "This document was successfully checked as XML!", then the document is well formed, meaning that it is free of syntactical errors. The document is also valid, meaning that your XML document follows all the rules of the DTD.
   - Ignore any warning messages. They are not relevant to our testing.
6. Close the browser and the file.

PAUSE. Keep the ShoppingList.xml file ready for the next exercise.

The **DTD** is used for validating both XML and XHTML documents. However, unlike XHTML, XML has many alternatives to DTD for creating document rules. The W3C XML **Schema** and RELAX NG are just two of the most popular new XML validators and are much more powerful than the DTD. They define not only the structure of the XML framework, but the content and attribute values as well. For example, the Schema can restrict the qty attribute to numeric values, while the DTD can only describe it as being character data. We will now use the W3C XML Schema to create our "language."

VALIDATE AN XML DOCUMENT USING SCHEMA

GET READY. We will continue with our ShoppingList.xml file in Visual Web Developer.

1. Open Visual Web Developer and create a new ASP.NET Web site using C#.
   - We will have to abandon our Notepad coding because Schema is much more complex than DTD. Instead, we will use Visual Web Developer, which has a built-in program to create a Schema from our DTD. After we create our Schema, we can make a few minor changes to help us understand how Schema differs from DTD.
   - We will not actually be using C# or Visual Basic in the site, which makes the Language selection irrelevant.

2. Open the **Add New Item** dialog box from the icon on the task bar and select the XML file **Template**. Use the default values and press the **Add** button.

3. Copy the code from our ShoppingList.xml file (from the last exercise) to this new file. Warning: Do not make a duplicate of the first line of code; we only need one XML declaration.
   - The next step is to create the Schema using our DTD rules. It is obviously best to make sure the XML document is well formed before converting it.
   - IntelliSense is now available to help with our XML syntax. You should make sure there are no errors in the document before creating a Schema.

4. Click on the XML pull-down menu and click **Create Schema**.
   - The first thing you will notice is that the Schema document is much larger than the DTD. It provides more detail, which allows us to have more control over our language.
   - Another major difference is that Schema is coded using XML syntax rather than the special DTD syntax. This normally makes a Schema easier to read than a DTD because we do not need to learn a completely new syntax.
   - Like DTD, Schema does not hold data, just the rules.
   - To have the XML file point to the new schema file, we need to place the file into the App_Data directory.

5. From the File menu, use **SaveXMLFile.xsd as** to save the file in a location of your choice. Note the location because we will come back to it later.

6. Remove the XMLFile.xsd from the editing window by clicking the **x** directly to the right of the tabs (not the top-right x, which will close the entire IDE window).

7. In the **Solution Explorer** window, right-click the WebSite path (at the top of the list) and click **Add Existing Item**.

8. From the **Add Existing Item** dialog box, find the **XMLFile.xsd** file you saved in Step 5. Then press the **Add** button.
   - The XMLFile.xsd should have been placed in the Solution Explorer list of files.
   - We will now make the switch from DTD to Schema.

9. Remove the DTD from the XML file XMLfile.xml, and add the attributes to the shopping list element for validation and to point to the Schema file.
   - The new file should now have XML code and a pointer to the Schema:

   ```
   <?xml version="1.0" encoding="utf-8" ?>

   <shoppinglist xmlns:xsi="http://www.w3.org/2001/
   ```

```
     XMLSchema-instance"
       xsi:noNamespaceSchemaLocation="XMLFile.xsd">
       <title>Sample</title>
       <item>
         <food>Milk</food>
         <unit qty="1">Gallon</unit>
       </item>
       <item>
         <food>Eggs</food>
         <unit qty="2">Dozen</unit>
       </item>
     </shoppinglist>
```

- Make sure IntelliSense has nothing underlined.

10. Add the tags to create a new element named unit2 under the first pair of unit tags to see what IntelliSense does with them:

    <unit2></unit2>

11. Hold the mouse over the squiggly underline to see the error message. Then erase the unit2 tags.

    - IntelliSense will use the Schema to alert you that the item element does not allow a child element named unit2.

    - At this point, the rules for our Schema are the same as those we had for the DTD.

    - We will now change the Schema so that the qty attribute will only accept numbers. Since it is possible to have a half gallon of milk, 0.5 gallons, we need to use a numeric data type that includes a decimal point.

    - First, we will place characters in the qty attribute to make sure the existing Schema will validate it. Remember that it is currently defined as character data (#PCDATA), because the DTD is unable to define it as numeric. The Schema converted this DTD rule as a String.

    - We will now change a Schema rule.

12. From the **Solution Explorer window**, double-click the **XMLfile.xsd** file and verify that Schema is expecting a string for the qty attribute:

    <xs:attribute default="1" name="qty"

    type="xs:string" />

13. Click the **XMLFile.xml** tab and change your XML file by replacing the "1" with '**One**' in the qty attribute:

    <unit qty='One'>Gallon</unit>

    - You should not have any errors with this change because '**One**' is a string type as defined.

    - It can be a little confusing at first to use XML syntax to define the rules for our XML document. The Schema lists rules for the XML document using attributes. In order to know what attribute the Schema is defining, you must find the attributes called "name."

14. Click the **XMLFile.xsd tab** and find the name attribute called "**qty**." Then change the Schema by replacing "string" with "**float**" for the "type" attribute:

    <xs:attribute default="1" name="qty"

    type="xs:float" />

- This will change the rule for qty, limiting it to numbers.

15. Click the **XMLFile.xml** tab to go back to the XML file.

- IntelliSense should now reject the 'One.'

16. Fix the error by replacing the 'One' with the number "1."

17. Spend some time changing various Schema values, including element definitions, to see what IntelliSense does with your changes.

PAUSE. Close Visual Web Developer.

Although our Schema is larger and more complex than the DTD, it is easier to read once we learn how it uses the XML syntax. For example, the number of acceptable item elements allowed is easily found: minOccurs="0" and maxOccurs="unbounded".

To make a comprehensive Schema to cover all possible rules of our tiny XML file will take much more time than is available for this lesson. For larger Schemas, you will find that many additional Schema rules are available. Of particular interest is the rule that can be created using regular expressions. These are created with another set of rules that are as large as the Schema rules. Covering all the Schema rules and any of the regular expressions is beyond the scope of this lesson.

Since the W3C XML Schema and RELAX NG standards are so similar and since the W3C XML Schema is included in Visual Web Developer, we will limit our discussions to the W3C XML Schema, commonly referred to simply as Schema with a capital S.

CERTIFICATION READY
When would it be better to use Schema rather than DTD, and how does the construction of the documents differ?
2.1

■ Distinguishing between DataSet and DataReader Objects

THE BOTTOM LINE

The **DataSet** and **DataReader** objects provide the properties and methods that enable the Web developer to retrieve data from a database on the server. The DataSet, along with supporting objects, can also be used to change the database. To take advantage of these objects, you need to have a fundamental understanding of databases.

Understanding Databases

After an introduction to databases, we will be installing Microsoft SQL Server and Microsoft SQL Server Management Studio. A database will then be created and filled with data. Finally, we will use the DataSet and DataReader objects to display our data.

To understand databases, we must first understand data. One of the most common, and misleading, definitions of data is that it is "raw facts"; it could just as easily be defined as "processed opinions." Data, which is actually plural, are anything that can be stored electronically: text, music, sounds, photos, movies, etc. Data are simply electronically stored stuff.

Data are not normally in a form that is easily deciphered by humans and most often require a computer program to process and convert the information into a useable form. This is what our program will do. It will read data that we place into a database, convert it into usable information, and display it in the browser.

A database is used to store data in a structured, well-organized, and well-managed facility. The primary structure of the database is the table. It holds data in rows and columns, similar to a spreadsheet. However, the rows of data that are stored in a table are called "records" and the individual cells are called "fields." Each column of fields is given a unique name when the table is constructed. The nameless records, or rows of data, are stored after the table is constructed. However, the rows are indirectly named using a primary key. At least one field name is chosen as the primary key in order to guarantee that each record it contains can be uniquely identified.

Each table holds tightly related data. For example, a sales company that has a sales force selling things may want to create three tables: one for the salespeople, one for the things they sell, and one to store the details of the sales. Notice how these three tightly related groups of data are related to one another. Data organized in this way are called a relational database.

Retrieving data from one of these tables typically results in a spreadsheet-like structure as well. However, the resulting grid of information may include sums, averages, or other processed data from one or more tables. The field names may be lost in this process and the records from the original tables may have undergone some manipulation. For these reasons, the results are simply referred to as rows and columns rather than records and fields. Briefly, fields are defined by the table, and records populate the fields. Tables, with their fields and records, can then provide us with information in the form of rows and columns.

A special high-level language, Structured Query Language (SQL), controls most of the activity in today's databases. IBM developed SEQUEL, the predecessor to SQL, in the 1970s, which soon became SQL to prevent a trademark infringement. Unlike SEQUEL, SQL is pronounced using its individual letters. However, enough time has elapsed since the days of SEQUEL that it is no longer improper to say "see-kwul" for the newer SQL.

Our code will use as little SQL as possible. You will only copy brief bits of SQL code into your program when required.

The next step is to set up a database management system to use in our lesson.

INSTALLING THE DATABASE MANAGEMENT SYSTEM

Visual Web Developer 2008 Express works well with Microsoft SQL Server 2008 Express. All Express editions are available free from the Microsoft Web site. Be sure to include the "With Tools" option when selecting the download file for SQL Server. This includes the Management Tools, which can be installed later if necessary.

As the installation process begins, a series of questions is asked. When this data-gathering process is complete, a tree view is shown that lists all the options selected. Once you agree to the settings, the real installation begins. The following is a list of some of the options that were selected for the installation used with this lesson:

- All Features were selected
- Named instance is SQLEXPRESS
- Server Configuration
  - Account Name is "NT ATHORITY\SYSTEM"
  - Password was left blank
  - Startup Type was left as "Automatic"
- Windows authentication mode was selected
  - This allows the use of SQL Server without the logon process
  - This can always be changed later
- Add Current User was used for Specifying the SQL Server administrator

Once your options are recorded, a summary is given for verification. Figure 3-7 shows the configuration used for creating our lessons.

Figure 3-7

Summary of the SQL Server installation used for the lessons

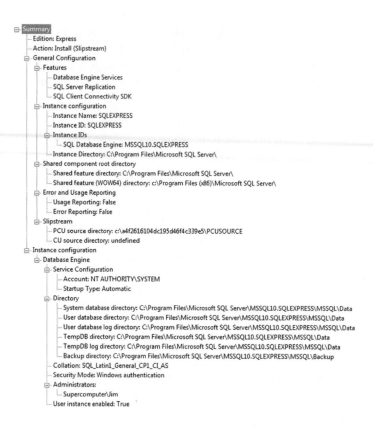

If SQL Server 2008 Express was not installed with the SQL Management Studio (SSMS), it can be downloaded and installed separately. However, do not be alarmed if the installation process menu leads you into reinstalling the server. Proceed with the reinstallation and it will eventually recognize the existing server and simply add the tool without reinstallation.

Even though the SQL Server 2008 Setup window, shown in Figure 3-8, says "Ready to Install SQL Server 2008," it is going to install the SSMS feature for SQL Server 2008 Express. Notice that "Ready to Install" is highlighted on the left, which is below the normal installation steps for SQL Server, and that the installation summary list is much shorter than the full installation displayed in Figure 3-7.

Figure 3-8

The SSMS feature is ready to be installed for SQL Server 2008 Express

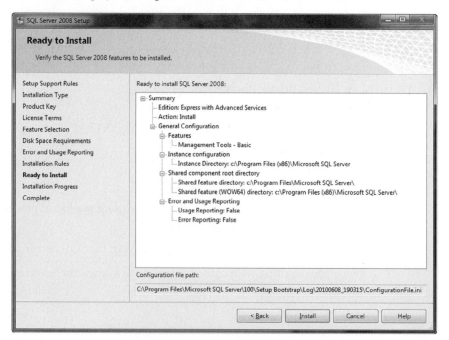

Once you have the database and SSMS installed, we will create a database and populate it with some data.

CREATE THE SAMPLE DATABASE

GET READY. We will be using Microsoft SQL Server 2008, SQL Management Studio, and Visual Web Developer.

1. Start Microsoft SQL Management Studio (SSMS)
   - SSMS can be found in the Start menu inside the Microsoft SQL Server 2008 directory and is displayed as shown in Figure 3-9.

Figure 3-9

Logging in to SSMS using the default values

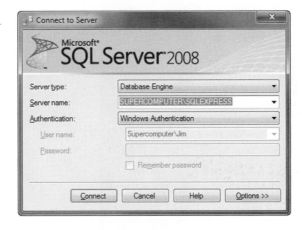

2. Press the **Connect** button to start the first window, which will look similar to the one in Figure 3-10.

Figure 3-10

Creating a new database in SSMS

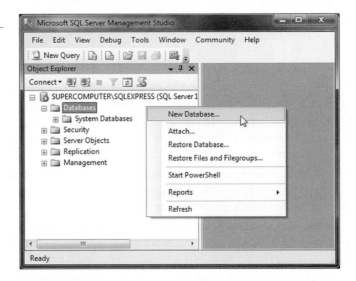

3. Click on the **Databases** expansion button.
   - The System Databases are obviously located in the system directory.
   - We will be creating our own database, but not within this system directory.
4. Right-click on **Databases** and click **New Database**.

5. Type in the name of your database, **Sample**, and press the **OK** button. Leave all the default values.

   • This will return you to the main SSMS window.

6. Expand the **Sample** database and right-click **Tables** to add a new table, as shown in Figure 3-11.

Figure 3-11

Adding a new table to the Sample database

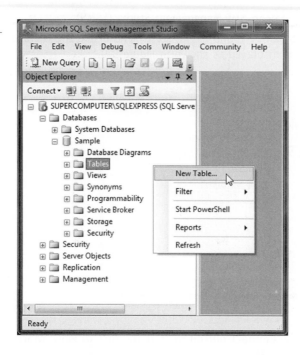

7. In the Properties window, name the table **ShoppingList**.

   • We will create a shopping list that only includes food. For each food item, we will define the unit and quantity. We will use **Food, Unit,** and **Qty** as the names for our fields in the table.

   • For each field, we also have to consider how memory will be used to store this data. Rules for selecting the proper data type can be rather complex. The following is a sample of what we need to consider for our Sample table.

   • The default **Nchar(10)** data type is fixed-length unicode. This will limit the field to 10 characters. Because it is Unicode, it will also require two bytes or 16 bits per character.

   • A valid alternative is to use **Varchar(50)**. Varchar is more popular because the data are variable in length. Varchar also is ASCII encoded for the characters where each character uses a single byte or 8 bits per character.

   • We will use Varchar(50) for the Food and Unit fields.

   • Numbers will be used to record the values placed in the Qty field. We need to consider partial units, such as the half gallon of milk we used before, that will require a decimal point. Several numerical data types use decimal points. We will use a small easy-to-use data type called float.

   • These data type selections are shown in Figure 3-12.

Figure 3-12

The nearly completed table definitions

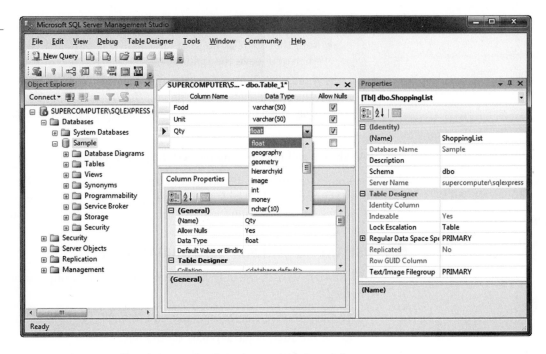

8. When completed, press the **Save** button on the toolbar.

9. Right-click the new table name and click **Edit Top 200 Rows** as shown in Figure 3-13.

Figure 3-13

Getting prepared to add new records to the table

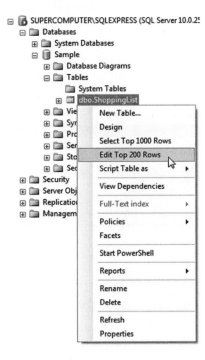

10. Enter the data by overwriting the NULL values, as shown in Figure 3-14.

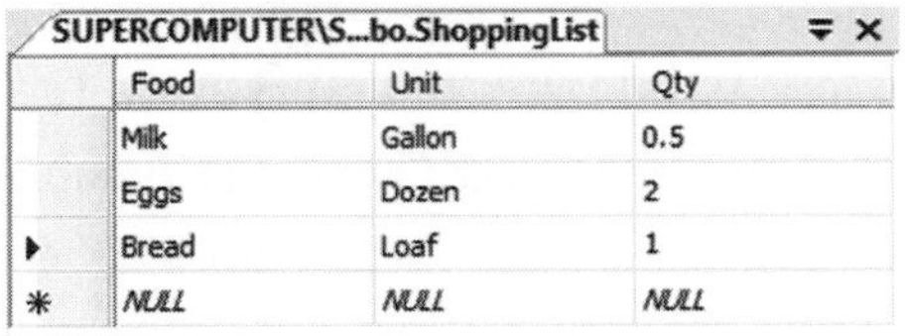

Figure 3-14

The completed table with data

	Food	Unit	Qty
	Milk	Gallon	0.5
	Eggs	Dozen	2
▶	Bread	Loaf	1
*	NULL	NULL	NULL

- Please do not be creative at this point; just enter the given values.
- Note that there is no save button. The data in the field is saved automatically when you leave the field.
- A red circle with an exclamation point will appear in the fields as you change their values. This icon is alerting you that the data has been changed. The icon will go away when you move to the next record or save the database.

11. Close the SSMS application.

PAUSE. We will not be using the SSMS application for the rest of the lesson.

One more step needs to be completed before using the Visual Web Developer. It enables us to see the ShoppingList table within our application. SQL server runs in the background as a Windows service. To connect to this service, we must first make sure it is running.

 USE THE SQL SERVER CONFIGURATION MANAGER

GET READY. We will use only Microsoft SQL Server Configuration Manager for this brief exercise.

1. Open the SQL Server Configuration Manager from the Windows Start menu.
2. Select **SQL Server Services** on the left.
3. Select **SQL Server Browser** on the right.
4. Right-click under **Start Mode** and make sure it is set to **Automatic**, as shown in Figure 3-15.
   - If grayed out, right-click SQL Server browser (top one on the list), click properties, click the Service tab, and change the Start Mode to Automatic. Now you can complete this step.
   - Turning on the SQL Server Browser service allows the database to be connected through a dynamic TCP/IP port. This should eliminate connection problems related to port numbers.

Figure 3-15

Setting SQL Server Browser to Automatic

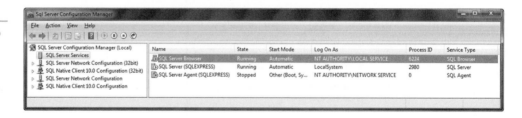

5. Close the application.

PAUSE. We will not be using SQL Server Configuration Manager for the rest of the lesson.

Now we can proceed to Visual Web Developer and write an application using our database.

 CONNECT THE DATABASE TO THE IDE

GET READY. We will be using Microsoft Visual Web Developer 2008 Express Edition again.

1. Start Visual Web Developer.
2. Create an entirely new ASP.NET Web site using Visual C#.
3. Click **Tools** from the menu and select **Connect to Database . . .**
4. Click the **Change . . .** button and select **Microsoft SQL Server** as shown in Figure 3-16.
   - We will not be using the default, which connects to a file rather than a service.

Figure 3-16

Microsoft SQL Server is
selected as our data source

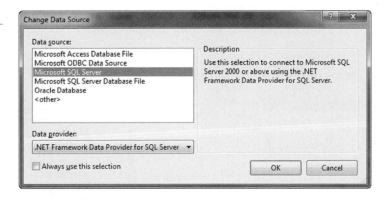

5. Press the **OK** button.

6. In the **Add Connection** dialog box, click the down arrow for the **Server name:** drop-down list box.

   • It is normal to take awhile for the list box to drop.

7. Select the server name\instance name of your SQL Server installation.

   • Most likely, you will only have a single choice.

8. Select Sample from the list of database names available on your database server, as shown in Figure 3-17.

   • Again, it may take some time for the list box to drop.

Figure 3-17

The completed database
connection dialog box

9. Press the **Test Connection** button to make sure the connection can be made.

   • If the connection was not successful, you may have security issues to address on your system.

10. Assuming the test was successful, press the **OK** button.

11. From the Database Explorer window, expand the tree to find the ShoppingList table and double-click it, as shown in Figure 3-18.

Figure 3-18

Expanded Tables tree with an opened table editor

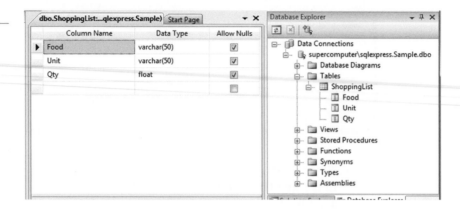

• Double-clicking the table opens it up so that you now have full control over both the data and the table structure through Visual Web Developer.

• Before the DataSet object will work properly for updating the table, a primary key constraint must be set.

12. Right-click on the drop-down list button to the left of the Food field and click **Set Primary Key**, Set Primary Key, as shown in Figure 3-19.

Figure 3-19

Setting the primary key

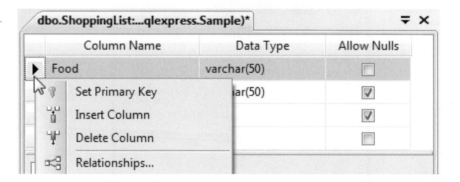

• Notice that the **Allow Nulls** constraint has been unchecked. Nulls are unknown values created by assigning nothing to fields when creating new rows. Primary keys require that all rows be uniquely identified. By setting the Food column as the primary key, we have essentially told the database management system that each Food field in the Food column is responsible for "naming" the row.

• The DataSet object will have trouble with tables not having a primary key assigned. When it uses the DataAdapter to update the database records from changes made in the DataSet, the database must know exactly what rows to update. It will not be able to locate the rows without knowing their "names," which the primary key provides.

13. Close the current tab and press the **Save** button to make this change permanent.

• Be careful to close the tab, not Visual Web Developer.

14. Go back to the Database Explorer window, right-click the **ShoppingList** table, and click **Show Table Data**, as shown in Figure 3-20.

Figure 3-20

Expanded tables tree with the opened data editor

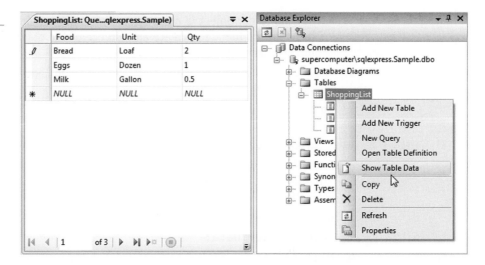

- All the data from the table can be changed in the Visual Web Developer IDE. Notice that the Save button in the toolbar is grayed out. Saving is done automatically when you click anywhere outside of the field you are changing.

- You overwrite the NULL values to add new rows. Right-click the left column of the grid to find more functionality, such as deleting a row.

- You may make changes to the table for practice, but put it all back when you are done. Remember, there is no "Undo" button.

15. Close the current tab.

PAUSE. Keep Visual Web Developer open for the next exercise.

Finally, we are ready to place the data onto a Web page. We will start by having our Web page show the data from the table with the least possible effort.

 CONNECT THE TABLE TO THE WEB PAGE

GET READY. We will continue using Microsoft Visual Web Developer.

1. Open the **Design** view of the Default form.
2. Single-click the name **ShoppingList** in Database Explorer and drag it to the form and drop it.
3. Run the program. Then close the browser.

PAUSE. Keep Visual Web Developer open for the next exercise.

Although this was a very easy way to place data on the form, it is difficult to make the necessary changes to meet the requirements of most Web page designs. A better way is to write the code yourself rather than using the code generated by Visual Web Developer. This not only gives you more control over the display, it allows you to create dynamic pages. As an added bonus, it allows your code to be used for other projects.

We will now use some of these objects to get control over the display and make the page more dynamic.

 USE THE DATAREADER OBJECT

GET READY. We will continue using Microsoft Visual Web Developer.

1. Go to **Design** view and remove the two controls from the form.

- The DataReader Object is not a typical control found in the Toolbox that can be placed on the form. You create an instance of the object in code and program its properties and methods.

2. Place a button on the form and write the following code for its click-event procedure. Ignore the error that IntelliSense gives you for SqlConnection.

```
SqlConnection con = new SqlConnection();
```

- The error would go away if you typed the entire namespace, **System.Data. SqlClient.SqlConnection**, but there is an easier way to address this problem.

3. To limit your typing, place the two namespaces in the code-behind just under the existing "using" statements. Be careful not to delete the existing using statements or you will lose the locations of objects in your code.

```
using System.Data.SqlClient;
```
```
using System.Data;
```

4. Run the new code to test for errors and click the button. Close the browser.

- Clicking the button should produce no noticeable difference at this point because the program simply creates a connection object.

- It is important to test all the small changes to an application as it is being developed. The results may not show that we did anything, but it will certainly let us know when something is not correct.

- Now that we have the database connection object, we need to connect it to our database. The only way the connection object is going to know anything about our database is to provide it with a connection string.

5. Append the following line of code to our event procedure:

```
con.ConnectionString=" ";
```

- Notice that we left the string blank. This is temporary. Finding the correct words for this string takes some thought. It is critical to get it right because it provides all the information needed to connect your application to the database, including the name of the server, authorized users, passwords, etc. However, we can connect the table quickly by using the same string we used when we dragged the table to the form.

6. Go back to **Design** view and drag the ShoppingList table from the Data Explorer window to the form.

7. Single-click the **SqlDataSource** control and go to the **ConnectionString** property in the **Properties** window.

- This is the connection string used when we first connected to the database. We will just borrow it.

8. Copy the value of the **ConnectionString** property and paste it between the empty quotation marks in the last line of code in the Click **event** procedure:

```
con.ConnectionString="Data
Source=SUPERCOMPUTER\SQLEXPRESS;Initial
Catalog=Sample;Integrated Security=True";
```

- Unless you have a supercomputer, your connection string will look different.

9. Place a second backslash in the string:

```
con.ConnectionString="Data
Source=SUPERCOMPUTER\\SQLEXPRESS;Initial
Catalog=Sample;Integrated Security=True";
```

10. Again, remove the gridview and SqlDataSource controls from the form.

- This technique will work for now, but connection strings need to be thoroughly understood and tweaked before deploying a site.

- Notice that an error showed up in the code. The backslash in C# is used to create special characters. Any character following a backslash in C# is treated differently from a standard character. In this case, we do not want special treatment. We just want the backslash. Therefore, we place another backslash in the special character position to let the compiler know that the backslash is what we really want.

11. Run the new code to test for errors. Make sure to click the button. Close the browser.

- We need to open and close the connection to make sure the connection string works.

12. Append the following code to the event procedure:

con.Open();

con.Close();

13. Run the new code to test for errors. Make sure to click the button. Then close the browser.

- To retrieve data from the database, we need to use SQL. An SQL statement will be sent to the server using an SqlCommand object.

14. Between the **Open()** and **Close( )**, place the command that tells the database exactly what data we want to retrieve:

SqlCommand cmd = new SqlCommand

("Select * from ShoppingList", con);

- This Select statement returns all the rows from the table.
- The asterisk is used to return all the fields (columns) from the table without having to list all the individual field names.

15. Run the new code to test for errors. Make sure to click the button. Close the browser.

- We will use the DataReader to quickly retrieve the data that was ordered by the SQL statement.
- The reader is used in two phases. The first is to retrieve the data from the database and place it into memory. The second is to bring the data to the control one row at a time using its Read method.

16. Follow the SqlCommand with the new instance of the DataReader object along with the closing of the reader:

SqlDataReader reader = cmd.ExecuteReader();

reader.Close();

17. Run the new code to test for errors. Make sure to click the button. Close the browser.

- We can finally use the Read method to bring the data into our Web page. The Response.Write method will be used to display it.

18. Place the following code between the ExecuteReader and Close methods of the DataReader:

reader.Read();

Response.Write(Convert.ToString(reader[0])

+ "<br>");

19. Run the new code to test for errors. Make sure to click the button. Close the browser.

- We should now have something written to the form.
- To get the rest of the data, we need to use multiple Read and Write methods. Each Read method reads a single piece of data and each Write method writes a single item.

20. Complete the event procedure with the following code:

protected void Button1_Click(object sender,

EventArgs e)

```
{
    SqlConnection con = new SqlConnection();
    con.ConnectionString="Data Source=
    SUPERCOMPUTER\\SQLEXPRESS;Initial Catalog=
    Sample;Integrated Security=True";
    con.Open();
    SqlCommand cmd = new SqlCommand
    ("Select * from ShoppingList", con);
    SqlDataReader reader = cmd.ExecuteReader();
    reader.Read();
    Response.Write(Convert.ToString(reader[0])
    + "<br>");
    reader.Read();
    Response.Write(Convert.ToString(reader[0])
    + "<br>");
    reader.Read();
    Response.Write(Convert.ToString(reader[0])
    + "<br>");
    reader.Close();
    con.Close();
}
```

21. Run the program and press the button. Close the browser.

    • Bread, Eggs, and Milk should have been displayed at the top of the page.

    • The only thing we can do with the DataReader is read. Since we have three rows of data, we used three read statements. After each read statement, we wrote out the data before the next read. Otherwise, the read buffer would be overwritten by the next read and only provide us with the last row. If we had added any more read statements, the program would have crashed because we would have run out of data.

    • The zeros in the reader array represent the first column of the data returned by the SQL statement. Because our SQL statement retrieves all the data, the first column maps directly to the table.

22. Replace the zeros in the reader with 1's. Run the code and close the browser.

    • You are now seeing the second column of data identified as column 1.

23. Replace the zeros in the reader with 2's. Run the code and close the browser.

    • You are now seeing the third column of data identified as column 2.

    • If you use 3, the program will crash because we do not have any more columns in the table to read. Writing the code to trap these errors is beyond the scope of this lesson.

PAUSE. Keep Visual Web Developer open for the next exercise.

Although some coding was involved, the DataReader provides us with a high-speed alternative to data retrieval. It reads the data and delivers it to the application one row at a time. It never rereads and never stores more than one row. Sometimes the DataReader is referred to as a "fire-hose" connection.

Typically, the DataReader is used in a loop. On each read, the DataReader method returns true or false depending on the success of the read. The code to read each row will repeat as long as the return value remains true. By using a loop, you will shorten the amount of code necessary to read the data. If you had 100 records, which would be a small database, using a loop would greatly reduce the lines of code in your program.

Pressing the button multiple times does not add additional output to the Web page. This is because the page is reprocessed by the server each time, giving us the same results.

The complementary object to the DataReader is the ExecuteNonQuery object. It can do anything to the database except read. SQL commands are written for this object and sent to the database management system (DBMS). These commands are most often used for inserting, updating, and deleting data. Using this object requires learning SQL, which is again beyond the scope of this lesson.

Even with the DataReader, we are not completely free from SQL. We used it earlier with a very simple statement that retrieved all the data from the table when the instance of the reader was created: `"Select * from ShoppingList"`.

Unlike the DataReader, the DataSet object can be used for both reading and writing when working alongside the DataAdapter object. Together, they can Create, Read, Update, and Delete (CRUD) records with minimal use of SQL.

Using the DataSet Object

> The DataSet object is a mini in-memory database. It is a complex object that is capable of managing multiple database tables in a similar manner to SQL Server.

Even though this object has about as much functionality as an entire database management system, it is primarily used as a temporary client-side database for the application to work in sync with the data at the server. Since we are working in a disconnected environment, a workaround like this is needed because a continuous connection to the database is not possible.

Another object, the DataAdapter, is used together with the DataSet to help with database management on ASP.NET Web sites. The DataAdapter is a go-between for the DataSet and the database. Like the DataReader, the DataAdapter uses an SQL query to retrieve the data, but the DataAdapter uses its Fill method to populate the DataSet rather than reading one row at a time.

When data are altered within the DataSet object, they can be synchronized with the database by using the DataAdapter's Update method.

We will now use the DataSet along with the DataAdapter to retrieve the same data we did with the DataReader.

 USE THE DATASET OBJECT TO DISPLAY DATA

GET READY. We will continue using Microsoft Visual Web Developer.

1. Place another button on the form.
   - We will use the same connection object that we used for the first button.
2. Copy some of the click-event procedure code from the first button you placed on the form to the clipboard. Select the lines of code from the first line, up to and including the line **con.Open()**. This should only include the first three lines of code. Paste this code into the event procedure of our new button.
3. Type in or copy **con.Close();** at the end of your event procedure.
4. Test the program for errors, press your new button, and close the browser.
   - We will transfer the data using the DataAdapter rather than the Command object as we did with the DataReader.
   - A new instance of the DataAdapter object named **da** will be created.
   - A new instance of the DataSet named **ds** will be created.
   - Finally, the DataAdapter's Fill method will fill the DataSet.

5. Place the following code between the open and close statements in the event procedure of the second button:

```
SqlDataAdapter da = new SqlDataAdapter
("Select * from ShoppingList", con);
DataSet ds = new DataSet();
da.Fill(ds, "LocalData");
```

6. Test the program for errors, press your new button, and close the browser.
   - Now we need to display the data from the DataSet.

7. Place the following code after the **da.Fill** and the **close()** in the event procedure of the second button:

```
Response.Write(ds.Tables[0].Rows[0][0].ToString()
+ ", ");
Response.Write(ds.Tables[0].Rows[0][1].ToString()
+ ", ");
Response.Write(ds.Tables[0].Rows[0][2].ToString()
+ "<br>");
Response.Write(ds.Tables[0].Rows[1][0].ToString()
+ ", ");
Response.Write(ds.Tables[0].Rows[1][1].ToString()
+ ", ");
Response.Write(ds.Tables[0].Rows[1][2].ToString()
+ "<br>");
Response.Write(ds.Tables[0].Rows[2][0].ToString()
+ ", ");
Response.Write(ds.Tables[0].Rows[2][1].ToString()
+ ", ");
Response.Write(ds.Tables[0].Rows[2][2].ToString()
+ "<br>");
```

8. Run the program. Close the browser.
   - The sequential code we used here should help you visualize how the program progresses through the table. However, it is not common to write code for the DataSet in this manner. Rather, a foreach loop would be used to iterate through a variable number of rows in the DataSet. This technique normally requires fewer lines of code as well.
   - The zero in the Tables property represents the first table in the array of table names. The numbers in the Rows property represent a two-dimensional table of rows and columns, as shown in Table 3-2.

TAKE NOTE*

Rather than using numbers for the table and columns, the DataSet can also use the names used in the data source.

Table 3-2

A visual representation of the rows and columns of the Rows property in a DataSet object for a table

[0][0]	[0][1]	[0][2]
[1][0]	[1][1]	[1][2]
[2][0]	[2][1]	[2][2]

PAUSE. Keep Visual Web Developer open.

We will now make a minor change to the DataSet and re-sync it to the site database.

 USE THE DATASET OBJECT TO SAVE DATA

GET READY. We will continue using Microsoft Visual Web Developer.

1. Place another button on the form.
   - We will use the same connection as in the first button for the second button so the second button can be used to update the table.
2. Copy the code from the first button you placed on the form from the beginning, up to and including the line starting with **da.Fill**;, and place it into the event procedure of our new button.
3. Type in or copy **con.Close()**; at the end of your event procedure.
4. Test the program for errors, press your new button, and close the browser.
   - Now we need to change the data in the DataSet and save it permanently in the database.
   - It was not logical to shop for a half gallon of milk in a gallon container. We will fix the database by changing the unit to **Half Gallon** and quantity to **one**.
5. Type the following code between the **Fill** method of the data adapter and the **con.Close()**; line:

```
ds.Tables["LocalData"].Rows[2][1] = "Half Gallon";
ds.Tables["LocalData"].Rows[2][2] = "1";
da.Update(ds, "LocalData");
```

   - Be careful of the subtle differences between the da and ds in the code.
6. Run the program and press the second button to display the current data.
   - The program is almost ready to update the database. The missing object is the Command Builder that is used to create the SQL statements for our updates.
7. Place the following code between the DataAdapter and DataSet:

```
SqlCommandBuilder cmdBldr = new SqlCommandBuilder(da);
```

   - The complete code for the third button is:

```
SqlConnection con = new SqlConnection();
con.ConnectionString = "Data Source=
SUPERCOMPUTER\\SQLEXPRESS;Initial Catalog=
Sample;Integrated Security=True";
con.Open();
SqlDataAdapter da = new SqlDataAdapter
("Select * from ShoppingList", con);
SqlCommandBuilder cmdBldr =
new SqlCommandBuilder(da);
DataSet ds = new DataSet();
da.Fill(ds, "LocalData");
ds.Tables["LocalData"].Rows[2][1] = "Half Gallon";
ds.Tables["LocalData"].Rows[2][2] = "1";
da.Update(ds, "LocalData");
con.Close();
```

8. Run the program and press the second button to display the current data.

9. Press the third button followed by the second button to see the changes to the data. Close the browser.

PAUSE. Shut down Visual Web Developer.

You now have the foundation to expand this to a usable site. What we have done should be enough to help you understand some basic DataSet capabilities and how the DataReader compares to them.

Choosing the Data Object Based on Application Requirements

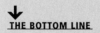
THE BOTTOM LINE

The two main contenders are the DataReader and the DataSet. The DataReader is the simpler object that reads one record at a time. It is unable to make changes to the database. The DataSet is a container for data. It can save changes back to the database on the server. These are some of the considerations to address in determining the best object for the application.

The DataSet is simply a set of tables. However, when combined with other controls, as we have seen with the DataAdapter and CommandBuilder, it begins to have more functionality. A common control used with the DataSet is the GridView, where a simple connection tying them together gives the DataSet even more functionality. Some less common objects that can be used with the DataSet are the DataRelation object that relates the tables, the UniqueConstraint object that enforces data integrity, and the ForeignKey constraint that enforces referential integrity. Whether you understand these terms or not, the point is that the DataSet is the center of a host of objects that can be used together to create a fully functional in-memory database environment.

The DataReader is very simple compared to the DataSet. It is designed to retrieve data as quickly as possible. Unlike the DataSet, it requires you to provide the destination for this data, such as a display, variable, array, another table, etc. It is limited to reading one row at a time and is unable to reread.

CERTIFICATION READY
When would it be better to use the DataReader than the DataSet, and how would the construction of the code differ?
2.2

The choice of which to use depends on what needs to be done with the data after they are available to the program. If the purpose is to display them on the page, the DataReader is the obvious choice. If the data need to be changed, either will work as long as the DataReader is used alongside the ExecuteNonQuery object for saving changes. This choice will require a good understanding of SQL. If the same rows of data will be referenced many times, the DataSet might be a better choice because the data will automatically be available in memory. The data from the DataReader would have to be saved into a variable, an array, or a control such as a list box. The DataSet also has other capabilities not covered here, such as a sorting method and the ability to work with XML. Rather than memorizing which control is best for a given situation, learn the capabilities of each control and choose wisely.

Calling a Service from a Web Page

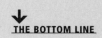
THE BOTTOM LINE

A *Web Service* is an application programming interface (API) that allows service-oriented applications to access Web-based service providers. Microsoft uses its ASP.NET-based *Windows Communication Foundation (WCF)* framework to easily create and consume such services.

In the early days of personal computing, desktop computers ran applications that handled their own data needs. Every application also stored and transported data in its own proprietary format. Eventually, computers were given network capability and databases were connected to share data. Applications were written to connect to specific database management systems. This required an understanding of the database management system and the database application used to share the data. To separate the database from the applications, XML was used to convert data into a common format. This reduced programming on the client side to working with XML, even though data came from multiple databases and database applications. Web services soon arrived and used these technologies to isolate the data from the applications.

WCF is the latest of these services. It has more features and protocols than the standard Web Service. WCF continues the move toward providing data in a way that reduces the need for applications to have an understanding of the data source.

We will create a simple service and test it with a WCF Services testing application.

 CREATE A BASIC WINDOWS COMMUNICATION FOUNDATION (WCF) SERVICE

GET READY. We will continue using Microsoft Visual Web Developer.

1. Start Visual Web Developer, but do NOT create a new Web site.

2. Open the **New Web Site** dialog box, but do NOT create a new Web site.

3. Select **WCF Service** from the Template and use the C# language.
   - This should take you to the Service.cs editing window.
   - In our previous Web page development session, we used Visual Web Developer to produce Web pages using a Web form. We pressed a button on the form that opened the code behind the form. This code could be written in a programming language such as C#. We also had the option of editing the form in HTML. Because the WCF Service has no Web form, the pages we use are very different.
   - In this page, we will write the code that delivers data from our WCF Service. A function is defined that then becomes a method of the service class. It is given a return value, a string with a message, to be delivered when this method of the service is invoked. If not defined as public, the function is not exposed as a method and remains a local function not seen by the client.

4. Place the following code between the last two curly braces at the end of the code:

```
public string Question()
{
  return "Will everyone see this?";
}
```
   - This code returns an invoked method of the service.

5. Go to the **Solution Explorer** window and double click the **IService.cs** file.
   - Notice that the code for IService.cs in this template is much more involved than what the generic Web site gave us. At this point, you may start to think that running such a simple service as ours on this complex platform may be more than we need. You could conclude that it might be more efficient to write it from scratch using a simple text editor and bypass all this overhead. However, although the code would most likely be much smaller, using this template is far easier. In fact, comments are even placed in the code to help guide us through the project.

6. Add the following code just under the **"// TODO: Add your service operations here"** comment:

```
[OperationContract]
string Question();
```

- The Operations Contract exposes the function to the Web as a method of the service. It relies on the Service.cs file for the data.
- We have now defined and exposed our data.

7. Go back to the **Service.cs** tab and start the service as you would an application.

- It will not run properly if you run it from the IService.cs window.
- Since our service is named Service, the top of the Web page should say **Service Service** followed by **You have created a service**, as shown in Figure 3-21.
- A program provided by Visual Studio named WcfTestClient.exe can be used to test this service.

Figure 3-21

Starting your service

8. Find the **WcfTestClient.exe** file and run it. The path may be a little different on your computer.

```
C:\Program Files\Microsoft Visual Studio 9.0
\Common7\IDE\WcfTestClient.exe
```

Or

```
C:\Program Files (x86)\Microsoft Visual Studio
9.0\Common7\IDE\WcfTestClient.exe
```

9. From the file menu, click **Add Service...** as shown in Figure 3-22.

Figure 3-22

Adding your service to the test area

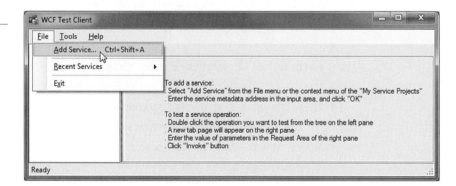

10. If the service does not appear, copy the URL from the browser and paste it into the drop-down list box in the **Add Service** dialog box. Then press the **OK** button.

- It should take a few seconds to connect to the service.

11. Once the connection is established, double-click **Question ( )** and click the **Invoke** button and then the **OK** button, as shown in Figure 3-23.

Figure 3-23

Starting to test the service

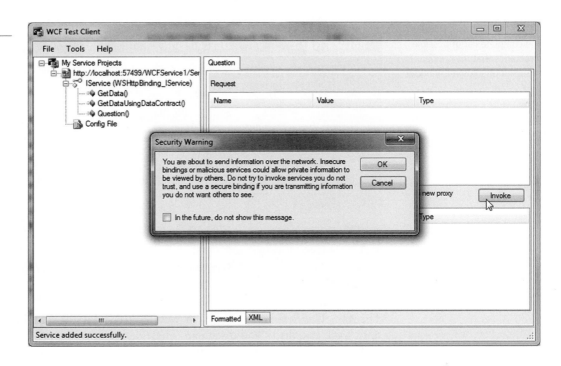

- You should now see the return value of your Question( ) method.
- If there are more methods to run, you could double-click them as well. Each method creates another tab across the top of the right side of the window.

12. Close the testing program.

13. Close the browser.

PAUSE. Keep Visual Web Developer open.

Although we found that it is very easy to create a WCF, we have only touched the surface. To create and deploy a WCF requires much more experience than you have gained here. The primary point of this exercise is that you understand that creating a service is very different from creating a Web page.

Examining App_WebReferences

Notice that there are two directories in our Solutions Explorer window. These directories are not only the defaults for our WCF Service, they are two of a special set of ASP.NET folders. The names should never be changed.

Because ASP.NET already knows these names, it can run faster by not having to look them up in another structure such as a configuration file or the registry. App_WebReferences is just one of these special directories. It holds files such as the Web Services Description Language (WSDL) files and discovery files. Table 3-3 shows the possible directories needed by ASP.NET. The App_WebReferences directory has no reason to exist at this point and will not be displayed in our Solutions Explorer Window.

Table 3-3

The complete list of possible directories that may appear in the Solution Explorer window

Folder Name	Description
Bin	Binary files such as third-party dll's that added to the application
App_Browsers	Browser capabilities
App_Code	Source code; limited to a single language such as C# or Visual Basic
App_Data	Data files such as XML and non-server database files such as MS Access
App_GlobalResources	Resource files that you want to be available for the entire application
App_Local Resources	Resource files that you want to be available for a single page
App_Themes	Supports applications that use themes; themes are "skin" files for controls
App_WebReferences	Files that link Web services to the applications

The **App_WebReferences folder** is a Web services folder. It contains files having the extensions wsdl, xsd, disco, and discomap. These define the reference to the Web services that the Web applications use. The .wsdl file is an XML file that describes WCF Services and how to access them. Being XML, the specifications of the service, in our case a string named Question, can be read by both humans and applications. Since we only tested the service, this XML file was not created.

 EXAMINE THE DEFAULT WCF FILES

GET READY. We will continue using Microsoft Visual Web Developer.

1. Look at the Solution Explorer window.
   - We have four files in the Solution Explorer to understand. Two are in an App_Code folder. These two are similar to our code-behind because they are written in C#. The Service.cs file is where we write the code that provides the processing for our service and the IService.cs file is the interface for these services.
   - Since we are already familiar with these two files, we will examine the other two.

2. Go to the **Solution Explorer** window, double-click the **Service.svc** file, and note its contents:

   ```
   <%@ ServiceHost Language="C#" Debug="true"
   Service="Service" CodeBehind=
   "~/App_Code/Service.cs" %>
   ```

   - This is the complete contents of the Service.svc file.
   - The one directive this file contains includes a CodeBehind attribute pointing to the Service.cs file. The Services.cs is code-behind, not for a form but for the service file.

3. Open the **web.config** file.
   - We have seen this file before, but this time we can see something that is relevant to our service.

4. Locate the **<system.serviceModel>** tag. Use (Ctrl) + (F) to find it quickly.
   - This is the location of the names to be changed according to the comments near the top of the Service.cs and IService.cs files. You may want to go back to these files to see the comments.

PAUSE. Close Visual Web Developer.

We will now locate some of the elements in this file and see what they store.

Examining the <system.serviceModel> Element

The **<system.serviceModel> element** is located near the bottom of the web.config file. It holds the specifications for all your hosted services.

The <system.serviceModel> element is broken down into three sections using the <services>, <bindings>, and <behaviors> elements. Refer to the web.config file as we describe this element below.

The <services> element contains one or more <service> elements for each of the services the application hosts. Each <service> element provides the specifications for that service. The two attributes are name and behaviorConfiguration. The name attribute holds the fully qualified name of the hosted service and the behaviorConfiguration attribute holds the name of the behaviors of the service.

Within each <service> element is an <endpoint> element. Our program exposed an Endpoint. Although we had just the one, the purpose of a WCF Service is to expose collections of Endpoints. An Endpoint is the portal for communication to be consumed by clients. The client is a program that exchanges messages with Endpoints. The client may also expose an Endpoint to establish two-way communication. We stopped at the testing phase for the client because the programming involved to create a client is beyond the scope of this lesson.

An Endpoint consists of three parts of a message: the where, the how, and the what. This information is stored in the three attributes: address, binding, and contract. The address attribute is expressed as a URL and identifies the location of the service. The binding attribute defines the protocol, encoding, and security used for the message. There are four types of contracts available. The service contract describes the operations the client can perform on a service. Data contracts define the data types used. Fault contracts define error handling. Message contracts let the service interact with the messages.

Our web.config file now shows that we have two more elements buried with the <service> element. These are the <identity> and <dns> elements that let the service know that we are running this from our own computer, the localhost.

If we had a <bindings> element, it would be used for communication settings such as adjust buffers, limit connections, and set timeouts.

The <behaviors> element modifies or extends service or client functionality by using the <serviceBehaviors> or <endpointBehaviors>.

The svcutil.exe will generate the output.config file to be used in the client application. The file can be created by locating svcutil.exe and running it with the given URL. The file is an XML-based configuration file. But unlike web.config, the only element under the root is <system.serviceModel>. It holds the configurations to be used on the client side of the service, such as the value for the address <hitpoint> attribute holding the URL that you used to run the program.

Although there is much more to learn about these settings, at least we now know that the web.config file holds a lot of information about our service under the <system .serviceModel> element.

SKILL SUMMARY

IN THIS LESSON YOU LEARNED TO:

- Read and write XML data.
- Apply XML rules.
- Validate an XML document using DTD.
- Validate an XML document using Schema.
- Create a simple database.
- Use the SQL Server Configuration Manager.
- Connect a database to a Visual Web Developer.
- Connect a database table to a Web page.
- Use the DataReader object.
- Use the DataSet object to display data.
- Use the DataSet object to save data.
- Create a basic Windows Communication Foundation (WCF) Service.
- Examine the default WCF files.
- Examine the App_WebReferences directory.
- Examine the <system.serviceModel> element.

■ Knowledge Assessment

Multiple Choice

Circle the letter or letters that correspond to the best answer or answers.

1. What is the *primary* purpose of XML?
   a. To provide the additional syntax rules for XHTML
   b. To transfer data between the Web server and database
   c. To improve the functionality of Web pages
   d. To structure hierarchical data

2. What informs us of a broken DTD rule in a Web page?
   a. Any browser
   b. A Schema Validator
   c. IntelliSense
   d. All of the above

3. How does the Schema compare to the DTD?
   a. The Schema is more powerful than a DTD
   b. The Schema is simpler than a DTD
   c. Both use XML syntax to record the rules
   d. Both are used to validate XHTML documents

4. What is NOT true about the Primary key of a database table?
   a. A table is unable to store data without the primary key
   b. It is one of the many available database constraints
   c. It essentially "names" each row in the table
   d. It must be unique and not Null

5. How does the DataReader object compare to the DataSet object?
   a. The DataReader reads all the data with a single method, while the DataSet reads a single row at a time as it moves forward
   b. The DataReader is more powerful but reads more slowly than the DataSet
   c. The DataSet uses the DataAdapter and the DataReader does not
   d. The DataSet uses SQL to retrieve data, while the DataReader reads it directly without the need for SQL

6. How is a DataSet object used to change the source data?
   a. It uses the SQL method
   b. It uses the Update method of the DataAdapter object
   c. It uses SQL through the Command object
   d. It automatically changes the source as changes are made in the object

7. What is the primary use for the DataAdapter object?
   a. To fill the DataSet with data
   b. To connect the DataReader to the database
   c. To adapt our controls to a variety of databases
   d. To adapt our data into a format that will fit into a DataSet

8. What is a valid advantage or disadvantage to using Visual Web Developer to create a WCF Service?
   a. Visual Web Developer is the only way to create a WCF Service
   b. It creates more efficient code than could be created with a text editor
   c. It is easier to create a WCF Service with Visual Web Developer than with a text editor
   d. It is easier to create a WDF Service with a text editor than with Visual Web Developer

9. What is NOT true about App_WebReferences?
   a. It is a default directory for a WCF Service
   b. It keeps the Web site from having to look for some needed files
   c. It is just one of many App_directories
   d. It must always be available to ASP.NET

10. Which element is a grandchild of one of the three child elements of the <system.serviceModel> element of the web.config file?
   a. <endpoint>
   b. <services>
   c. <bindings>
   d. <behaviors>

Fill in the Blank

Complete the following sentences by writing the correct word or words in the blanks provided.

1. The _____ markup language is the superset of XML.

2. Every XML document must have one and only one _____ element.

3. Both XML and _____ require that every tag have an ending tag.

4. The _____ validator not only defines the structure of an XML document, it defines the content and attribute values.

5. Both the DataSet and DataReader objects require the _____ object to make the connection to the data source.

6. The DataReader object can use the SqlCommand object to send the SQL statement while the DataSet would use the _____ object.

7. Once the SQL statement is sent to the server, the DataReader uses the _____ method to execute the statement.

8. The _____ method is used by the DataReader to retrieve individual rows sent from the server.

9. The _____ .exe file is used to test the client side of a WCF Service.

10. The special directory used by Visual Web Developer to hold WCF Service files is called _____.

■ Competency Assessment

Scenario 3-1: Creating and Verifying an XML File

Your school has a closet full of CDs used for classroom presentations. Your job is to organize them in an XML file that will be used by several applications, from ordering new CDs to checking them out. The name of the root element is to be cdlib with a single child element named cd. The cd has the child elements title, authors, subjects, courses, length, and check-outs. There can be many authors, subjects, courses, and checkouts. Add your own elements for checkouts.

Add a DTD to the file that verifies that the root element only contains cd elements and that each of the cd elements is the only element allowed and in the same order listed above. Verify that the title and length elements are listed once and only once per cd, the authors are listed at least once, and the subjects, courses, and checkout elements appear zero or more times. The checkouts element is up to your discretion.

Scenario 3-2: Creating a Database

XML is great for storing small amounts of hierarchical data but falls short when more demand is placed on the data storage requirements. This is now the case with our CDLibrary .xml file. Use SSMS to create a database named CDLibrary. Eventually this database will have several related tables holding all our CD-related data. We will start by creating a single table named CD with the fields related only to the CD itself. Name the fields CDid, CDName, PurchaseDate, PurchasePrice, Department, and Obsolete. Choose appropriate data types for each field. You should consider CDid to be numeric and the Obsolete field to be Boolean. Use SSMS to populate the table with at least three records.

■ Proficiency Assessment

Scenario 3-3: Display Database Data on a Web Page

Use ASP.NET to display your table in a presentable form so that the page shows what each row represents in a more readable form than the field names. You may use the DataReader object or the DataSet object. Document your page with a comment explaining the reason for choosing one object over the other.

Scenario 3-4: Choosing to Use a Web Page or WCF Service

A new bank has been started to serve a very small community. You are in charge of designing the online user interfaces for both the clients and bank employees. For the following people, determine whether you will consider a Web page, WCF Service, or both for their online banking needs. Explain the pros and cons for each decision related to Clients, Tellers, Loan Officers, Bank Managers, and the Bank President.

✳ Workplace Ready

Creating a Database-Driven Web Page

Suppose you are working for a small manufacturing company that changes products every few months. It barely has a Web presence and you are the one who was volunteered for the job of maintaining its Web page. Your reluctance for this responsibility is due to the fact that it takes time to make the product specification changes to the Web page, especially when the only tool provided is Notepad.

Now that you have seen what you can do with Microsoft Visual Web Developer and SQL Server, you realize that your Web page can easily be database driven and decide to take the plunge. After your Web page conversion, with a few additional changes you've always wanted to see, your monthly changes are now as simple as changing a database table. The results are then automatically displayed in the Web page.

Of course, you now keep the details of this Web site maintenance task to yourself, to keep others from wanting to take this terribly inconvenient job from you.

LESSON 4

Working with Data

LESSON SKILL MATRIX

SKILLS/CONCEPTS	MTA EXAM OBJECTIVE	MTA EXAM OBJECTIVE NUMBER
Understanding DataSource Controls	Understand DataSource controls	2.4
Binding Controls to Data by Using Data-Binding Syntax	Bind controls to data by using data binding syntax	2.5
Managing Data Connections and Databases	Manage data connections and databases	2.6

KEY TERMS

connection object

connection pool

data-aware controls

database connections

data-bound controls

DataSource controls

LinqDataSource control

ObjectDataSource control

SqlDataSource control

transaction object

XmlDataSource control

Karen is now finding a couple of problems with her online database application. One is that the database code is so tightly integrated with HMTL that it is becoming hard to manage. The second arises when several updates to the database need to be made together. If one of them has an error, the other updates are no longer relevant because they cannot stand alone. Any successful updates must then be reversed. For example, when an inventory item is added to the database, it needs to update the inventory table at the same time that it updates the vendor table.

Microsoft Visual Web Developer can easily address these problems and more.

■ Understanding DataSource Controls

THE BOTTOM LINE

A requirement for most modern Web sites is that they be dynamic. Static pages are not often revisited. One of the most efficient ways to accomplish this is by connecting Web pages to a database, and ASP.NET provides all the controls you need.

Most of the Microsoft *DataSource controls* are capable of reading data as well as changing the data at the source. Once you understand how the DataSource controls retrieve data (the focus of this lesson), it will be much easier to understand how to increase the functionality of your own pages by allowing them to make changes to the data source.

Understanding the LinqDataSource Control

> The *LinqDataSource control* is the latest control used for the communication between ASP.NET Web pages and the database. It can be applied without having to type a single line of code. The developer can opt to have all code written automatically by ASP.NET.

SQL has been the standard for relational databases for many years. However, the syntax of the language has not been so standard. Every provider of data—SQL Server, Oracle, MySQL, etc.—uses varying rules. This means that whenever a database is needed or changed for an application, the language must be considered. Microsoft is making an attempt to change this by introducing Language INtegrated Query (LINQ).

Many developers are finding that this technology has more advantages than simply providing a common database language. It not only supports typical database functions like retrieve, update, insert, and delete, but it supports the advanced features of database management like relationships, constraints, transactions, views, and stored procedures. However, because it is still new, it is not yet widely used.

 USE THE LINQDATASOURCE CONTROL

GET READY. Visual Web Developer, SQL Server, and the Sample database from Lesson 3 will be used for this exercise.

1. Using Visual Web Developer, create a new ASP.NET Web site using C#.
2. Go to the **Design** view of the Default.aspx form and add the **LinqDataSource** from the Data category of the Toolbox.
   - You can click on the View Designer button or right-click on the Default.aspx object to get to the Design view.
   - We now need to add a new template to the page before we can configure the data source for the LinqDataSource control. The next step is included only to show the consequences of an attempt to configure the LinqDataSource without the template.
3. Click the **small arrow**, called the "smart tag," located on the side of the LinqDataSource control and select **Configure Data Source**.
   - The drop-down list box in the dialog box will be empty because this dialog box must have a file that is located in either the App_Code or Bin directory that contains a valid class.
4. Click the **Cancel** button in the dialog box.
   - We will now use the LINQ to SQL Classes template to hook up to the database.
5. Use **Add New Item** to select the **LINQ to SQL Classes** template, as shown in Figure 4-1. Make sure to select Visual C#. You can use the menu bar, choose Website, and then Add New Item.

Figure 4-1

Adding the LINQ connection

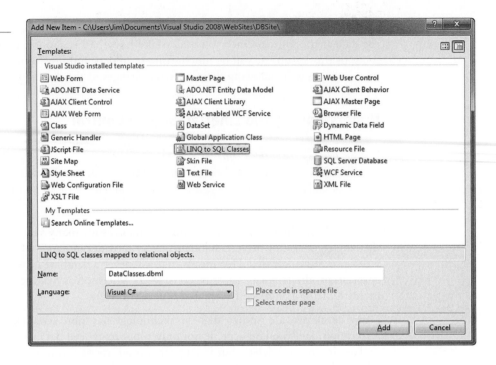

- Notice the name DataClasses.dbml, which is a DataBase Markup Language that is used internally when the application runs.

6. Click the Add button.

- The dialog box, shown in Figure 4-2, lets you know that ASP.NET will send a file to the APP_Code directory. This directory and its contents will then be displayed in the Solution Explorer window.

Figure 4-2

Placing the LINQ file into the App_Code folder

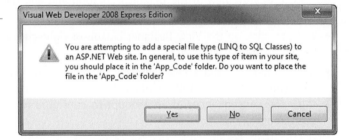

7. Click the **Yes** button in the dialog box and give it some time to process.

- A new window representing this file should now appear as shown in Figure 4-3.

Figure 4-3

Directions that appear after starting LINQ

- A set of new DataClasses files, provided you left the default name, should now be listed in the App_Code directory of the Solution Explorer window. Before using this window, we will need to make a connection to our database using the IDE. Only a single step will be used because this has been done in several previous lessons.

8. From the Tools menu, click **Connect to Database** as you did in Lesson 3.

9. Once the Database Explorer window displays the table name, open the tree view to the **ShoppingList** table by clicking on the plus signs, as shown in Figure 4-4, and drag it to the left pane of the new window that appeared when adding the LINQ item. We will not be dragging anything to the right pane.

Figure 4-4

Dragging the database table to the left pane

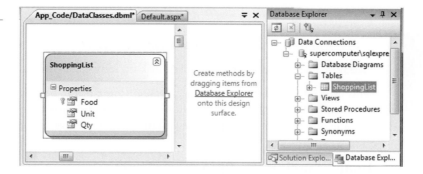

- We will now define the specifics for the data needed.
- Before the control can see the table, you will need to build the site.

10. Click on the **Build** menu and select **Build Web Site**.

- You will not see any changes. This simply ensures that the IDE recognizes your changes.

11. Go back to the Default form. Click on the **smart tag** of the LinqDataSource control and select **Configure Data Source**.

- This time we have a context object named DataClassesDataContext.

12. Click the **Next** button.

- The Configure Data Source is known as "Query by Example." This is a way to write SQL statements using point and click rather than writing the statements by hand. The clicked information is used by ASP.NET to create the query string for you. This query string is what the database management system uses to know which data you want retrieved. We only have one table and the asterisk means that we want all field names.

13. Do not make any changes to this dialog box and click the **Finish** button.

- To see the code that was generated, you might want to view the code-behind in the DataClasses.designer.cs file by double-clicking it in the Solution Explorer window.

14. Click the **Default.aspx** tab and run the application to test for errors. Then close the browser.

- Although we now have a connection, we have not provided a way to display the data.

15. Go to the **Design** view of the Default page and drag the GridView control from the Data category of the Toolbox onto the form.

16. In the **smart tab** of the GridView control, select **LinqDataSource1** for the Data Source, as shown in Figure 4-5.

Figure 4-5

Connecting the GridView control

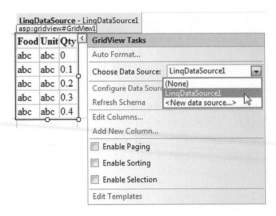

17. Run the application and make sure there is data. Close the browser.

PAUSE. Close Visual Web Developer but keep it available for the next exercise.

This exercise should have made you aware of some of the benefits of this control. Because of its unifying capabilities with multiple databases and programming languages, it will soon become one of the most popular techniques in data source connectivity.

Understanding the ObjectDataSource

> Unlike the LinqDataSource, the **ObjectDataSource control** does not retrieve data from a database. The purpose of this object is to move any needed data connections along with any needed Input/Output activities of the database, or any other data source, to a location outside the Web page.

A Web page does not need to know where the data is coming from nor where it is going. All the page needs to do is ask the ObjectDataSource for the data when it needs it and send it to the ObjectDataSource to save changes.

This separation is logically referred to as a movement from two-tier to three-tier architecture. The two-tier architecture consists of the Web page as one of the tiers and the Web server as the other. Database activities are integrated into both tiers.

With three-tier architecture, the database activities are separated from one or both of the two tiers. A typical three-tier system separates the Web server from the database server. The ObjectDataSource focuses on separating the Web page code from the database code. Removing the database-related code from the Web page allows the developer to focus on the user interface. Database needs are now limited to the simple calls for Creating, Reading, Updating, and Deleting records. These activities are often referred to as CRUD. The code that is used to create the database connections and database communication is removed from the Web page and placed into the middle tier.

This middle tier allows Web developers to make major changes to the data source such as moving from one database management system to another, which nearly always requires a different SQL syntax, or possibly from a database to an XML source. The goal is to keep the Web page from knowing anything has changed. From the Web page's point of view, the ObjectDataSource is simply a black box that handles all the data requirements.

The following steps will take you through the process of creating this three-tier architecture using the familiar SqlConnection, DataAdapter, and DataSet objects to retrieve data in the middle tier. The ObjectDataSource will then be used to transfer the data to the Web page.

USE THE OBJECTDATASOURCE CONTROL

GET READY. Visual Web Developer, SQL Server, and the Sample database will be used for this exercise.

1. Make sure SQL Server is still running and that you have the Sample database available.

2. Create a new ASP.NET Web site using C#.

3. Go to the **Design** view and add the **ObjectDataSource** from the Data category of the Toolbox to the form.

4. Click on the **smart tag** of the control and select **Configure Data Source**.
   - Notice that the drop-down list box in the dialog box is empty. It is empty because we have no APP_Code or Bin directory. Even if we did, one of them would need a file with a valid class.
   - As in the last lesson, ASP.NET places the App_Code directory into the Solution Explorer window when necessary. This will happen again when we create our own external class.

5. Click the **Cancel** button on the dialog box.

6. Open the **Add New Item** dialog box and select **Class**. Make sure C# is selected and click the **Add** button.
   - A dialog box should pop up asking if you want ASP.NET to save a file in the APP_Code folder.

7. Click the **Yes** button.

8. From the **Design** view of the Default form, Click on the **smart tag** of the ObjectDataSource again and select **Configure Data Source**.

9. Click the down arrow by the drop-down list box for the business object and select the only available item.
   - The name of the class will be Class1 unless you changed the name when you created it.

10. Click the **Next** button on the dialog box.
    - Notice that there are no methods available for us in this dialog box. However, it gives some suggestions about using the DataSet and DataReader to help us to create methods.

11. Click the **Cancel** button on the dialog box.
    - We now have to edit our new class and create a method that the ObjectDataSource will be able to use.

12. From the **Solution Explorer** window, double-click your new class file, **file1.cs**, located in the App_Code folder.
    - You should now be looking at the code making up the middle tier between the database and the Web page.
    - We will use the same database connection we used earlier to retrieve the data from the ShoppingList table.

13. Edit the code for the Class file. Make sure you change the connection string to match your system.

TAKE NOTE* An easy way to find the correct connection string is to open Microsoft SQL Server. On the Connect to Server dialog box, there will be an item called Server Name. Next to it will be the connection string for your system. You can copy and paste it into your code. However, you will need to add a backslash character (\) before the SQL Express part of the code because it will only have one.

```csharp
using System;
using System.Collections.Generic;
using System.Linq;
using System.Web;
//Data namespaces added
using System.Data.SqlClient;
using System.Data;
public class Class1
{
  public Class1()
  {
  }
  public DataTable GetFood()
  {
    SqlConnection con = new SqlConnection();
    con.ConnectionString =
    "Data Source=SUPERCOMPUTER\\SQLEXPRESS;Initial
    Catalog=Sample;Integrated Security=True";
    con.Open();
    SqlDataAdapter da = new SqlDataAdapter
    ("Select * from ShoppingList", con);
    DataSet ds = new DataSet();
    da.Fill(ds, "Tier2Data");
    con.Close();
    return ds.Tables[0];
  }
}
```

- This is the code used for the middle tier.

14. Although not always necessary, click the **Save** button and build the site.
    - To build the site, bring down the Build menu and click **Build Web Site**.
    - It is a good habit to save periodically in case of power failures, etc. Building the site will alert you to syntax errors not caught with IntelliSense.

15. Run the program. Close the browser.
    - This was just a check for errors. Nothing should show on the browser.
    - We now need to finish connecting the ObjectDataSource and add a new control to the form to see the data.

16. Go the **Design** view of the Default page, click on the **smart tag** of the ObjectDataSource, and select **Configure Data Source**.

17. From the dialog box, select your class name again and click the Next button.
    - This time the "Choose a method" drop-down list box should have the name of your method. Also, notice the tabs that allow you to connect to any of the CRUD functions that you may want to write for the table.

18. Select the **GetFood** method and click the **Finish** button.
    - You should run the program again to check for errors.

19. From the Data category of the Toolbox, place the **GridView** control on the form.
    * The GridView is just one of many controls available to us for presenting the data.
20. Click the **smart tag** of the GridView and click the **ObjectDataSource** as the Data Source.
21. From the same menu of the smart tag, select **Edit Columns** and verify that the **Auto-generated fields** check box is checked.
22. Run the application. Close the browser.
    * The data should have shown up on the Web page.
    * If this produces an error that points to con.open( ); , verify that the connection string has been configured to your computer and not the one in step 13.

PAUSE. Close Visual Web Developer.

CERTIFICATION READY
What is the fundamental difference between the ObjectDataSource and the LinqDataSource controls?
2.4

Notice that we accessed the database with the code we used before. The only reason we used the ObjectDataSource control was to move the data source processing code out of our Web page. The ObjectDataSource control complements the SqlConnection object; it does not replace it.

 USE THE XMLDATASOURCE CONTROL

GET READY. We will continue using Visual Web Developer, SQL Server, and the Sample database.

1. Use **Add New Item** to create a new Web form on your site using C#.
2. Use **Add New Item** to create a new XML file using C#. **XML File** is the last template in the Add New Item dialog box.
3. Copy the contents of the **ShoppingList.xml** file used in Lesson 3 to this new page, or type in the following text:

```xml
<?xml version="1.0" encoding="utf-8" ?>
<shoppinglist>
    <title></title>
    <item>
        <food>Milk</food>
        <unit qty='1'>Gallon</unit>
    </item>
    <item>
        <food>Eggs</food>
        <unit qty='2'>Dozen</unit>
    </item>
</shoppinglist>
```

* Make sure you do not create a duplicate of the first line of code.

4. Run this from the current editing window to make sure it is well formed. Close the browser.
    * If the XML is displayed, it is well formed. Otherwise, check for typing errors.
5. Go to the **Design** view of your new Web page and add the **XmlDataSource** and **GridView** controls to the form. They are located in the Data category of the Toolbox.
    * The GridView control not only displays data from a database, it can also present XML data. In order to do so, the SqlDataSource control needs to be replaced with the XmlDataSource control.

6. Click the **smart tab** of the GridView control and set **Choose Data Source** to the XmlDataSource control.

   • Notice that once the XmlDataSource control has been selected and the menu expanded to include **Configure Data Source**. This allows you to configure the data source from either control.

7. Using the smart tab from either control, click **Configure Data Source**.

8. From the dialog box, click the Browse button to find the Data file. Select the XML file and click the **OK** button.

9. Click the **OK** button on the Configure Data Source dialog box.

10. Attempt to run the application, which will show a Server Error. Close the browser.

    • The database table is stored in a layout that the GridView control understands. However, XML data are not so easily read. The tag names mean nothing to either of our controls.

    • For these controls to see the rows and columns of the XML data, the data in the XML file need to be adjusted. The data must be laid out flat and all content must be in the form of attributes.

    • The XML file must remain well formed as these adjustments are made. The data for the GridView must be in the form: <element **attribute="data" attribute2="data2" [etc.]** />

11. Return to the XMLFile.xml editing window and change your XML file to match the following text:

    ```
    <?xml version="1.0" encoding="utf-8" ?>
    <ShoppingList>
    <item Food ="Milk" Unit ="Gallon" Qty ="2" />
    <item Food ="Eggs" Unit ="Dozen" Qty ="1" />
    </ShoppingList>
    ```

    • The browser will now be able to display XML data when it is presented in this row/column format.

12. Run this from the current editing window to make sure it is well formed. Close the browser.

13. Click the **Defalut.aspx** tab and run it again.

    • This time you should see the data in table format.

14. Click one of the **smart tags** of the controls on the form and click **Refresh Schema**.

    • If the controls understand the new format, the data should now be displayed in the GridView on the form.

    • We transformed this document by hand. However, if you have a document with thousands of elements, you have the option to use code to create a file called a Transform file.

15. Go back to the Configuration Data Source dialog box of either control.

    • Notice the **Transform File:** text box. It is used to select a file that gives the rules for transforming an XML document into a different format. However, writing these rules in the file is beyond the scope of this lesson.

16. Click the **Cancel** button on the dialog box.

PAUSE. Close Visual Web Developer, but keep it available for the next exercise.

In its simplest form, the *XmlDataSource control* is a rather crude control because it is incapable of deciphering the language of XML. However, when used with a file that provides the rules, it becomes a complex powerhouse for handling XML documents.

CERTIFICATION READY
How can any well-formed XML document be converted into another well formed XML document so it can be read by the XmlDataSource control?
2.4

USE THE SQLDATASOURCE CONTROL

GET READY. We will use Visual Web Developer, SQL Server, and the Sample database for this exercise.

1. Make sure SQL Server is still running and that you have your database available.
2. Create a new ASP.NET Web site using C#.
3. Connect to the **Sample** database using the Tools menu and clicking **Connect to Database**. Remember to change to Microsoft SQL Server before looking for the database and table.
4. Open the **Design** view of the new form.
5. From the **Database Explorer** window, open the tree to the **ShoppingList** table and drag it to the form.
6. Run the application. Close the browser.

PAUSE. Close Visual Web Developer, but keep it available for the next exercise.

CERTIFICATION READY
What databases can be used to provide data for your Web page when using the SqlDataSource control?
2.4

The ***SqlDataSource control*** enables you to connect and interact with any database supported by ADO.NET. Although we have used this control in previous lessons, it was applied by writing code. This time, we simply used its drag-and-drop feature along with the GridView control to demonstrate the ease of connecting a database table to a Web page with minimal data manipulation.

■ Binding Controls to Data by Using Data-Binding Syntax

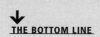
THE BOTTOM LINE

Up to now, we have used wizards and dialog boxes to bind our data source controls to our data display controls. To make your page a little more dynamic, you may want to perform the data binding in code. We will now create all connections manually in code. The focus in the coding will be on clarity rather than efficiency.

We will create a new Web site with a single GridView and four buttons. Each button will submit a different database query on the same table and bind that data to the same GridView. The first two buttons will use the SqlConnection object with the DataSet. The third button will use the SqlConnection object with the DataReader. The last button will use the SqlDataSource control.

 USE DATA-BINDING SYNTAX

GET READY. We will use Visual Web Developer, SQL Server, and the Sample database for this exercise.

1. Make sure SQL Server is still running and that you have your database available.
2. Create a new ASP.NET Web site using C#.
3. Go to the code-behind window by double-clicking the form and add the following namespaces to the code just below the ones already present:

```
using System.Data.SqlClient;
using System.Data;
```

4. Go to **Design** view and place the GridView control and four buttons on the form.

5. In the Click event procedure for the first button, use the code from an earlier lesson. If you type in the following code, make sure to match the name of the computer to yours and verify the name of your database server.

Button 1: SqlConnection with DataSet: Displays all data

```
SqlConnection con = new SqlConnection();
con.ConnectionString = "Data
Source=SUPERCOMPUTER\\SQLEXPRESS;Initial
Catalog=Sample;Integrated Security=True";
con.Open();
SqlDataAdapter da = new SqlDataAdapter
("Select * from ShoppingList", con);
SqlCommandBuilder cmdBldr = new
SqlCommandBuilder(da);
DataSet ds = new DataSet();
da.Fill(ds, "LocalData");
```

6. Run the application, click the first button, and close the browser to check for errors.

7. Add the following code immediately after the **da.Fill** method:

```
GridView1.DataSource = ds;
GridView1.DataBind();
```

- The first line sets the DataSource property of the GridView control to use our instance of the DataSet object, ds. The DataSet is considered the source, whether it comes from a database or is loaded manually.
- The **DataBind( )** method of the GridView control uses the name that was just placed into the DataSource, ds. It executes code to make the connection and display the data.

8. Run the application and click the first button. Close the browser.

- The GridView control should now show the data.

9. Copy the contents of the event procedure of the first button and paste it to the event procedure of the second button.

Button 2: SqlConnection with DataSet: Displays the number of rows in the table

10. Change the SQL statement of the second event procedure code:

From: `"Select * from ShoppingList"`

To: `"Select count(*) as [Number of rows] from ShoppingList"`

11. Run the application and alternate clicking the two buttons. Then close the browser.

- Each button should produce a different result because of the SQL statement. As mentioned earlier, there are more efficient ways to do this, but as you can see, it is possible to bind controls manually in code rather than depending on wizards and dialog boxes.

12. Copy the contents of the event procedure of the first button and paste it to the third button.

Button 3: SqlConnection with DataReader: Displays two columns of data

13. Edit the third button's event procedure:

```
SqlConnection con = new SqlConnection();
con.ConnectionString = "Data
Source=SUPERCOMPUTER\\SQLEXPRESS;Initial
```

```
Catalog=Sample;Integrated Security=True";
con.Open();

SqlCommand cmd = new SqlCommand("Select Food,
Qty from ShoppingList", con);
SqlDataReader reader = cmd.ExecuteReader();

GridView1.DataSource = reader;
GridView1.DataBind();
```

14. Run the application and click the buttons. Then close the browser.
   • Each button should produce a different result because of the SQL statement.
   • It makes no difference whether we use the DataSet or DataReader. The data from either can be bound to the GridView control. For such a small amount of data, you will not notice the increased speed of the DataReader over the DataSet.
   • Rather than using the SqlConnection object to connect to the data and having to use the DataSet or DataReader, we will greatly simplify the code by using an instance of the SqlDataSource control. Again, all our development will be in code.

15. Place the code in the event procedure of the fourth button. You might want to copy parts from elsewhere in the program.

Button 4: SqlDataSource: Displays the sum of the Qty fields

```
SqlDataSource SqlCon = new SqlDataSource();
SqlCon.ConnectionString = "Data
Source=SUPERCOMPUTER\\SQLEXPRESS;Initial
Catalog=Sample;Integrated Security=True";

SqlCon.SelectCommand = "Select sum(Qty)
as [Sum of Qty] from ShoppingList";
GridView1.DataSource = SqlCon;
GridView1.DataBind();
```

16. Run the application and click the buttons. Then close the browser.
   • Again, each button should produce a different result because of the SQL statement.

PAUSE. Close Visual Web Developer, but keep it available for the next exercise.

This does not have to be an all-or-nothing proposition. For example, if you want to use the query-by-example feature of the SqlDataSource control, you can place the SqlDataSource on the form, set the SelectCommand property using the dialog box, and use the code to do the rest. In this case, no instance name of the SqlDataSource object (SqlCon) will be available in the code for the binding. The ID property of the SqlDataSource control that was placed on the form will need to be used to set the GridView.DataSourceID property.

Understanding Data-Aware Controls

> The simplest definition of ASP.NET **data-aware controls** is that they are all the controls having the DataSource and DataSourceID properties. **Data-bound controls**, on the other hand, are data-aware controls that have been bound to a specific data source.

It is not required for all data-aware controls to be data bound. It is also possible to bind controls that are not data aware. Binding controls that do not have the DataSource or DataSourceID properties can often be quite challenging. The distinction between data-aware and data-bound controls is not always recognized; the term "data bound" is often used for both.

⊙ USE A DATA-AWARE CONTROL

GET READY. We will use Visual Web Developer, SQL Server, and the Sample database for this exercise.

1. Make sure SQL Server is still running and that you have your database available.
2. Create a new ASP.NET Web site using C#.
3. From the **Standard** category of the Toolbox, place the **ListBox** control on the form.
4. Click the **smart tab** and click **Edit Items**.
5. Add three new Members and edit the text for each with **One**, **Two**, and **Three**, as shown in Figure 4-6.

Figure 4-6

Adding items to an unbound data-aware control

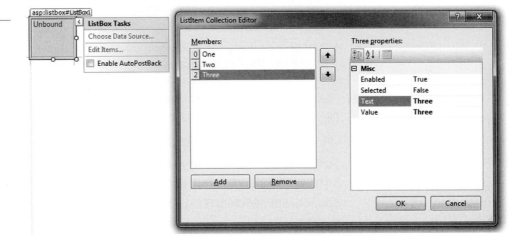

6. Then click the **OK** button.
7. Make sure the ListBox is selected and look at the property window. Notice the value that is in the DataSourceID property.
   - Because the DataSourceID property is blank and no code populated either the DataSourceID or DataSource properties, this control remains unbound.
8. Run the application. Then close the browser.
   - Notice that the ListBox control is very useful even when it is not bound.
   - We will now convert the data-aware ListBox to a data-bound control.
9. Place the SqlDataSource control on the form.
10. Click the **smart tab** of the SqlDataSource control and configure the data source to show all the data in our table.
    - You may have to click the asterisk check box when creating the SQL statement.
11. Click the **smart tab** of the list box and click **Choose Data Source**.
12. From the dialog box, select the **SqlDataSource** control as the data source.
13. Select **Food** and **Qty** from the drop-down list box settings and click the OK button.
    - Notice that the ListBox control on the form now says **Databound**.
    - We now have a data-aware control that is also data bound.
14. Run the application. Then close the browser.
    - The list box should now show the selected data.

PAUSE. Close Visual Web Developer, but keep it available for the next exercise.

There are many data-aware controls listed in the Toolbox. All of these controls are very complex and most are designed to be used with their provided dialog boxes and to be data bound.

Standard Category

- DropDownList
- ListBox
- CheckBoxList
- RadioButtonList
- BulletedList
- AdRotator

Data Category

- GridView
- DataList
- DetailsView
- FormView
- Repeater
- ListView

Navigation Category

- Menu
- TreeView

CERTIFICATION READY
How do you turn a control into a data-bound control in ASP.NET?
2.5

It would take an entire chapter to cover each of these dialog boxes because each has a specific purpose. As you start working with ASP.NET, you should make a point to become familiar with these controls. They can save you hours of unnecessary work.

Managing Data Connections and Databases

↓ **THE BOTTOM LINE**

There is an abundance of continually changing data that Web sites are able to access. This data comes in many forms, from text files to very large and complex databases. Managing the connections of the hundreds of users who could be simultaneously reading and writing this data on a single Web site is no small feat. This lesson will introduce various data sources, the options available to the Web developer for connecting the Web pages to the data sources, and a technology used for Web sites that enables them to handle the overhead of hundreds of connections opening and closing without bringing down the site. We will also introduce an object that allows the execution of multiple SQL statements as a single unit to ensure that each one completes successfully.

ASP.NET uses ADO.NET to handle all of its *database connections*. The compiled code that ASP.NET generates from your .NET programs and objects is called *managed code*. Managed code is created to run on Microsoft's Common Language Runtime (CLR) rather than creating an executable that is limited to a particular hardware platform. However, this does not mean that the older unmanaged COM objects, such as OleDB and ODBC, cannot be used for .NET programs.

ADO.NET also allows us to write provider-independent code so the program is able to connect to a variety of data sources. Several of the .NET database connections are also referred to as data providers because each is designed to work with specific database management systems. In fact, many of our lessons have been using the SqlConnection object, which is a data provider for Microsoft SQL Server.

Microsoft's Component Object Model (COM), introduced in 1993, is a technology that enables software components to communicate. The database is only one of the many components that COM manages.

COM objects are still available for use in ADO.NET because they are often the only solution available for communication with specific data sources. There are also special situations that make the COM solution more suitable than the ADO.NET data provider. COM-Interop is the tool used in the background that allows managed code to interact with the previously unmanaged COM code. ADO.NET manages the COM objects so they will comply with the CLR specifications. We will modify our database connection to use these legacy objects.

 EXAMINE DATABASE CONNECTIONS

GET READY. We will use Visual Web Developer, SQL Server, and the Sample database for this exercise.

1. Make sure SQL Server is still running and that you have your database available.

2. Create a new ASP.NET Web site using C#.

3. Double-click the form and start typing in the following namespace ending in a period, as shown in Figure 4-7:

   System.Data.

   • It is just as easy for ASP.NET developers to use the COM objects as it is to use the .NET objects through IntelliSense.

Figure 4-7

IntelliSense lists ADO.NET namespaces for both new and old ways of database communication

4. Erase what you just typed and replace it with the namespace shown in Figure 4-8, again ending with a period:

   System.Data.Odbc.

   • ODBC (Open Database Connectivity) is one of the oldest currently used ways to connect to a database. As the name implies, it is designed to connect to databases. In order to connect to a specific database, the appropriate database driver must be used. One reason ODBC is still used today is that it has been around so long that its database drivers are well known by developers and can be trusted to do the job with little risk of failure.

Figure 4-8

Using ADO.NET to connect to ODBC

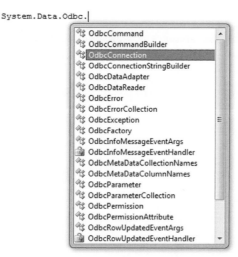

`System.Data.Odbc.|`

5. Erase what you just typed and replace it with the following namespace, again ending with a period as shown in Figure 4-9:

`System.Data.OleDb.`

- OleDB (Object Linking and Embedding Database) is an improvement over ODBC in that it expands its connectivity to sources beyond databases such as spreadsheets. OleDB is also faster than ODBC. Microsoft intended to replace ODBC with OleDB. However, as long as there are data sources that can only be accessed through ODBC, this replacement cannot happen.

Figure 4-9

Using ADO.NET to connect to OleDB

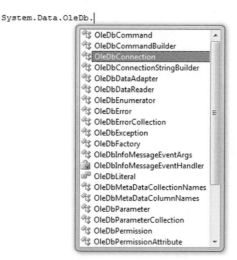

`System.Data.OleDb.|`

PAUSE. Close Visual Web Developer.

There are many ways to provide data for ADO.NET applications. These fall into two basic categories, direct connections to specific data sources or the more general connections that provide connectivity to a variety of data sources. The direct connections, such as the SQLConnection, are faster and more efficient than the general connections. However, these more general connections, such as ODBC and OleDB, have the important role of connecting to many of the legacy data sources.

Table 4-1 lists some of the databases and data sources that are supported by the direct connection object, .NET. It also lists the databases and data sources of two of the most popular general connections, OleDB and ODBC. These two data providers exist primarily to support legacy data sources.

Table 4-1

Data providers available for the connection object and the data sources they support

.NET	OleDB	ODBC
Microsoft SQL Server	SQL Server SQL Server via SQLXMLOLEDB	SQL Server
MySQL (written by CoreLab)	MySQL	MySQL
ODBC Providers		
OleDB Providers		
Oracle Provider (written by Microsoft)	Oracle (written by Microsoft)	Oracle (written by Microsoft)
Oracle (written by Oracle)	Oracle (written by Oracle)	Oracle (written by Oracle)
Oracle Provider (Written by CoreLab)		Oracle Rdb
Postgres SQL Direct (written by CoreLab)		
Sybase ASE	Sybase Adaptive Server Enterprise Sybase Adaptive Server Anywhere	Sybase Sybase SQL Anywhere
VistaDB Provider	Microsoft Jet (used for MS Access)	Access
	AS/400 (written by IBM)	AS/400
	AS/400 and VSAM (written by Microsoft)	AS/400
	Excel	Excel
	Text Files	Text
	Visual FoxPro	Visual FoxPro
	Active Directory Service	dBASE
	Advantage	Informix
	Commerce Server	Interbase (written by Easysoft)
	DB2	Interbase (written by InterSolv)
	DTS Packages	Lotus Notes
	Exchange	Mimer
	Internet Publishing	Paradox
	Index Server	Teradata
	Microsoft Project	
	Pervasive	
	Simple Provider	
	SQLBase	
	OLAP Services	
	UniData and UniVerse	

Notice that Table 4-1 reveals several data sources having all three data providers. Also, notice that there are data sources that rely solely on OleDB or ODBC. Although the older data providers are no longer needed for the newer data sources, the dependency that the older data sources have on the legacy data providers has prevented them from being dropped from current development platforms.

The list of data sources and their providers in Table 4-1 is not intended as a technical reference. Further research is required to find the correct solution to your data source connection.

More advanced applications may have a requirement to isolate application code from the data connection code beyond using the ObjectDataSource object. Large applications may have millions of lines of code with embedded database connections. The task of changing to a different database management system might be large enough that the changeover can never be justified. One solution is to simply include all the database providers and program the application to select the one that is required.

Another solution is to use the higher-level ADO.NET data classes that ADO.NET uses to create the specific data provider classes for the databases such as SQL Server. However, this technique requires a high level of expertise and many lines of code, which are beyond the scope of this lesson. Figures 4-10 and 4-11 show IntelliSense list boxes holding some of the tools used for this provider-independent .NET-managed code.

Figure 4-10

The classes that create specific data providers

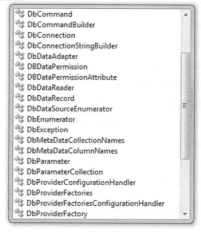

Figure 4-11

Interface classes used with the Db classes in Figure 4-10

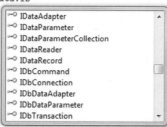

Although the ASP.NET data providers, including ODBC and OleDB, are not the only way we can connect to data sources, they are the most common and should be well understood in order to make wise decisions about which is best for the given needs and architecture of the data storage.

We will now use our Sample database to apply some of the various connections that we just discussed.

 USE THE OLEDBCONNECTION OBJECT

GET READY. We will use Visual Web Developer, SQL Server, and the Sample database for this exercise.

1. Create a new ASP.NET Web site using C#.
2. Go to the **Design** view of the form and place two buttons and the GridView control on the form.
3. Place the following namespace near the top of the code-behind just under the existing namespaces:

   using System.Data.OleDb;

4. Type in the code below and place it in the click event procedure for the first button:

   ```
   OleDbConnection con = new OleDbConnection();
   GridView1.Caption = "OleDb";
   con.ConnectionString = "Provider=SQLNCLI10;Server=
   SUPERCOMPUTER\\SQLEXPRESS;Database=Sample;
   Trusted_Connection=yes";
   con.Open();
   OleDbCommand cmd = new OleDbCommand();
   cmd.Connection = con;
   cmd.CommandText = "Select * from ShoppingList";
   OleDbDataReader reader = cmd.ExecuteReader();
   GridView1.DataSource = reader;
   GridView1.DataBind();
   reader.Close();
   con.Close();
   ```

   • Do not forget to modify your connection string as you have done in previous exercises in this lesson.

5. Run the program to make sure the data shows up in the GridView control.

PAUSE. Do NOT close Visual Web Developer. Keep it running for the next exercise.

The second button will use the ODBC object for comparison in the next exercise.

 USE THE ODBCCONNECTION OBJECT

GET READY. We will continue using Visual Web Developer, SQL Server, and the Sample database.

1. Place the following namespace near the top of the code-behind just under the existing namespaces:

   using System.Data.Odbc;

2. Type in the code below and place it in the click event procedure for the second button:

   ```
   OdbcConnection con = new OdbcConnection();
   con.ConnectionString =
   ```

```
"Driver={SQL Server Native Client 10.0};
Server=SUPERCOMPUTER\\SQLEXPRESS;Database=Sample;
Trusted_Connection=yes";
con.Open();
OdbcCommand cmd = new OdbcCommand();
GridView1.Caption = "Odbc";
cmd.Connection = con;
cmd.CommandText = "Select * from ShoppingList";
OdbcDataReader reader = cmd.ExecuteReader();
GridView1.DataSource = reader;
GridView1.DataBind();
reader.Close();
con.Close();
```

- You may want to use the copy/paste feature of the editor.
- Notice that the code for the two buttons is nearly identical. Other than the OleDB and ODBC prefixes for the Connection and DataReader objects, the connection string is the only significant change. In fact, the connection string is the most important property of the connection object because it controls how all the communication will be handled for the data source.

3. Run the program and click the buttons. Close the browser.

- The buttons should give you the same results with the exception of the ODBC and OleDB headings.

PAUSE. Close Visual Web Developer, but keep it available for the next exercise.

The connection string can become so complex that ADO.NET includes a ConnectionStringBuilder class to define the properties explicitly for the SqlConnection object. This is an alternative to using a single property to hold all the data included in the string. The list of ConnectionStringBuilder properties is shown in Table 4-2.

Table 4-2

Properties of the ConnectionStringBuilder for building an SqlConnection connection string

NAME	DESCRIPTION
ApplicationName	Gets or sets the name of the application associated with the connection string.
AsynchronousProcessing	Gets or sets a Boolean value that indicates whether asynchronous processing is allowed by the connection created by using this connection string.
AttachDBFilename	Gets or sets a string that contains the name of the primary data file. This includes the full path name of an attachable database.
BrowsableConnectionString	Gets or sets a value that indicates whether the ConnectionString property is visible in Visual Studio designers. (Inherited from DbConnectionStringBuilder.)
ConnectionReset	Gets or sets a Boolean value that indicates whether the connection is reset when drawn from the connection pool.
ConnectionString	Gets or sets the connection string associated with the DbConnectionStringBuilder. (Inherited from DbConnectionStringBuilder.)

(continued)

Table 4-2

(*continued*)

NAME	DESCRIPTION
ConnectTimeout	Gets or sets the length of time (in seconds) to wait for a connection to the server before terminating the attempt and generating an error.
ContextConnection	Gets or sets a value that indicates whether a client/server or in-process connection to the SQL Server should be made.
Count	Gets the current number of keys that are contained within the ConnectionString property. (Inherited from DbConnectionStringBuilder.)
CurrentLanguage	Gets or sets the SQL Server Language record name.
DataSource	Gets or sets the name or network address of the instance of the SQL Server.
Encrypt	Gets or sets a Boolean value that indicates whether the SQL Server uses SSL encryption for all data sent between the client and server if the server has a certificate installed.
Enlist	Gets or sets a Boolean value that indicates whether the SQL Server connection pooler automatically enlists the connection in the creation thread's current transaction context.
FailoverPartner	Gets or sets the name or address of the partner server to connect to if the primary server is down.
InitialCatalog	Gets or sets the name of the database associated with the connection.
IntegratedSecurity	Gets or sets a Boolean value that indicates whether User ID and Password are specified in the connection (when false) or whether the current Windows account credentials are used for authentication (when true).
IsFixedSize	Gets a value that indicates whether the SqlConnectionString Builder has a fixed size. (Overrides DbConnectionStringBuilder .IsFixedSize.)
IsReadOnly	Gets a value that indicates whether the DbConnectionStringBuilder is read-only. (Inherited from DbConnectionStringBuilder.)
Item	Gets or sets the value associated with the specified key. In C#, this property is the indexer. (Overrides DbConnectionStringBuilder .Item[String].)
Keys	Gets an ICollection that contains the keys in the SqlConnectionStringBuilder. (Overrides DbConnectionStringBuilder.Keys.)
LoadBalanceTimeout	Gets or sets the minimum time, in seconds, for the connection to live in the connection pool before being destroyed.
MaxPoolSize	Gets or sets the maximum number of connections allowed in the connection pool for this specific connection string.
MinPoolSize	Gets or sets the minimum number of connections allowed in the connection pool for this specific connection string.

MultipleActiveResultSets	Gets or sets a Boolean value that indicates whether multiple active result sets can be associated with the associated connection.
NetworkLibrary	Gets or sets a string that contains the name of the network library used to establish a connection to the SQL Server.
PacketSize	Gets or sets the size in bytes of the network packets used to communicate with an instance of the SQL Server.
Password	Gets or sets the password for the SQL Server account.
PersistSecurityInfo	Gets or sets a Boolean value that indicates if security-sensitive information, such as the password, is not returned as part of the connection if the connection is open or has ever been in an open state.
Pooling	Gets or sets a Boolean value that indicates whether the connection will be pooled or explicitly opened every time the connection is requested.
Replication	Gets or sets a Boolean value that indicates whether replication is supported using the connection.
TransactionBinding	Gets or sets a string value that indicates how the connection maintains its association with an enlisted System.Transactions transaction.
TrustServerCertificate	Gets or sets a value that indicates whether the channel will be encrypted while bypassing the certificate chain to validate trust.
TypeSystemVersion	Gets or sets a string value that indicates the type of system the application expects.
UserID	Gets or sets the user ID to be used when connecting to SQL Server.
UserInstance	Gets or sets a value that indicates whether to redirect the connection from the default SQL Server Express instance to a runtime-initiated instance running under the account of the caller.
Values	Gets an ICollection that contains the values in the SqlConnection StringBuilder. (Overrides DbConnectionStringBuilder.Values.)
WorkstationID	Gets or sets the name of the workstation connecting to SQL Server.

CERTIFICATION READY
Why does ASP.NET still support the old ODBC and OleDB data connections?
2.6

The database *connection object* is the closest object to the data source. We have now used three connection objects to connect to our database—the SqlConnection, OleDB and ODBC—without making major changes to the syntax. Although the last two older connection objects cause a performance hit, it was not noticed in the example. This is only a concern for much larger and busier sites.

Understanding Connection Pools

Because of the disconnected nature of the Internet, many database connections can be created and destroyed in a single session. Each connecting process is one of the most resource-intensive activities in your application. To help speed things up, ADO.NET uses connection pooling.

CERTIFICATION READY
What do connection pools do to help the performance of the database when it is connected to a Web page?
2.6

A *connection pool* is a collection of open data connections that Web applications presumed were closed. Behind the scenes, however, ADO.NET has taken the "closed" connections and kept them open. By default, there are 100 such connections in the pool. If the same connection is needed again, an unused and still-open connection is assigned to the application.

All .NET data providers support connection pooling. This includes SQL Server, OleDB, ODBC, and Oracle. Although there are many settings available for us to use to fine-tune the service, most applications work fine with the defaults. If changes are made, third-party applications are available to monitor the changes in performance or you can write your own simulations.

Understanding Transaction Objects

A *transaction object* allows multiple SQL statements to be processed as a group. If any of the statements in the group fail, all the statements in the group that have been processed will be rolled back and the whole transaction is aborted. ASP.NET includes the transaction object that allows us to do this in code.

Before looking at transaction objects, we must understand the concept of the transaction. For a simple financial transaction such as buying a cup of coffee, you pay an employee and expect coffee in return. An example of a failed transaction would be if you paid for the cup of coffee just before the shop closed and the employee went home before returning with your coffee. Transactions are all-or-nothing propositions. Any location that sells coffee will guarantee that you receive your purchase or you get your money back. Moving this into the world of databases, getting your money back is equivalent to having a SQL transaction rolled back.

The official definition of a database transaction uses the term "Properties." Do not confuse this with the properties of the transaction object. The properties that define the goals of a perfect transaction via the ACID test are shown in Table 4-3.

Table 4-3

Properties of the ACID test for transactions

Atomic	There is no such thing as a partial transaction. Every step of the transaction must be completed.
Consistent	A transaction will not be considered successful if it produces any errors in the database.
Isolated	During a transaction process, changed data cannot be seen by other transactions. Other transactions only see the data before it is changed.
Durable	Upon successful completion, the results are permanent. Any undo's are turned over to the backup system.

As much as developers would like to achieve perfect transactions, the definition is simply a goal. It is unreasonable to achieve them on a busy system because so many locks would have to be in place that the database would slow to a crawl. A trade-off must be made between speed and the increased risk of data corruption. Since we are the only users of the sample database, we will not be addressing this issue.

A simple demonstration of the syntax needed for a database transaction will now be created. We will use our ShoppingList table in a scenario that requires two SQL statements to be executed as a single transaction.

The scenario:

We need the two dozen eggs that are currently included in our shopping list. However, it would be preferable if half of them were green. No matter the color, the requirement stands at two dozen eggs. If we reduce the current quantity of eggs on the list to one dozen before adding the green eggs, we will temporarily reduce the total number of eggs on the shopping list to one dozen. If another user, the shopper, reads the list before the transaction is completed, the required two dozen eggs will not be there. If we add the one dozen green eggs before reducing the original order of two dozen, we will temporarily have three dozen eggs on the list. Our program needs to reduce the existing order of eggs and place the new order of green eggs without the chance of someone reading the shopping list before both SQL statements are successfully executed.

We need to get a better understanding of the framework required for transaction objects before jumping into programming transactions. We will read the table, insert a new record (5 pounds of ham), add a try-catch error handler, and finally, execute the transaction.

 USE THE TRANSACTION OBJECT

GET READY. We will use Visual Web Developer, SQL Server, and the Sample database for this exercise.

1. Make sure SQL Server is still running and you have your database available.
2. Create a new ASP.NET Web site using C#.
3. Go to the **Design** view of the form and place two buttons and the GridView control on the form.
   - This time we will place text on the buttons.
4. Single-click the **first button** and use the Properties window to place the text **Show** on the button.
5. Single click the **second button** and place **Run** on the button.
6. Double-click the **Show** button for the code-behind.
7. Place the namespaces at the top with the others:

   ```
   using System.Data.SqlClient;
   using System.Data;
   ```

8. Place the following code into the **Show** button's click event procedure:

   ```
   SqlConnection con = new SqlConnection();
   con.ConnectionString = "Data
   Source=SUPERCOMPUTER\\SQLEXPRESS;Initial
   Catalog=Sample;Integrated Security=True";
   con.Open();
   SqlCommand cmd = new SqlCommand();
   cmd.Connection = con;

   cmd.CommandText = "Select * from ShoppingList";
   SqlDataReader reader = cmd.ExecuteReader();

   GridView1.DataSource = reader;
   GridView1.DataBind();

   reader.Close();

   con.Close();
   ```

   - Do not forget to modify your connection string as you have done in previous exercises in this lesson.

9. Run the program to make sure the GridView shows the data from the table, as seen in Figure 4-12. Then close the browser.
   - If the table does not display two dozen eggs, edit the table directly by using the Tools menu to connect to the database or optionally use SQL Management Studio. Follow the same procedures we have used in previous lessons.

Figure 4-12

The list with the two dozen eggs

10. Create the click event procedure for the **Run** button, copy the code from the **Show** button, and test the program.
    - A framework is needed for the transaction to trap any errors in the SQL statements. We will insert a new record into our table and then attempt to insert the same record again. The framework will catch this error and prevent creating a duplicate record.

11. Make all the following changes to the **Run** button between

    `cmd.Connection = con;` and `con.Close();`:

    ```
    SqlConnection con = new SqlConnection();
    con.ConnectionString = "Data
    Source=SUPERCOMPUTER\\SQLEXPRESS;Initial
    Catalog=Sample;Integrated Security=True";
    con.Open();
    SqlCommand cmd = new SqlCommand();
    cmd.Connection = con;
    cmd.CommandText = " Insert into ShoppingList
    Values('Ham', 'Pounds',5)";
    cmd.ExecuteNonQuery();

    con.Close();
    ```

12. Run the program and click the **Show** button. (Do not close the browser.)
    - You should see the current records of the table.

13. Click the **Run** button and wait for the table to update. (Do not close the browser.)
    - Nothing should have changed on the Web page.

14. Click the **Show** button again to see the changes as shown in Figure 4-13. (Do not close the browser.)
    - The changes should now appear on the Web page.

Figure 4-13

The results of adding the ham to the shopping list

15. Click the Run button again and watch the program crash. Close the browser.

- The primary key constraint will not allow you to enter duplicate ham orders. We will now catch this error and let the user know that this is not allowed, rather than letting the program crash.

16. Place a **label** on the form and change the text property to **Welcome**.

17. Place the following **try/catch** structure around the existing **Run** button code and add the label assignment:

```
try
{
    cmd.CommandText = " Insert into ShoppingList
    Values('Ham', 'Pounds',5)";
    cmd.ExecuteNonQuery();
}
catch
{
    Label1.Text = "NonQuery Failed";
}
finally
{
    con.Close();
}
```

- The command that we are evaluating will go inside "try", the error message will go inside "catch", and anything inside "finally" will be executed following the try or the catch.

- The command will place the message on the label if it fails. Since we do not have feedback at this time to describe exactly what happened, we have to use our own generic failure message. If you want to pursue this later, there is a way to write the code to deliver the failure message generated by the database management system.

18. Run the program and click the **Run** button. Close the browser.

- Notice that the label shows the failure message rather than crashing the program.

- We will now place the Insert and Update SQL commands within a transaction.

19. Change the **Run** button's code as shown below:

```
SqlConnection con = new SqlConnection();
con.ConnectionString = "Data
Source=SUPERCOMPUTER\\SQLEXPRESS;Initial
Catalog=Sample;Integrated Security=True";
con.Open();
SqlCommand cmd = new SqlCommand();
cmd.Connection = con;

SqlTransaction tran = con.BeginTransaction();
cmd.Transaction = tran;

try
{
    cmd.CommandText = "Insert into ShoppingList
    Values('Green Eggs', 'Dozen',1)";
```

```
        cmd.ExecuteNonQuery();
        cmd.CommandText = "Update ShoppingList set Qty=1
        Where Food = 'Eggs'";
        cmd.ExecuteNonQuery();
        tran.Commit();
        Label1.Text = "Transaction Successful";
    }
    catch
    {
        tran.Rollback();
        Label1.Text = "Transaction Failed";
    }
    finally
    {
        con.Close();
    }
```

20. Run the program and click the **Show** button. (Do not close the browser.)

- This should bring up the table's current values.

21. Click the **Run** button, wait a bit, and then click the **Show** button again.

- You should now see the changes as shown in Figure 4-14.

Figure 4-14

One dozen regular eggs and one dozen green eggs guaranteed by the transaction

Transaction Successful

| Show | Run |

Food	Unit	Qty
Bread	Loaf	1
Eggs	Dozen	1
Green Eggs	Dozen	1
Ham	Pounds	5
Milk	Half Gallon	1

22. Close the browser.

- We will now show the results of a rollback. One of the SQL statements will be valid and the other not. In the rollback, neither statement will make a permanent change to the table.

23. In the **Run** button code, replace the number **1** with the number **2** in both cmd .CommandText statements following the Dozen and following the Qty:

```
cmd.CommandText = "Insert into ShoppingList
Values('Green Eggs', 'Dozen',2)";
cmd.CommandText = "Update ShoppingList set Qty=2
Where Food = 'Eggs'";
```

24. Run the program, click the **Show** button, the **Run** button, and then the **Show** button. Close the browser.

- We will get an error message in the Label control because the insert command violated the primary key constraint again. The second command properly used an update and was successful. However, the table was rolled back to its original condition when the Commit method caused the transaction to fail and the code within the catch ran the Rollback method and sent the failure message to the label. The result is that the table remained the same.

- The fix is to change the insert statement to an update for the green eggs.

PAUSE. Close Visual Web Developer.

Here is a summary of the four steps to the transaction.

CERTIFICATION READY
Why would databases be prone to corrupted data if the functions that transaction objects provide were not available?

2.6

1. Start the transaction.
   - We tied a new instance of the transaction object to our SqlConnection, con, and our SqlCommand, cmd.
2. Issue all the transaction commands.
   - Within the try block of code, we ran both SQL statements.
3. Commit the transaction if all commands were successful.
   - Also with the try block of code, we ran the commit method to attempt to finalize both SQL statements.
4. Roll back if any commands failed.
   - Within the catch block of code, we rolled back all SQL statements if the commit method failed.

TAKE NOTE * If there is a loss of power or a computer crash before the commit method is reached, SQL Server will automatically roll back all uncommitted transactions when it restarts.

SKILL SUMMARY

IN THIS LESSON YOU LEARNED TO:

- Use the LinqDataSource control.
- Use the ObjectDataSource control.
- Use the XmlDataSource control.
- Use the SqlDataSource control.
- Use data-binding syntax.
- Use a data-aware control.
- Examine database connections.
- Use the OleDB connection object.
- Use the OdbcConnection object.
- Use the connection pool.
- Use the transaction object.

Knowledge Assessment

Multiple Choice

Circle the letter or letters that correspond to the best answer or answers.

1. Which control is designed for separating the Web site from the database code?
   a. LinqDataSource
   b. ObjectDataSource
   c. XmlDataSource
   d. SqlDataSource

2. Which control allows you to connect to ADO.NET but is limited to the query language of the connected database?
   a. LinqDataSource
   b. ObjectDataSource
   c. XmlDataSource
   d. SqlDataSource

3. Which control is the latest way to connect to a database?
   a. LinqDataSource
   b. ObjectDataSource
   c. XmlDataSource
   d. SqlDataSource

4. Which control is used for hierarchical data?
   a. LinqDataSource
   b. ObjectDataSource
   c. XmlDataSource
   d. SqlDataSource

5. What is a data-aware control?
   a. A control that is data bound
   b. Any presentation control
   c. Any Web-based control that can be connected to a database
   d. A control that has the two required data source properties

6. Which data connection object connects to the fewest databases?
   a. .NET
   b. OleDB
   c. ODBC

7. Which data connection is the oldest?
   a. .NET
   b. OleDB
   c. ODBC

8. Which data connection is the most universal in the types of its data sources?
   a. .NET
   b. OleDB
   c. ODBC

9. Which statement is NOT true regarding the connection pool?
   a. The .NET, OleDB, ODBC, and Oracle providers all use the connection pool.
   b. Connection pools keep connections open longer than normal.
   c. The connection pool control is found in the Data category of the Toolbox.
   d. There are 100 connections in the default connection pool.

10. What is the purpose of the transaction object?
    a. It allows SQL statements to be run from the Web page.
    b. It allows SQL statements to write to the database.
    c. It gives the Web site the ability to handle financial transactions.
    d. It is used to tie multiple SQL statements together.

Fill in the Blank

Complete the following sentences by writing the correct word or words in the blanks provided.

1. The _____ control uses a non-proprietary version of SQL.

2. The _____ control provides a way for coding an application to retrieve data from a variety of sources without being concerned about the details.

3. The _____ control enables you to connect and interact with any database supported by ADO.NET.

4. The XmlDataSource pulls data from the _____ of an XML file.

5. The _____ method of the GridView binds data to the control.

6. A data-aware control has the _____ and _____ properties to simplify data binding.

7. The _____ is a property of the connection object responsible for providing the object with information such as the driver, server, password, etc.

8. The C# structure _____ is necessary to take advantage of the transaction object.

9. The _____ transaction method is called when a transaction fails.

10. A _____ _____ is used to reduce the number of times a data connection opens and closes.

■ Competency Assessment

Scenario 4-1: Creating an Online Inventory Management System (Part I)

Regal Fruit Cooperative has ten drivers who have to deliver bins to their members' orchards in the summer months. These bins come from six storage locations located many miles apart. Drivers need to record how many bins have been removed from which location in order to know how many bins are located at each in order to distribute them more efficiently. This system also prevents a driver from pulling into an empty lot.

The inventory activity is currently performed in the office. However, the office staff is not always available. Since Internet-connected computers are available to the drivers at all times, the plan is to have the drivers record their own loads at each site when they pick up the bins.

Your job is to create a simple user interface for the truck drivers. They will see how many bins are located at each location. Their inputs will include their driver ID number, the storage location ID, the coop member ID, and the number of bins delivered. Other information, such as the date, is optional. The new count will be placed on a separate location on the screen to reflect the change.

Scenario 4-2: Creating an Online Inventory Management System (Part II)

Create the database to be used with Scenario 4-1. Although this database could be normalized (broken into multiple tables) we will create a single table for this scenario. Create a separate field for the primary key, which will not be displayed on the screen.

■ Proficiency Assessment

Scenario 4-3: Creating an Online Inventory Management System (Part III)

Connect the database you created in Scenario 4-2 to the user interface you created in Scenario 4-1 to display the data when the page loads.

Scenario 4-4: Creating an Online Inventory Management System (Part IV)

Add data manipulation functionality to the scenarios above. The user should be able to insert new records, and update and remove existing records. Optionally, add report and print functionality.

✳ Workplace Ready

Creating an Online DVD Inventory and More

Suppose you have an extensive DVD collection holding instructions for all phases of work for your employees. If they want to see what is available, they would normally have to contact you. If this inventory was stored on a local database, they would still need to have contact with this database. Using a tool like Visual Web Developer, you could easily place your inventory online for all your employees to share. With this technology, you could eventually give your employees access to the videos online without having to come in to pick them up.

As you work through these lessons, you will find an increasing number of uses for this technology at the workplace.

Working with Client-Side Scripting

LESSON SKILL MATRIX

Skills/Concepts	MTA Exam Objective	MTA Exam Objective Number
Understanding Client-Side Scripting	Understand client-side scripting	4.1
Understanding Ajax Concepts	Understand AJAX concepts	4.2

KEY TERMS

Ajax

ASP.NET AJAX

ChildrenAsTriggers

client-side libraries

client-side scripting

DOM

EnablePartialRendering

Extender control

JavaScript

ScriptManager

ScriptManagerProxy

Scripts collection

Services collection

Timer control

triggers

UpdateProgress

VBScript

XMLHttpRequest

Now that Karen has the database under control, she finds that some pages take longer to load than expected. Even something as trivial as changing a small image on the page requires the whole page to be redrawn.

This lesson will present her with a couple of ways to fundamentally change the way a page responds to a user. One is to continue using postback, but limit the postback to the area of her page containing the image. The other is to have the browser do all the work, eliminating postback altogether and using client-side scripting. Either technique can be used to speed up her Web pages.

Understanding Client-Side Scripting

THE BOTTOM LINE

So far, we had the server run our programs and recreate the Web pages, and had the pages posted back to the browser for display. An alternative to postbacks is having the browser process programs rather than the server. This is called *client-side scripting*. It allows the page to respond immediately to user activities rather than waiting on the server to build a new page and send it to the browser.

One would assume that having your computer run programs from the Internet is dangerous. This, of course, is true for desktop applications, but not as much for browser-run scripts. Since the browser is in charge of the application, it has much more control over malware attacks than if the local operating system was running it as a desktop application. However, since the browser is acting as a virtual operating system for client-side scripts, malware attacks are becoming more focused on this platform because the popularity of client-side scripting is on the rise. This does not mean we should abandon client-side scripting any more than we should abandon the Internet. The benefits of using client-side scripting far outweigh the dangers of threats like JavaScript malware.

Do not confuse JavaScript with Java. *JavaScript* is embedded into HTML for the browser to run when Java applets are downloaded along with HTML as separate files. These files are run on the locally installed Java Virtual Machine. JavaScript is text-based commands while a Java applet is compiled code generated from a complex high-level language that only a computer can read. Java is a full-fledged object-oriented programming language that can also create stand-alone applications. Although both are relatively secure because neither is allowed to write to local storage devices, the Java Virtual Machine has exhibited better control over malware attacks using Java than browsers attempting to control these attacks via JavaScript.

Since we are working with client-side scripting, the following two exercises do not need to connect to a Web server. This means that postbacks do not need to be addressed. We also do not need to be concerned about the Java Virtual Machine because we will not be doing exercises using Java. All the code will be run on a browser where the code may be interpreted differently depending on the browser used. Even though the sample code uses IE (Internet Explorer), you may want to try different browsers to see how they handle the code differently.

⊙ WRITE JAVASCRIPT

GET READY. We will be using a simple text editor for this exercise.

1. Open your Web browser and make sure JavaScript is enabled.
   - JavaScript needs to be enabled for JavaScript-enabled pages to display properly.
   - To enable scripting: Open a browser window and go to the Tools menu item. Choose **Internet Options,** choose **Custom Level,** go to **Active Scripting,** and click the **Enable** option. Click the **OK** button, click the **OK** button on the next window, close the browser window, and reopen it.
2. Using Windows Explorer, create a text file and rename it **hi.html.**
   - Remember to have Windows show file extensions so you do not create a hi.html.txt file.

ANOTHER WAY

You can also create the text file in the Notepad Accessory. When saving the file put the file name in quotes—"hi.html". The quotes will cause the file to be saved with the html extension and will avoid the .txt extension being added to the file name.

3. Right-click on the file name and select **Edit** from the pop-up menu.

- If the Edit selection does not show, you can rename it with the txt extension, open it in your text editor, and then do a save as using html for the name of the file extension.

4. Place the following code in the file:

```
<input type="button" onClick="alert('Hi');"
value="Say Hi" />
```

- For now, we will not consider the strict XHTML specifications and focus on the objectives.
- The JavaScript is embedded into this HTML code as the onClick attribute.
- All JavaScript within the Web page will run as soon as the page loads unless we use an event handler, as we did with the code above. Here we included the onClick event handler that will allow the code to run only when we click the button.

5. Save the file but leave the editor open.

6. Run the program by double-clicking the file icon in Windows Explorer. Press the button when the browser opens, as shown in Figure 5-1, and click the **OK** button. Leave the browser open.

 **ANOTHER WAY** You can also run a script directly from the browser by using the File menu, selecting Open, and locating the file.

Figure 5-1

JavaScript making the Web page interactive

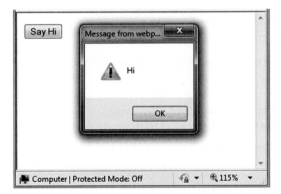

7. Edit the file and capitalize alert to **Alert**.

8. Save the file, refresh the browser and press the **Say Hi** button.

- JavaScript will no longer execute the code for the button.
- JavaScript is case sensitive.

9. Undo the capitalization and make sure the button works again.

- The alert("Hi") part of this code is a JavaScript method that would normally have been placed within the body of a script element rather than embedded as we did above. It is important to keep the HTML code separate from the script.
- We will now make our own function named **hiAlert( )** and place it between script element tags.
- The **onClick** event handler will then call our function to run the JavaScript code rather than running it directly in HTML.

10. Change the code as shown below, paying close attention to upper- and lowercase characters:

```
<script>
function hiAlert()
{
alert('Hi again');
}
</script>
<input type="button" onClick="hiAlert( )"
value="Say Hi" />
```

- Notice that the alert message changed slightly. This is to make sure you know that the browser is running the new code.

11. Press the **save** button on the editor and the **refresh** button on the browser.
    - The only difference you should notice is that the message of the alert changed.
    - Again, this is very simplified. For example, since the default scripting language for browsers is JavaScript, the type attribute `<script type="text/javascript">` is not needed but is normally included for code readability. Of course, we are also excluding all the XHTML elements such as html, head, and body.

12. Type in the complete version of the code, which would normally be seen in a deployed Web page. Save the file, update the browser, and then test the program.

```
<!DOCTYPE html PUBLIC "-//W3C//DTD XHTML 1.0
Transitional//EN"

"http://www.w3.org/TR/xhtml1/DTD
/xhtml1-transitional.dtd">

<html xmlns="http://www.w3.org/1999/xhtml">

<head>

<meta http-equiv="Content-type"
    content="text/html;charset=UTF-8" />
<title>JavaScript Sample</title>
<script type="text/javascript">
function hiAlert()
{
alert('Hi, from the completed Web page');
}
</script>
</head>
<body>
<input type="button" onClick="hiAlert()"
value="Say Hi" />
</body>
</html>
```

- Now that we have a complex page in which HTML is mixed with script, we will simplify the HTML by placing the code into its own file.

13. Create a new text file in the same directory as the HTML file, rename it **Hi.js**, and open it up for editing using a text editor such as Notepad.

- The file extension normally used for JavaScript files is .js but any extension can be used.

14. Cut out the code from between the script element tags (leave the tags) in the HTML file and paste it into the new Hi.js file. Then change the alert message again to show that the new code is running.

```
function hiAlert()
{
alert('Hi, from the script file');
}
```

- This is all the code that the Hi.js file should have.

15. Save the JavaScript file.

16. Place the **src** attribute in the opening <script> tag in the HTML file to provide the document with the name of the JavaScript file to use.

```
<script type="text/javascript" src="Hi.js"></>
</script>
```

17. Verify the changes you made in the hi.html file.

```
<!DOCTYPE html PUBLIC "-//W3C//DTD XHTML 1.0
Transitional//EN"

"http://www.w3.org/TR/xhtml1/DTD/
xhtml1-transitional.dtd">

<html xmlns="http://www.w3.org/1999/xhtml">

<head>

<meta http-equiv="Content-type"
    content="text/html;charset=UTF-8" />

<title>JavaScript Sample</title>
<script type="text/javascript"
src="Hi.js"></></script></head>

<body>

<input type="button" onClick="hiAlert()"
value="Say Hi" />

</body>

</html>
```

18. Save the HTML file.

19. Refresh the browser and press the button on the page.
- When the button is pressed, triggering the onClick event handler, the hiAlert( ) function is called. The browser then looks for the file designated by the src attributes and runs the function.

PAUSE. Close the HTML file, the JavaScript file, and the browser.

These samples only show the basic structure of how to use HTML with JavaScript. As with CSS, we have a choice of placing the code in line with HTML, separated from HTML within the page, or in an external file. In addition, as with CSS, using inline JavaScript should be avoided in favor of separating the scripting code from HTML.

WRITE VBSCRIPT

GET READY. We will be using a simple text editor for this exercise. You will also be required to use Internet Explorer because no other browser will recognize VBScript.

1. Open your Web browser and make sure VBScript is enabled.
   - VBScript should normally be disabled because malware is able to abuse it.
2. Using Windows Explorer, create a text file and rename it **Hello.vbs**.
3. Right-click on the file name and select edit from the pop-up menu.
4. Type the following code into the file, save it, and close the file:
   MsgBox "Hello"
5. Double-click the file's icon and click your button when the message pops up.
   - We will now embed our VBS message box into an HMTL document.
6. Rename the file to **Hello.html.**
7. Double-click the file's icon. Close the browser.
   - Notice that the message box did not pop up. This is because HTML only treats it as text. We need to let HTML know that this text is VBScript.
8. Edit the **Hello.html** file to match the following code:

```
<script type="text/vbscript">
Function hiAlert()
  MsgBox "Hello"
End Function
</script>
<input type="button" onClick="hiAlert()"
value="Say Hi" />
```

9. Save the file but leave it open for more editing.
   - Compare this script with the script used in Step 10 of the previous exercise using JavaScript. HTML uses JavaScript as the default language for the <script> tag, making the type attribute optional. Since we are using VBScript, the type attribute is no longer optional: VBScript must be specified as the language.
   - Notice that the onClick attribute is used to execute code when the button is clicked. An alternative to using HTML's onClick attribute is to replace the onClick attribute with the name attribute. VBScript can then use this name and create an event handler so we can write event procedure code. Since the function is already named hiAlert, we will use this name for the name of the button. The function name is then changed to a typical Visual Basic event procedure.
10. Double-click the file's icon and click your button when the message pops up. Close the browser.
    - This step was just to make sure the script still runs.
11. Edit the **Hello.html** file to match the following code:

```
<script type="text/vbscript">
Function hiAlert_OnClick()
  MsgBox "Hello"
End Function
</script>
<input type="button" name="hiAlert"
value="Say Hi" />
```

12. **Save** and **Close** the file.
   - The Visual Basic code used for scripting predates that used on the .NET platform. The syntax for event handlers is integrated into the name of the procedure. It begins with the name of the object, then an underscore, followed with the name of the event followed by a set of empty parentheses.
   - Notice that onClick is now **OnClick**. Even though VBScript is not case sensitive, the first letter of the names we use is typically capitalized.
13. Double-click the file's icon, and click your button when the message pops up. Then close the browser.
   - This step was just to make sure the script still runs.

PAUSE. Close the HTML file.

Although ***VBScript*** is an alternative to JavaScript for enhancing HTML, it is not used nearly as often. The most important reason for this lack of popularity is that it can only be run with Internet Explorer. However, VBScript is popular with network administrators because of its ability to create stand-alone applications.

As in CSS and JavaScript, an external file can also be used to separate the VBScript code from the HTML page.

Understanding Client-Side Scripting and DOM

JavaScript is manipulating ***DOM*** on the client-side while the server requests are processing in the background. DOM defines the structure of the Web page and all its components.

All XML documents adhere to the XML Document Object Model (DOM) specification. When the XML structure holds HTML data, it becomes XHTML. The browser reads the XML document populated with XHTML data for the Web page to know what to display on the document and where to place it. This becomes the Document Object Model, or just DOM, that the client-side scripting code manipulates. The browser then changes the display to reflect the changes to this DOM without completely re-creating the page or having to contact the Web server unnecessarily.

Since the HTML DOM is an XML document, all the rules of XML apply. The first or top-level element is the root. Note: XML mixes the metaphors of a family tree and a tree growing in the woods. The next layer of elements is the child elements of the root. The root is the parent element of these child elements. All the child elements of the root, at the same level, are siblings. Child elements can have children of their own. However, if an element has no children, the element is referred to as a leaf.

We can use the browser to see the underlying DOM structure of any Web page. For Internet Explorer, we can download its Developer Toolbar from Microsoft.com and install it.

 EXAMINE THE DOCUMENT OBJECT MODEL

GET READY. We will be using Microsoft Internet Explorer with the Developer Toolbar.

1. If the Developer Toolbar for IE is not installed, find the download from Microsoft.com and install it.
2. Open or create the **Hello.html** file with the following code with Internet Explorer:

```
<script type="text/vbscript">
Function hiAlert_OnClick()
  MsgBox "Hello"
End Function
```

```
</script>
<input type="button" name="hiAlert"
value="Say Hi" />
```

3. From the Tools menu of IE, click **Developer Tools.**
   - Remember that Developer Tools must be installed.
4. From the **View** menu, open the **Source -> DOM (Page)**, as shown in Figures 5-2 and 5-3.

Figure 5-2

Using the Developer Tools in IE 8 to view the Web page from the DOM point of view

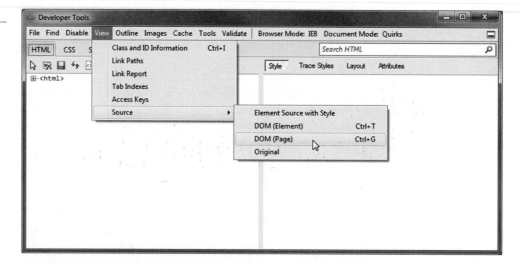

Figure 5-3

The DOM for the simple Web page as seen by IE 8

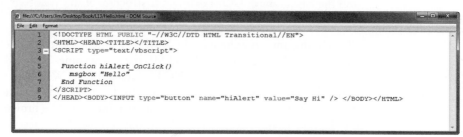

- Notice that DOM makes some assumptions for the DOCTYPE by automatically placing it at the top of the document. DOM does not always match your source code to ensure that the browser is able to use it.
- Any changes to DOM will instantly change what is displayed on the form.

5. While the Browser, Developer Tools, and DOM Source windows are open, open the **Hello.html** file for editing.
6. Change the **Hello.html** file to replace MsgBox "Hello" with **hiAlert.value = "Hello"** as shown below:

```
<script type="text/vbscript">
Function hiAlert_OnClick()
  hiAlert.value = "Hello"
End Function
</script>
<input type="button" name="hiAlert"
value="Say Hi" />
```

- The change you make here will change the text on the button from "Say Hi" to "Hello" rather than pop up a message box.

7. Save the **Hello.html** file and refresh the browser.
   - The refresh only updates the Developer Tools windows but not the DOM Source window.

8. Close the DOM Source window and use the Developer Tools to reopen it.
   - The DOM Source window should now display the changes in your Hello.html file.

9. From the browser, press the **Say Hi** button. (Leave the browser window open.)
   - The button should now say Hello.
   - Notice that the value of the button in the DOM Source window still says has value= "Say Hi."

10. Close the DOM Source window and use the Developer Tools to reopen it.
    - Notice that we used the name attribute to identify the element. Using the ID attribute would have worked just as well for our purposes. Using the name attribute works well for changing many objects with a single line of code because many elements can share the same name. For specifying individual elements, the ID attribute would be a better choice. If we were to use ID rather than name in this exercise, we could have placed id="B1" in the INPUT element and replaced **hiAlert.value = "Hello"** with **B1.value = "Hello"**.
    - When the server was making comprehensive changes to the page, DOM was being completely replaced as well. This required the whole page to be recreated. Our small change to DOM only requires a partial-page postback. The code we will be adding to the page, as we continue the exercise, will reveal that the entire page is NOT doing a postback.

11. Add the following code to the top of the Hello.html file without making any changes to the existing code:

    ```
    <script type="text/javascript">
    alert("Welcome");
    </script>
    ```

12. Refresh the browser.
    - The alert should pop up immediately upon refresh.

13. Press the **Say Hi** button.
    - Notice the alert did not reappear but pressing the refresh button will pop up the alert again.
    - The alert would reappear when the button is pressed if we had a postback.

PAUSE. You can now close all the windows.

JavaScript and VBScript are used by the browser to manipulate the DOM and to make calls to the server for server-side processing if necessary.

TAKE NOTE*

Ajax can use any browser-based scripting language other than JavaScript, such as VBScript.

CERTIFICATION READY

What does client-side scripting provide for Web pages that Active Server Pages (ASP) does not?

4.1

■ Understanding Ajax Concepts

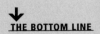
THE BOTTOM LINE

JavaScript is limited to client-side scripting. Although this makes pages dynamic, JavaScript is unable to communicate directly with the server. To work with the server, it makes calls to a server-side scripting language. Unlike a typical page request, however, JavaScript does not have to wait for the new page; in fact, it does not even ask for a new page. It sends and retrieves data from the server for the data to update the page. To make things even better, it can keep processing while these requests are being handled by the server. This concept is called *Ajax*.

The term Ajax was coined by Jesse James Garret, founder of Adaptive Path, in his 2005 article *Ajax: A New Approach to Web Applications*. Adaptive Path used the term as shorthand for Asynchronous JavaScript + XML. Ajax is neither an acronym nor a technology; it is a group of existing technologies used to speed up server requests. Garret was not the only one to use these technologies; he was just the one to popularize the term. According to Garret's article, these are the required technologies:

- Standards-based presentation using XHTML and CSS
- Dynamic display and interaction using the DOM
- Data interchange and manipulation using XML and XSLT
- Asynchronous data retrieval using XMLHttpRequest
- JavaScript binding everything together

The following is a list of the individual Ajax technologies used in his definition:

- **XML:** Extensible Markup Language defines a structure that can hold data. Ajax often uses XML for returning data from the server. However, HTML, text, JSON, or any other desired structure can be used. JSON is an optional technology, used in place of XML, whose name stands for JavaScript Object Notation.

- **XHTML:** Extensible Hypertext Markup Language is HTML code that adheres to XML syntax.

- **CSS:** Cascading Style Sheets define the display of a Web page. Even though CSS is included in the Ajax definition, it is not required.

- **XSLT:** This is a language for manipulating XML and CSS. Even though XSLT is included in the Ajax definition, it is not required. We will not cover XSLT in this lesson.

- **DOM:** Document Object Model is the XML structure used to store the Web page. Every Web page has one. We will be exploring this concept in more detail in this lesson. Manipulating DOM alone is often confused with Ajax, but it is nothing more than Dynamic HTML (DHTML).

- **XMLHttpRequest:** *XMLHttpRequest* is a client-side object that requests XML data from the Web server when JavaScript asks for it. Once the request is made, the browser continues asynchronously as though nothing happened. The request is processed in the background while the user is using the browser. When the XML data is returned, JavaScript will process the data and most likely make a change in DOM for the user to see.

- **JavaScript:** The key technologies that make Ajax so powerful are DOM and XMLHttpRequest. A client-side scripting language communicates asynchronously with a server-side scripting language via XMLHttpRequest as the user interacts with the Web page. When the user *triggers* an event on the Web page, the client-side scripting language processes a function that can change the DOM, which creates a dynamic Web page. With Ajax, the client-side code can reach out and grab data from the server without the user being aware and change the DOM using this downloaded server data. Since this is done asynchronously and without having to render the whole page, the Web application has the appearance of a desktop application. The names of the technologies to accomplish this are somewhat irrelevant when defining the term Ajax.

There are many technologies involved in Ajax. Although two of them, XSLT and CSS, will not be covered in this lesson, you should nevertheless have an introduction to XSLT and understand the importance of CSS. Extensible Stylesheet Language Transformations

(XSLT) is an XML-based language that is commonly used to transform an XML document into a new CSS-embedded XHTML document that will be displayed in the browser. From Lesson 1, you learned that CSS is the technology used to describe page content. These two technologies are responsible for the vast majority of DOM changes to create dynamic displays.

Using ASP.NET AJAX

The ASP.NET implementation of Ajax, which is spelled with all capitals (***AJAX***), includes several objects. The ScriptManager, UpdatePanel, and XMLHttpRequest objects are key to asynchronous communication with the server while only parts of the Web page are executing the postbacks.

TAKE NOTE *
The all-caps version of Ajax (AJAX) refers to Microsoft's implementation of Ajax. Thus, Ajax for ASP.NET is ASP.NET AJAX, not ASP.NET Ajax.

Only a handful of AJAX Extensions are listed in the Visual Web Developer Toolbox shown in Figure 5-4. This lesson will cover them all. However, some will be covered in more depth than others.

Figure 5-4

The complete list of AJAX Extensions

➤ **SET THE ENABLEPARTIALRENDERING PROPERTY OF THE SCRIPTMANAGER CONTROL**

GET READY. We will be using Microsoft Visual Web Developer 2008 Express for this exercise.

1. Start Visual Web Developer and create a new Web site.
2. Select the ASP.NET Web site template using C#.
3. Go to **Design** view and place the **ScriptManager** on the form from the AJAX Extensions category of the Toolbox.
   • The ScriptManager control should be the first control placed on the form.
4. Place two labels and a button on the form as shown in Figure 5-5.

Figure 5-5

The form for the first AJAX-enabled page

ScriptManager - ScriptManager1
Label
Label
Button

5. Double-click the form to add the following code:

```
protected void Page_Load(object sender,
EventArgs e)
{
  if (IsPostBack)
    Label1.Text = "PostBack!";
  else
    Label1.Text = "Welcome to AJAX!";
}
```

6. Double-click the button to add the following code:

```
protected void Button1_Click(object sender,
EventArgs e)
{
    Label2.Text = DateTime.Now.ToString();
}
```

- The timestamp that is returned to the Web page comes from the server. In our sample program, this will be the same as the local time. However, for a deployed site, the server time will often be in a different time zone. Server-side script is used to retrieve local time from the client's machine.

7. Run the program and press the button. (Keep the browser open.)
   - Notice that the button triggered a postback. The server rendered the entire page.
   - We will now use the UpdatePanel to isolate the button and the label from the page for an entire page rendering.

8. Close the browser and place an UpdatePanel control on the page from the AJAX Enabled category of the Toolbox.

9. Move the button and the second label into the UpdatePanel area as shown in Figure 5-6.

Figure 5-6

The second label and button are placed within the UpdatePanel

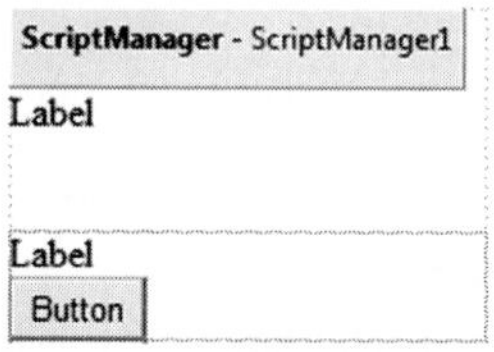

```
ScriptManager - ScriptManager1

Label


Label
Button
```

10. Run the program again and press the button. Then close the browser.
    - Notice that the first label still displays the Welcome message. This confirms that the server did not render the entire page.
    - If, for some reason, you do not wish to have the UpdatePanel do a partial render, you can easily resort back to the full-page postback by turning off the *EnablePartialRendering* property of the ScriptManager control.

11. Turn off the **EnablePartialRendering** property of the ScriptManager control by setting it to **False** as shown in Figure 5-7.

Figure 5-7

Turning off the AJAX
functionality of the page

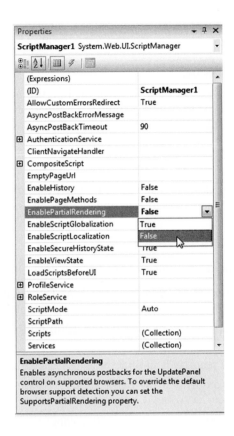

EnablePartialRendering
Enables asynchronous postbacks for the UpdatePanel
control on supported browsers. To override the default
browser support detection you can set the
SupportsPartialRendering property.

12. Test the change by running the program.

- Notice that we now have full-page postback with the EnablePartialRendering property set to False.

13. Close the browser.

14. Set the **EnablePartialRendering** property back to **True** and run the program again to verify that we again have partial-page rendering. Then close the browser.

PAUSE. Keep Visual Web Developer open. We will continue with this Web page in the next exercise.

All areas of the form that will take advantage of partial rendering must have all related objects placed within UpdatePanels. In our case, we have a single UpdatePanel with a button that updates a label. Another button and label, or any other set of controls, can be placed in other UpdatePanels to isolate rendering from the rest of the form.

Understanding ScriptManager and ScriptManagerProxy

As seen in the previous exercise, the ScriptManager control is responsible for controlling the activities of AJAX on a form. Every ASP.NET AJAX page must have its own ScriptManager control unless the site is using a master page. In that case, all pages will use the ScriptManager of the master page.

If an individual page needs to do something different from what the ScriptManager on the master page defines, a **ScriptManagerProxy** control can be placed on that page to make the necessary changes unique to the page. In addition, because only a single ScriptManager or its proxy is allowed on a page, there is no reason to manually bind any of the AJAX controls that are placed onto the page.

CERTIFICATION READY
Why is setting the EnablePartialRendering property to True an important step in ensuring that your Web page is supporting the concept of Ajax?
4.2

The following exercises are based on some of the AJAX controls that are automatically bound to the ScriptManager control. These are the Timer, UpdatePanel, and UpdateProgress controls.

USING THE TIMER CONTROL

The *Timer control* is used to delay scripts. When the interval property is set in milliseconds and the Enabled property is set to true, the code in the timer's event procedure will run repeatedly on every cycle set by the interval.

For a single timing event, setting the Interval property to false is usually the procedure's first line of code.

The most common use for AJAX applications is to do a postback on an UpdatePanel at a given interval. We will automate our clock to update itself by using a timer.

 APPLY THE TIMER CONTROL

GET READY. We will continue with the previous exercise in our Visual Web Developer project.

1. Place a **Timer** control on the form from the AJAX Extensions category of the Toolbox. Place it within the UpdatePanel along with the label and button.

2. Change the **Interval** property of the timer to **1000 milliseconds** from the Properties window.
   - Since the **Interval** property is in terms of milliseconds, this value will give us 1 second.

3. Change the enabled property of the timer to **False**. (Leave the EnableViewState property as True.)

4. Double-click the **Timer** object and move (NOT copy) the code from the Button's event procedure into the timer's event procedure.
   - An easy way to do this is to select the text, click on the selected text, and drag it from the Button to the timer's event procedure.
   - The timer will now be responsible for placing the current time into the label.

5. Replace the Button's event procedure code to enable the timer with the following line of code:

   ```
   Timer1.Enabled = !Timer1.Enabled;
   ```

   - Clicking the button multiple times will toggle the timer on and off.

6. Run the program and click the button. Close the browser.
   - The time should now be updating the label every second.
   - Postback should still be limited to the UpdatePanel.
   - If you chose to toggle the timer on and off, clicking on the button the second time will shut the timer off.

PAUSE. Keep Visual Web Developer open. We will continue with this Web page in the next exercise.

The Timer object is handy for displaying a real-time clock. However, it may not always work as expected. The timer automatically begins another count down after the event procedure code has finished processing. Because the code directs the page to perform a postback, the overall time between seconds is slightly longer that the 1,000 milliseconds. This forces the display to periodically skip seconds.

The postbacks will also create a blinking display, which can be distracting to the user. A quick test is to change the interval to 2,000 milliseconds and watch the display slowly alternate the seconds from a series of even numbers to a series of odd numbers, depending on the processing and update speed.

USE THE UPDATEPROGRESS CONTROL

GET READY. We will continue with the previous exercise using our existing Visual Web Developer project.

1. Place an **UpdateProgress** object on the form from the AJAX Extensions category of the Toolbox. Place it outside of the UpdatePanel.

   • Normally, progress bars are not displayed until there has been a little delay. This prevents controls from blinking when the postbacks are fast. Since we want to see this control all the time, we will set it to zero.

2. Go to the properties window of the UpdateProgress control and change the **DisplayAfter** property from the default of a half second to **0 (zero) milliseconds**.

   • We need a message or animated gif to represent the progress of the update. For simplicity, we will use text.

   • Anything placed in the **UpdateProgress** object on the form will be used as feedback to the user during the wait for the update.

3. Place the text message of your choice into the UpdateProgress object.

   • We are almost ready. The problem is that the timer is a client-side control and is not waiting for the server to respond. For this simulation only, we will use the Sleep method from the system. Do not use this on an actual page.

4. Place the following as the first line in the timer's event procedure:

   ```
   System.Threading.Thread.Sleep(1000);
   ```

5. Run the program and press the button.

   • You should have a one-second delay for the Timer control and one second for the Sleep method. While the page is waiting for the update, your message should show on the page.

6. Close the browser.

   • The UpdateProgress object automatically monitors a specific UpdatePanel by its AssociatedUpdatePanelID property. If the AssociatedUpdatePanelID does not have a value, it will monitor all UpdatePanels on the form.

   • Although the next step is not needed because we only have a single UpdatePanel, we will do it for practice.

7. Associate the UpdateProgress object to the UpdatePanel by using the Properties window and selecting the **UpdatePanel** from the drop-down list box of the UpdateProgress object.

   • This will not change the way the page functions.

8. Rerun the program to make sure the page functions as before.

PAUSE. Close Visual Web Developer. We will use it again with a new site in the next exercise.

CERTIFICATION READY
Why is the Timer object often used with an UpdatePanel control?
4.2

The UpdateProgress control is used for user feedback with asynchronous postbacks whether it is for the entire page or for individual UpdatePanel controls. Before AJAX, Web pages were unresponsive during the postback process, making it impossible to inform the user of his or her progress.

USING CHILDRENASTRIGGERS AND UPDATEMODE PROPERTIES

These two properties are very important to understand in applying AJAX to a Web page. They work as a team, which make them much more difficult to apply than a single property.

ChildrenAsTriggers is a Boolean property of the UpdatePanel that, when set to True, is updated automatically when any of its child, or nested, UpdatePanels are updated.

UpdateMode is a string property of the UpdatePanel that can be set either to Always or to Conditional. An Always setting will update the panel whenever any other panel on the form is updated. A Conditional setting will only cause the UpdatePanel to trigger when explicitly called.

These two properties of the UpdatePanel must be addressed together because both are often changed to achieve the desired results. We will be creating a Web page with three UpdatePanels, one of which will be nested, and changing both of these properties for a basic understanding of their influences on neighboring UpdatePanels.

SET THE CHILDRENASTRIGGERS AND UPDATEMODE PROPERTIES OF THE UPDATEPANEL CONTROL

GET READY. We will use Visual Web Developer and a new Web site.

1. Start Visual Web developer and create a new Web site using C#, as we have done before.
2. Go to **Design** view and remove the **div** control from the form.
   • We removed the div control to keep the layout of the form as simple as possible.
3. Place the ScriptManager control on the form. It is found in the AJAX Extensions category of the Toolbox.
4. Place an UpdatePanel control on the form.
5. Place a Label, Button, and CheckBox within the UpdatePanel. For aesthetics, arrange them vertically.
6. Change the text property of the button to say **Parent**.
7. Place another UpdatePanel within the existing UpdatePanel.
8. Place another set of controls within this new nested UpdatePanel as you did with its parent.
9. Change the text property of the new button to say **Child**.
10. Place another UpdatePanel below and outside of the existing panels.
11. Place another set of controls within this new UpdatePanel as you did with the others.
12. Change the text property of the new button to say **Other**.
    • Notice that you have four distinct areas on the form, as shown in Figure 5-8. The first is the form and the second and last are update panels placed on the form. The third is an update panel that is nested within the first.

Figure 5-8

The form layout for testing regular and nested update panels

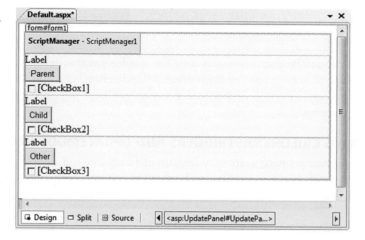

- If the control panels begin displaying **Error Creating Control** in the design window, as shown in Figure 5-9, simply click **View** from the pull-down menu and click **Refresh**. Then double-click each button to make sure the event procedures are still wired up correctly. If not, copy the code from the old event procedure and place it into the recognized event procedure. Then erase the entire event procedure that no longer works.

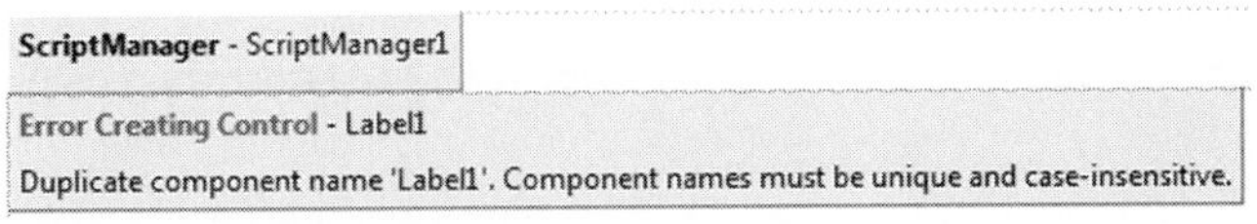

Figure 5-9

The form layout needing to be refreshed

```
ScriptManager - ScriptManager1

Error Creating Control - Label1
Duplicate component name 'Label1'. Component names must be unique and case-insensitive.
```

13. Use the following code for the click event procedure for the Parent button:

    ```
    Label1.Text = DateTime.Now.ToString();
    Label2.Text = DateTime.Now.ToString();
    Label3.Text = DateTime.Now.ToString();
    if (CheckBox1.Checked) UpdatePanel1.Update();
    ```

14. Use the following code for the click event procedure for the Child button:

    ```
    Label1.Text = DateTime.Now.ToString();
    Label2.Text = DateTime.Now.ToString();
    Label3.Text = DateTime.Now.ToString();
    if (CheckBox2.Checked) UpdatePanel2.Update();
    ```

    - You can copy and paste the first three lines, or create a procedure for them, or just type everything in.

15. Use the following code for the click event procedure for the Other button:

    ```
    Label1.Text = DateTime.Now.ToString();
    Label2.Text = DateTime.Now.ToString();
    Label3.Text = DateTime.Now.ToString();
    if (CheckBox3.Checked) UpdatePanel3.Update();
    ```

16. Run the program and click the buttons. Do not use the check boxes yet.
    - The current time should show up on all three labels when any of the buttons are clicked.
    - The button will crash the program if the check box in the same UpdatePanel is checked.
    - Notice that all UpdatePanels make a trip to the server to get the time, not just the one with the clicked button.
    - To start testing the effects that the ChildrenAsTriggers and UpdateMode properties have on UpdatePanels, we will start with all their combinations as shown in Table 5-1 (called a truth table) for the stand-alone UpdatePanel named Other.

	CHILDREN AS TRIGGERS	UPDATE MODE	RESULT
Other	True	Always	Automatically updates itself
			Explicit calls to the Update method will fail
Other	True	Conditional	Automatically updates itself
			Explicit calls to the Update method are allowed
Other	False	Always	Error! This combination is never allowed for any UpdatePanel
			It is unable to Always update when the Child updates Conditionally
Other	False	Conditional	Updates only on explicit Update method calls
			Does not automatically update

17. Verify the settings in the Properties window for the "Other" UpdatePanel's ChildrenAsTriggers and UpdateMode properties. They should match the first row of Table 5-1:

| True | Always |

18. Run the program and click the **Other** button.

 • The label in the Other UpdatePanel should display a timestamp from the server. (Ignore the Parent and Child panels for now.)

19. In the "Other" panel again, click the check box and then the button. Stop the program.

 • This will give you an error because the button explicitly calls the same panel to update. According to Table 5-1, this error is supposed to occur.

20. Change the setting of the "Other" UpdatePanel to match the second row in Table 5-1:

| True | Conditional |

21. Run the program and click the **Other** button.

 • As before, the label in the Other UpdatePanel should display a timestamp from the server. (Again, ignore the Parent and Child panels.)

22. In the "Other" panel again, click the check box and then the button. Stop the program.

 • As Table 5-1 says, this combination of properties allows the explicit Update calls.

23. Change the setting of the "Other" UpdatePanel to match the third row in Table 5-1:

| False | Always |

24. Attempt to run the program. Close the browser.

 • You should have gotten an error before the browser had a chance to display the page. With this combination of properties, you are telling the UpdatePanel to always update but then telling it not to update for child UpdatePanels. The child UpdatePanels do not have to exist for the browser to reject this combination.

25. Change the setting of the "Other" UpdatePanel to match the last row in Table 5-1:

| False | Conditional |

26. Run the program and click the **Other** button, but do not expect anything to happen.

 • The UpdatePanel will only update on an explicit call to the UpdatePanel's Update method.

27. In the "Other" panel again, click the check box before clicking the button.

- As Table 5-1 says, this combination of properties will only update the panel using explicit calls.

28. Close the browser.

- We will now include the parent and child relationship in our exploration of the UpdatePanels. Table 5-2 gives us the properties for all three UpdatePanels where the ChildrenAsTriggers property is set to False and the UpdateMode property is set to Always. Again, telling the UpdatePanel to always update but not including the child UpdatePanels does not work.

Table 5-2

Setting the properties to False and Always never works

	Children As Triggers	Update Mode	Update Without Call	Update Using Call	Updates Itself Plus
Parent	False	Always	Error	Error	Error
Child	False	Always	Error	Error	Error
Other	False	Always	Error	Error	Error

- **Update Without Call** means that the UpdatePanel will do a postback as normal and does not need to be called externally.
- **Update Using Call** means that the UpdatePanel can be called externally without errors.
- **Updates Itself Plus** means that the panel not only updates itself, it updates one or more named panels as well.

29. Verify that the settings in Table 5-2 will only result in an error.

30. Close the browser.

- We will now set the properties back to their default values. However, this time we will investigate all three UpdatePanels.
- As you can see from Table 5-3, the default settings do not allow us to explicitly call for an Update for any panel.

Table 5-3

Setting the properties to True and Always only works if not called

	Children As Triggers	Update Mode	Update Without Call	Update Using Call	Updates Itself Plus
Parent	True	Always	Y	N (Error)	All
Child	True	Always	Y	N (Error)	All
Other	True	Always	Y	N (Error)	All

31. Verify that the settings in Table 5-3 work the same way as the "Other" panel did earlier in this exercise.

32. Close the browser.

- To prevent a critical error by using the False/Always combination, Table 5-4 has been created where the UpdateMode is set to Conditional. The resulting truth table gets quite large when considering all three UpdatePanels.

Table 5-4

All eight combinations of the ChildrenAsTriggers property where the UpdateMode is set to Conditional

	CHILDREN AS TRIGGERS	UPDATE MODE	UPDATE WITHOUT CALL	UPDATE USING CALL	UPDATES ITSELF PLUS
Parent	False	Conditional	N	Y	Child
Child	False	Conditional	N	Y	
Other	False	Conditional	N	Y	
Parent	False	Conditional	N	Y	Child
Child	False	Conditional	N	Y	
Other	True	Conditional	Y	Y	
Parent	False	Conditional	N	Y	Child
Child	True	Conditional	Y	Y	
Other	False	Conditional	N	Y	
Parent	False	Conditional	N	Y	Child
Child	True	Conditional	Y	Y	
Other	True	Conditional	Y	Y	
Parent	True	Conditional	Y	Y	Child
Child	False	Conditional	N	Y	
Other	False	Conditional	N	Y	
Parent	True	Conditional	Y	Y	Child
Child	False	Conditional	N	Y	
Other	True	Conditional	Y	Y	
Parent	True	Conditional	Y	Y	Child
Child	True	Conditional	Y	Y	
Other	False	Conditional	N	Y	
Parent	True	Conditional	Y	Y	Child
Child	True	Conditional	Y	Y	
Other	True	Conditional	Y	Y	

33. Verify a sampling of the settings in Table 5-4 and notice some of the patterns below:
    - Half the combinations can only be updated using calls:
      ChildrenAsTriggers = False
    - Half the combinations allow updating without calls:
      ChildrenAsTriggers = True
    - All combinations allow updates using calls
    - The parent always updates the child
    - Even though ChildrenAsTriggers is set to True, the child does not update the parent. For this to occur, the Conditional setting must be set to Always
34. Close the browser.
    - Although we will get errors, Table 5-5 was created to observe the results of having ChildrenAsTriggers set to True for all our combinations of UpdatePanels.

Table 5-5

All eight combinations of the UpdateMode property where the ChildrenAsTriggers property is set to True

	CHILDREN AS TRIGGERS	UPDATE MODE	UPDATE WITHOUT CALL	UPDATE USING CALL	UPDATES ITSELF PLUS
Parent	True	Conditional	Y	Y	Child
Child	True	Conditional	Y	Y	
Other	True	Conditional	Y	Y	
Parent	True	Conditional	Y	Y	All
Child	True	Conditional	Y	Y	Other
Other	True	Always	Y	N (Error)	
Parent	True	Conditional	Y	Y	Child
Child	True	Always	Y	N (Error)	
Other	True	Conditional	Y	Y	Child
Parent	True	Conditional	Y	Y	All
Child	True	Always	Y	N (Error)	Other
Other	True	Always	Y	N (Error)	Child
Parent	True	Always	Y	N (Error)	Child
Child	True	Conditional	Y	Y	Parent
Other	True	Conditional	Y	Y	All
Parent	True	Always	Y	N (Error)	All
Child	True	Conditional	Y	Y	All
Other	True	Always	Y	N (Error)	All
Parent	True	Always	Y	N (Error)	Child
Child	True	Always	Y	N (Error)	Parent
Other	True	Conditional	Y	Y	All
Parent	True	Always	Y	N (Error)	All
Child	True	Always	Y	N (Error)	All
Other	True	Always	Y	N (Error)	All

35. Verify a sampling of the settings in Table 5-5 and notice some of the patterns below:
- All combinations allow updates to occur automatically without explicit calls
- Half the combinations allow updates using calls: UpdateMode = Conditional
- Half the combinations produce errors when attempting to update using calls: UpdateMode = Always
- Updates from any panel will update panels having UpdateMode set to Always

36. Close the browser.
- Although we could run through more of these truth tables, it is up to you to test your strategies when using nested UpdatePanels. Now you have a way to do this.

PAUSE. Close Visual Web Developer. We will use it again with a new site in the next exercise.

Understanding how setting these two properties can affect the functionalities of the UpdatePanels can be difficult because there are so many possible settings. For example, for just these three UpdatePanels, there are 64 ways to set these two properties.

One reason for using AJAX is to reduce server traffic. Setting UpdateModes to Always defeats this purpose because one UpdatePanel will cause all other UpdatePanels to update. Creating pages with nested UpdatePanels can also cause unnecessary updates. For these reasons, the general recommendation for UpdatePanels is to change all UpdateMode properties to Conditional, leave all ChildrenAsTriggers properties set to True, and never nest UpdatePanels. It is also good practice to call all UpdatePanels manually. These recommendations maximize the benefits of using AJAX.

USING TRIGGERS

The *Triggers* collection of the UpdatePanel control allows an event to respond to the UpdatePanel control without actually placing it in the UpdatePanel control. This provides more flexibility to the designer by allowing external events to either use or not use UpdatePanel control postbacks as needed.

 CREATE A TRIGGER

GET READY. We will be using Microsoft Visual Web Developer 2008 Express for this exercise.

1. Open Visual Web Developer and create a new Web site using C#, as we have done before.
2. Go to **Design** view and place the ScriptManager on the form from the AJAX Extensions category of the Toolbox.
3. Place a Label control on the form.
4. Place an UpdatePanel on the form, leave its ChildrenAsTriggers property as **True**, and set its UpdateMode property to **Conditional.**
5. Place a new label from the Standard category and an AJAX timer control from the AJAX Extensions category into the UpdatePanel. The form should now look like Figure 5-10.

Figure 5-10

The form demonstrating the Triggers collection of an UpdatePanel control

6. Set the Timer's Interval property to 1000.
   • The Timer's resolution is in milliseconds. We have just set it for 1 second.
7. Write the following code for the two UpdatePanel event procedures:

```csharp
protected void Page_Load(object sender,
EventArgs e)
{
    if (IsPostBack)
        Label1.Text = "PostBack!";
    else
        Label1.Text = "Welcome to AJAX!";
}
protected void Timer1_Tick(object sender,
EventArgs e)
{
    Label2.Text = DateTime.Now.ToString();
}
```

- Remember to double-click the form and to double-click the timer to create the event procedure structures; do not type them in.

8. Run the program, watch it for a while, and then close the browser.
   - Your Web page should now be running the clock using partial-page rendering.
   - The Welcome message should stay intact because the page is not doing postbacks.

9. Move both controls out of the UpdatePanel. Either cut and paste or drag and drop (using the pop-up tabs) will work.
   - The postback message should now show up, indicating that the partial-page rendering is no longer taking place. However, if the results are unchanged, the browser may be using the previous page from the cache. Simply closing the browser and running it again should do the trick. If not, clear the browser cache manually.
   - We will now use the Triggers property of the UpdatePanel so that the timer can trigger an update from outside the UpdatePanel.

10. Click on the UpdatePanel's **Triggers (Collection)** property from the Properties window and click the icon on the right side to open a dialog box.
    - The Triggers property is actually a collection of triggers.

11. Add the **AsyncPostBack** member, select the timer for the ControlID Behavior, and **Tick** for the EventName as shown in Figure 5-11.

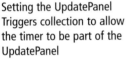

Figure 5-11

Setting the UpdatePanel Triggers collection to allow the timer to be part of the UpdatePanel

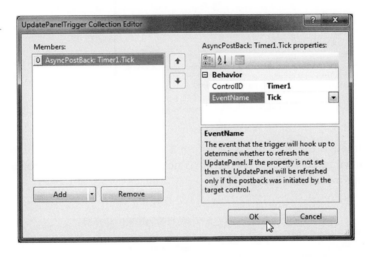

12. Place **Label2** back into the UpdatePanel.
    - The UpdatePanel Triggers property only works for triggering an update panel. To have the label involved in the postback, it must reside within the update panel.

13. Run the program again, watch it run, then close the browser.
    - The page should now run as though the timer has been placed into the UpdatePanel.

PAUSE. Close Visual Web Developer. We will use it again with a new site in the next exercise.

All the triggers in the collection of an UpdatePanel can trigger a postback. This allows the developer to physically place controls anywhere on the form. Otherwise, the controls would have to be placed in the proper UpdatePanels for controlling postbacks.

The ScriptManager also has properties that are collections. These are the *Scripts collection* and the *Services collection*, which make it easy to include external scripts and services into the Web page.

USING THE SCRIPTMANAGER FOR REFERENCING SCRIPTS AND SERVICES

The *ScriptManager* is more than a tool for partial-page postback. The ScriptManager is also used to manage scripts. One of the many responsibilities of the ScriptManager is to provide a reference to additional client-side JavaScript files and Web services. After a script or service is registered, the functions within these files can be called within your application.

Before the ScriptManager was available, referencing a script located in a separate JavaScript file or referencing a Web service was limited to adding the src attribute to the HTML `<script>` element. For example, to reference a JavaScript file named myScript.js, the HTML would be written as `<script src="myScript.js" type="text/javascript"> </script>`.

For scripts, the ScriptManager applies the ScriptReference object to register static script files or assembly-embedded scripts located on the Web site. The stand-alone JavaScript files use the path property of the ScriptManager for registration where assemblies need both the assembly name and the name of the script by using the assembly and name properties. These properties are found by clicking on the Scripts (Collection) property button in the Properties window, as shown in Figure 5-12.

Figure 5-12

The Scripts collection of the ScriptManager can register a list of JavaScript files

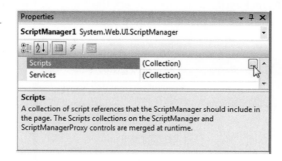

Although the myScript.js file is not a path, the Path property holds the name of the file as shown in Figure 5-13. If the file is not located in the same directory as the application, the path must be included.

Figure 5-13

The myScript.js file is to be registered

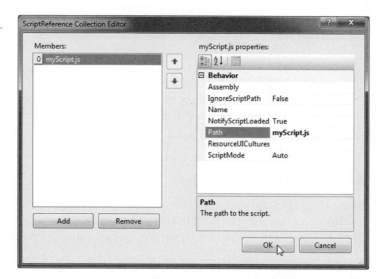

After pressing the OK button, you can see how the Script Collection Editor dialog box changed the source of your Web page from Source view.

```
<asp:ScriptManager ID="ScriptManager1"
runat="server">
  <Scripts>
    <asp:ScriptReference Path="myScript.js" />
  </Scripts>
</asp:ScriptManager>
```

Referencing services is very similar. Clicking on the Services (Collection) property button will produce a ServiceRegistration Collection Editor similar to the Script Collection Editor, as shown in Figure 5-14.

Figure 5-14

The myService.asmx file is to be registered

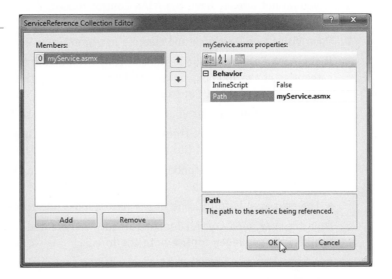

Since a service cannot be stored in an assembly, the name of the service and/or path is the only property available.

After pressing the OK button, you can see that the ServiceRegistration Collection Editor simply appended the service code to the ScriptManager element.

```
<asp:ScriptManager ID="ScriptManager1"
runat="server">
  <Scripts>
    <asp:ScriptReference Path="myScript.js" />
  </Scripts>
  <Services>
    <asp:ServiceReference Path="myService.asmx" />
  </Services>
</asp:ScriptManager>
```

Having all registrations centralized into a single location allows the ScriptManager to control every aspect of the scripts and services. One of the more important responsibilities is to prevent duplicates when a script or service is needed more than once and possibly in multiple locations.

Remember that some Web sites use a master page with a ScriptManager that manages the entire site. If a page needs ScriptManager settings different from the master, a ScriptManagerProxy control is placed on the page to make these alternative settings. Scripts from the ScriptManager and all ScriptManagerProxy controls are merged at runtime for the entire site to use. Services from the ScriptManager and all ScriptManagerProxy controls are also merged at runtime.

CERTIFICATION READY
What functionality does the Triggers collection provide to the UpdatePanel?
4.2

USING EXTENDER CONTROLS

AJAX 3.5 has the capability of converting any control into an *Extender control*. The new control can either be a stand-alone control, just like the other controls in the Toolbox, or a non-visible control that enhances existing controls.

We can create our own extender controls or download them from many sites on the Internet. A popular source for extender controls is the AJAX Control Toolkit located at codeplex.com.

 INSTALL AND USE EXTENDER CONTROLS

GET READY. We will be using Microsoft Visual Web Developer 2008 Express for this exercise.

1. If you do not already have the AJAX Control Toolkit, download it from codeplex.com and uncompress the files.

2. Open Visual Web Developer and create a new Web site using C#, as we have done before.

3. If the AJAX Control Toolkit has not already been added to your Toolbox, close all the categories of the Toolbox, right-click below the categories, and click **Add Tab**. Give the tab the name **AJAX Control Toolkit**.

4. Right-click the area under your new tab and click **Choose Items**.

5. From the **Choose Toolbox Items** dialog box, click the **Browse** button. Find and select the AjaxControlToolkit.dll file that you uncompressed. Then press the **OK** button.
   - This will place all the toolkit controls into the Toolbox for you to extend the functionality of the other controls.
   - The next step is to use one of the new stand-alone controls.

6. From the new AJAX Control Toolkit category you created in the Toolbox, place the **ToolkitScriptManager** control onto the form.
   - A ScriptManager control must always be the first control placed on the form to run Extender controls.
   - This set of Extender controls works best using the custom version of the ASP.NET ScriptManager called the ToolkitScriptManager.

7. Place the **Editor** control onto the form from the new AJAX Control Toolkit category of the Toolbox.

8. Run the program and test the editor.
   - Notice that you now have a fully functional word processor. Note that this is not technically a text editor because it has to contain formatting data.
   - You will have to write the code yourself for any file-handling routines such as saving.

9. Close the browser.
   - The hidden controls will now be addressed.

10. Click on the **Editor** control and open the smart tab.

11. Click the **Add Extender**.
    - This usage of the extenders may or may not work depending on the support for the control, the IDE, and the installation of the extender files.
    - We will not be applying these extenders to our controls for this exercise.

12. Cancel the **Extender Wizard** dialog box.

13. From the Standard category of the Toolbox, place any control onto the form.
    - Notice that the Add Extender selection shows up on anything placed onto the form.
    - Just because a control shows up and is selectable does not mean that it is appropriate. You will have to do the necessary research on the controls and extenders to use them properly.

PAUSE. Close Visual Web Developer. We will use it again in the next exercise.

Extender controls are typically free downloads, purchased controls, or personally created controls. You take a risk with free controls because they are often buggy or bloated. Purchased controls, of course, cost money but are usually of higher quality. You can also create controls yourself. While creating these controls can be difficult, it can ultimately be very rewarding.

Working with Client-Side Libraries

Client-side libraries hold client-side programming code, such as JavaScript, that is run in the browser. The files that make up the libraries must be downloaded and the code referenced from within the HTML page. Table 5-6 shows where you can download some of the most popular libraries.

Table 5-6

Some of the most popular client-side libraries

Library Name	URL (http://...)
Dojo	dojotoolkit.org
Google Chrome Frame	code.google.com/chrome/chromeframe
jQuery	jquery.com
MooTools	mootools.net
Prototype JS	prototypejs.org
Script.aculo.us	script.aculo.us
YUI	developer.yahoo.com/yui

JavaScript libraries can be put together for many purposes, from providing new and more complex controls called widgets, to simply making the task of writing JavaScript code less complex. JQuery is the latter. It is one of the most popular libraries because of its support of Unobtrusive JavaScript. Where CSS separates style from structure, Unobtrusive JavaScript separates behavior from structure. Microsoft has adopted the Unobtrusive JavaScript paradigm and has partnered with jQuery to integrate it into their new products.

As we have seen in Lesson 1, selectors are used to match patterns in DOM to identify the parts of the page that will be affected by CSS code. JQuery also uses selectors. However, these selectors identify the parts of the page that will be affected by JavaScript code.

The following exercise will show you how to use jQuery to run your two lines of JavaScript code.

 USE JQUERY TO MANAGE JAVASCRIPT CODE

GET READY. We will be using Microsoft Visual Web Developer 2008 Express for this exercise.

1. If you do not already have access to jQuery, navigate to http://jquery.com using your browser. You may want to select the uncompressed version to avoid unzipping it after the download. Click the **Download** button and save the file. Uncompress the zipped file if necessary. Although no installation is necessary, we will be placing a copy of the file into the project.

2. Open Visual Web Developer and create a new Web site using C# as we have done before.

3. Use Windows Explorer to find the downloaded jQuery file.

4. Drag the file from the Windows Explorer window to the Solution Explorer window of the IDE. Make sure it is in the root directory of the Solution Explorer window.

TAKE NOTE * If you are using the 2008 version of Microsoft Visual Studio or Web Developer, you need to install a hotfix for IntelliSense to work properly. The hotfix can be found at *http://code.msdn.microsoft.com/KB958502*

5. From **Design** view, open the HTML category of the Toolbox and place the **Input (Button)** control onto the form.

   • Since we are not interested in postback, we will use the HTML element.

6. Go to **Source** view of the **default.aspx** page and place the following code just under the two title tags, `<title></title>`:

```
<script src="jquery-1.4.2.js"
type="text/javascript"></script>
```

   • Make sure you change the version number to match your file download.

   • The scr attribute loads only the needed jQuery script in this part of your HTML file at runtime.

7. Run the program and click your button just to check for errors. Close the browser.

8. Place all of the following code, including the script tags, just under the script tag you previously placed:

```
<script type="text/javascript">
  $(document).ready
  (
    function()
    {
      alert("Document is ready!");
    }
  );
</script>
```

   • The $(document).ready prevents any scripts from running that are located between the parentheses until the entire page is loaded. Otherwise, scripts can fail because parts of the page that the script may need are not present.

   • The $ is used to signify that a jQuery selector follows. In this case, it is our Web page. It will fire when the page is ready.

9. Run the program and click your button just to check for errors. Then close the browser.

   • You should have gotten the pop-up message when the page finished loading.

10. Remove the alert function:

```
<script type="text/javascript">
  $(document).ready
  (
  );
</script>
```

11. Place a new function into your JavaScript:

```
<script type="text/javascript">
$(document).ready
  (
    function()
    {
      $("input").click
      (
        function()
        {
          alert("You are being transferred
          to MSN.com");
          document.location="http://msn.com/";
        }
      );
    }
  );
</script>
```

* The jQuery selector is used to find all the "input" elements of the form and execute the code within the parentheses when the click event fires. In this case, it only found one input element.

12. Run the program and click your button to execute your JavaScript code. Then close the browser.

* Notice that this page did not do any postbacks; it executed the script with the browser.

13. Run the program again but do not click the button.

14. Click the View pull-down menu on the browser and click Source.

* Notice that all your code was sent to the browser as is. This means that the code is being run directly by the browser, not the server. It also means that your source code is not secure; everyone can see it.

15. Close the source view and the browser.

PAUSE. Close Visual Web Developer.

As with the CSS selectors, you will need to do your own research on the vast pattern-matching possibilities available. You will also find that jQuery has much more to offer the developer than Unobtrusive JavaScript.

CERTIFICATION READY
Where do extender controls come from and how are they managed in Visual Web Developer?
4.2

SKILL SUMMARY

IN THIS LESSON YOU LEARNED TO:

* Understand client-side scripting.
* Write JavaScript code.
* Write VBScript code.
* Examine the Document Object Model (DOM).
* Understand the history of Ajax.

- Understand the technology and terminology of Ajax.
- Set the EnablePartialRendering Property.
- Use the ScriptManager and ScriptManagerProxy Controls.
- Use the Timer and UpdateProgress Controls.
- Set the ChildrenAsTriggers and UpdateMode Properties.
- Use Triggers for UpdatePanels.
- Understand ScriptManager Scripts and Services.
- Use Extender Controls and Client-Side Libraries.

■ Knowledge Assessment

Multiple Choice

Circle the letter or letters that correspond to the best answer or answers.

1. What best describes client-side scripting?
   a. It is script that is called by the Web server.
   b. It is script that gets compiled for the client.
   c. It is script that runs on the Java Virtual Machine.
   d. It is script that is run by a browser.

2. What is the difference between JavaScript and VBScript?
   a. JavaScript runs on the client while VBScript runs on the server.
   b. JavaScript runs on the server while VBScript runs on the client.
   c. JavaScript needs a hosting language where VBScript can stand alone.
   d. JavaScript can stand alone where VBScript needs a hosting language.

3. What is NOT true about the Document Object Model (DOM)?
   a. It is written in XML.
   b. It is located on the Web server.
   c. It is the code that generates the Web page.
   d. It is what client-side scripting languages manipulate.

4. What best describes Ajax?
   a. Ajax is an extension of ASP.NET.
   b. Ajax is an acronym for Asynchronous JavaScript And Xml.
   c. Ajax is the technologies used for asynchronously updating Web pages.
   d. All of the above.

5. To which control does the EnablePartialRendering property belong?
   a. ScriptManager
   b. UpdatePanel
   c. UpdateProgress
   d. All extender controls

6. What is the purpose of having a ScriptManagerProxy control on your pages?
   a. It makes exceptions to the ScriptManager settings.
   b. It is used in place of the ScriptManager for pages using JavaScript.
   c. It is used in place of the ScriptManager for pages using any client-side scripting.
   d. One ScriptManager per site means that all other pages must use the ScriptManagerProxy.

7. How does an UpdateProgress control differ from a standard progress control?
   a. It needs to have the ScriptManager present.
   b. It provides feedback during a postback process.
   c. It prevents the page from being unresponsive during postbacks.
   d. All of the above.

8. Which statement is true regarding ChildrenAsTriggers?
   a. Must be set to False when UpdateMode is set to Always
   b. Must be set to Always when UpdateMode is set to False
   c. Limits the triggering of an UpdatePanel to child elements
   d. Allows nested UpdatePanels to trigger their parents

9. Which statement is true regarding UpdatePanels?
   a. They can be nested.
   b. They update independently by default.
   c. They can be used as client-side controls.
   d. All of the above.

10. Which statement is true regarding the Scripts collection?
    a. It is part of the ScriptManager.
    b. Is the only way to include scripts on a Web page.
    c. It holds the script code to be included on the Web page.
    d. All of the above.

Fill in the Blank

Complete the following sentences by writing the correct word or words in the blanks provided.

1. The _____ event handler in an attribute for the HTML <input> element that calls a JavaScript function.

2. VBScript will not run on any browser except _____.

3. Although VBScript and JavaScript can be embedded into HTML, _____ can run as a stand-alone application as well.

4. _____ defines the structure of an XHTML Web page and is manipulated by client-side script.

5. The _____ control is often used with the UpdatePanel to automate postbacks at given intervals.

6. The _____ property of the UpdatePanel must often be changed to take full advantage of the ChildrenAsTriggers property of the same control.

7. The ScriptManager can hold a collection of Scripts and _____.

8. For UpdatePanels to work properly, the _____ control must be placed on the form before any UpdatePanels.

9. The programmer can create or download _____ controls, which can be stand-alone or enhance existing controls.

10. _____ is a popular client-side library from Microsoft.

■ Competency Assessment

Scenario 5-1: Using Visual Web Developer to Validate a Page

You decide that you want to start a new project using some of the code you saw on a Web site when browsing the Internet using Internet Explorer. You want to make sure the code is written to the XHTML standard, so you would like to validate it before moving on.

Use one of the latest versions of Internet Explorer to validate the page (any page) with its built-in Developer Tools for validating Web pages.

Scenario 5-2: Setting ChildrenAsTriggers and UpdateMode

Your project requires three control panels that are placed on the form three layers deep. This generates parent, child, and grandchild control panels. Because the truth tables for the ChildrenAsTriggers and UpdateMode properties in this lesson did not cover grandchildren, you will need to create your own truth table that includes them. This is required in order to have a better understanding of how these panels will perform before proceeding with your project. Create a table that produces a truth table for the three control panels where UpdateMode is set to Conditional for all three panels.

■ Proficiency Assessment

Scenario 5-3: Using an External VBScript file

You decide that you want to use VBScript instead of JavaScript for your project. You have several scripts to run and want to use separate files holding the VBScript code. To help understand this process, finish the VBScript exercise that we did in this lesson by separating the VBScript from the HTML code. Cut out the VBScript, place it in a separate file, and call it from the HTML page.

Scenario 5-4: Incorporating a Client-Side Library

You are part of a small Web development team who needs many controls that are not included in Visual Web Developer's Toolbox. You understand the hours of work to create these controls in-house and opt to use a pre-built client-side library.

Investigate the libraries in Table 5-6 and select the top two that you think will most likely help your team. Write a report comparing the two choices. Summarize the report by justifying your recommended choice.

 ## Workplace Ready

Creating a Web Page with UpdatePanels

Suppose you have a Web page that is connected to a database and the part of the page displaying data is the only part that ever changes. Having text and graphics covering the page means that the entire page must do a postback every time any of the data changes. There are many ways to handle this, including client-side scripting. Here the JavaScript (or VBScript) sends a request to the server for data. The server then needs to have a program written, typically in PHP, that will do more processing and send the data back. However, this requires a lot of programming and can be prone to errors.

An alternative that simplifies this process is placing the required database controls into an UpdatePanel and setting the EnablingPartialRendering property to True. This ensures that only part of your page will need to do a postback.

The bottom line is that either way, you will have significantly reduced the wait time for changing data and made your Web page perform more like a desktop application.

Troubleshooting and Debugging Web Applications

LESSON SKILL MATRIX

SKILLS/CONCEPTS	MTA EXAM OBJECTIVE	MTA EXAM OBJECTIVE NUMBER
Debugging a Web Application	Debug a Web application	3.1
Handling Web Application Errors	Handle Web application errors	3.2

KEY TERMS

<customErrors> element

DefaultRedirect attribute

HTTP Status Codes

requestLimit attribute

Trace.axd

Trace.IsEnabled property

Trace="true" on @Page directive

Keeping track of all the data manipulation that takes place in her Web site has been overwhelming for Karen. Although she can place Response.Write methods on all her pages and use other debugging tools, she finds that these techniques are just as hard to manage as the data she is tracking. What she needs is an easy way to follow the data throughout her site. The advanced tracing abilities found in this lesson will provide Karen with the tools she needs to fully understand what the Web pages are doing with the data. She will also discover that some very useful debugging tools are available to help her pinpoint misbehaving data.

■ Debugging a Web Application

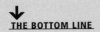
THE BOTTOM LINE

Debugging is an essential part of any program, whether it is a desktop or Web application. Because we have more than a single computer running Web applications, debugging can be particularly difficult. Errors from the code within an application are normally caught with the same tools used for desktop applications. However, some errors get past the error-trapping techniques in various applications on the client or server. These unhandled errors are addressed in this lesson.

Displaying the Appropriate Error Information to the Appropriate User

> When code is being processed in a Web page, it is inevitable that an error will eventually occur, no matter how well the code is written. While developers need as much information as possible to correct the situation, the details of the errors are not appropriate for the public. Who gets what information can be controlled with ASP.NET.

Rich error pages contain detailed information that is only useful to developers. Generic error pages contain rather useless information for the developer but at least indicate that there is a problem with the Web page. Because rich error pages display so much information, including parts of the source code, ASP.NET's default settings limit them to the local machine; all other users see the generic error pages. Even though showing the generic errors presents a low security risk, they may only confuse the end user. To enhance the user experience, ASP.NET allows the creation of custom error pages with appropriate levels of security using the *<customErrors> element*. Table 6-1 summarizes these error page settings.

Table 6-1

Two important attribute settings for the <customErrors> element

ATTRIBUTE	DESCRIPTION
defaultRedirect=" *URL*"	Overrides the generic error page with your custom page at the designated URL
mode="RemoteOnly"	Default: Rich error pages show on local machine; generic or custom error pages show on remote machines
mode="On"	Everyone sees generic or custom error pages
mode="Off"	Everyone sees rich error pages

It is standard practice to set the mode attribute to "Off" for development so developers can work on the site without having to use the local machine. Once deployed, the mode attribute is set back to "RemoteOnly" and the *defaultRedirect attribute* is filled with a URL to show custom error pages. Setting the mode attribute to "On" is rarely used because it would totally block developers from seeing the rich error pages.

 WRITE A CUSTOM ERROR PAGE

GET READY. We will be using Microsoft Visual Web Developer 2008 Express for this exercise.

1. Start Visual Web Developer and create a new Web site.
2. Select the ASP.NET Web site template using C#.
3. Place a Standard button on the form and write the code below for its event procedure to produce a runtime error:

```
int x = 0;
Response.Write(1 / x);
```

   - If 1/0 were used rather than 1/x, the editor would spot the division-by-zero error at design time. We want the error to be discovered at runtime.
4. Run the program and click the button. Close the browser.
   - The debugger should have taken you directly to the code that caused the error.
   - As always, you should have allowed the web.config file to enable debugging.
   - We will now modify the web.config file to disable debugging.

5. Double-click the **web.config** file from the Solution Explorer window, find the debug attribute of the <compilation> element, and change it to **false:**

   From: **<compilation debug="true">**

   To: **<compilation debug="false">**

   - A quick way to find this code is to use Quick Find, which is found on the Edit menu under Find and Replace. Type **<compilation debug="true">** into the dialog box and hit the **find next** button.
   - This needs to be changed so the <customErrors> element is allowed to operate. Otherwise, Visual Web Developer overrides it.

6. Run the program again and click the button. However, this time do not allow the web.config to be modified, as shown in Figure 6-1.
   - Since we are using default settings of the <customErrors>, you will now see the rich error page.

Figure 6-1

Leaving debugging turned off

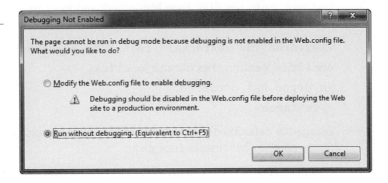

7. Close the browser.

8. Double-click the web.config file from the Solution Explorer window and find the <customErrors> element.

   <!--

   The <customErrors> section enables configuration of what to do if/when an unhandled error occurs during the execution of a request. Specifically, it enables developers to configure html error pages to be displayed in place of an error stack trace.

   <customErrors mode="RemoteOnly"
   ** defaultRedirect="GenericErrorPage.htm">**

   ** <error statusCode="403" redirect**
   ** ="NoAccess.htm" />**

   ** <error statusCode="404" redirect**
   ** ="FileNotFound.htm" />**

   </customErrors>

   -->

9. Uncomment the **<customerErrors>** code by moving the comment, -->, from just below the </customErrors> tag to just above the <customErrors mode=... > tag.
   - Notice that the code is commented out along with the descriptive text. This means that we will continue seeing the rich error page.
   - Notice that the defaultRedirect attribute is assigned a URL. Since we are running in RemoteOnly mode, only remote users will be directed to this URL, not you.

10. Run the program again and click the button. Do not allow the web.config file to be modified. Then close the browser.
    - As expected, you will see the same rich error page.

11. Change the mode from "RemoteOnly" to "**On.**"

12. Run the program again and click the button. Do not allow the web.config file to be modified. Close the browser.
    - Notice that we are back to the original error page.
    - Also notice that the defaultRedirect attribute has a URL. This means that we are not actually viewing the generic error page. We are viewing a default custom error page! This is where we can place our own custom error page.

13. Using **Add New Item,** add an HTML Page to our site using the default name **HTMLPage.htm.**

14. Go to the **Design** view of the HTML page and place a **TextArea** control on the form with text indicating that an error has occurred on the page. To add the text to the text area, go to the **HTMLPage.htm** object and open its code. Add the error message before the ending test area tag, as shown below:

    ```
    <textarea id="TextArea1" cols="20" name="S1" rows="2"
    onclick="return TextArea1_onclick()">
    An error has occurred.
    </textarea>
    ```

15. Change the **defaultRedirect** attribute of the <customErrors> element in the web.config file to point to our custom error page:

    ```
    From: <customErrors mode="On"
            defaultRedirect="GenericErrorPage.htm">
    ```

    ```
    To: <customErrors mode="On"
            defaultRedirect="HTMLPage.htm">
    ```

16. Run the program again and click the button. Do not allow the web.config file to be modified. Close the browser.
    - You should now see your custom error page.

PAUSE. Close Visual Web Developer. We will use it again in the next exercise.

Turning off the debug attribute of the <compilation> element in the web.config file allowed us to use ASP.NET's <customErrors> for controlling error pages. We are able to display the appropriate error information to the appropriate user. However, leaving the debug attribute as "true" provides a host of Visual Web Developer debugging tools that are well worth exploring in the future.

TURNING ON PAGE TRACING

Error pages are great for examining runtime errors that are caught by ASP.NET. However, not all errors are caught. Logical errors will perform fine but produce erroneous results. Programmers typically place code within a program to display various data as the program runs, but there is a cleaner way to accomplish this: tracing.

TRACE DATA IN A WEB PAGE

GET READY. We will be using Microsoft Visual Web Developer 2008 Express for this exercise.

1. Start Visual Web Developer and create a new Web site.
2. Select the ASP.NET Web site template using C#.

3. From **Design** view, change the Trace property to **"true"** for the **Default.aspx** page.

4. Open the **Source** view window.

   • Notice that the page directive at the top added the attribute *Trace="true"*.

   • If the trace value is changed to "false," the properties window will also change to false.

   • This page attribute can also be changed in code-behind using the trace property of the default page object.

5. Run the program. You may now allow the web.config file to be modified.

6. Scroll through the page to see what information you might find valuable.

   • One area that you might find useful lists the various state variables and their values. Another area even lists all the available server variables.

7. Close the browser.

8. Place two buttons on the form and give them the text **On** and **Off** using the properties window.

9. Type in the following event procedure for the **On** button:

   `Trace.IsEnabled = true;`

   • The *Trace.IsEnabled property* can be used to get or set tracing in ASP.NET.

10. Type in the following event procedure for the **Off** button:

    `Trace.IsEnabled = false;`

    • Notice that if we extend the namespace to `Page.Trace.IsEnabled = false;`, we are changing the same Trace as the attribute of the page used in the page directive: `<%@ Page Trace="true"... %>`.

11. Run the program. You may still allow the web.config file to be modified.

12. Click the **On** and **Off** buttons to toggle tracing.

    • This can be helpful when debugging in order to see what the page looks like without tracing turned on. It also can reduce the amount of code you need to remove before deployment.

13. Close the browser.

PAUSE. Close Visual Web Developer. We will use it again in the next exercise.

As with the error pages, tracing is limited to the local machine by default or expanded for all users. However, with such detailed information, the security risk is much higher and is not advised.

 TRACE DATA IN A WEB APPLICATION

GET READY. We will be using Microsoft Visual Web Developer 2008 Express for this exercise.

1. Start Visual Web Developer and create a new Web site.

2. Select the ASP.NET Web site template using C#.

3. Add the following line of code to the web.config file just under the <system.Web> tag:

   `<trace enabled="true" requestLimit="20" />`

   • The *requestLimit attribute* gives you control over the maximum number of trace requests to store on the server.

4. Run the program. You may allow the web.config file to be modified. Keep the browser open.

5. Open another browser window, copy the URL from your empty page, and use it for the URL of your new browser window.

6. Append **trace.axd** to your second page URL and press the **Enter** key.

   • If your URL happens to end with `Default.aspx`, repeat this step but delete `Default.aspx` before appending `trace.axd`.

7. Click the **View Details** link in the new page.
   - *Trace.axd* opens a trace window for whatever page is open on the other browser window.
8. Close both browser windows.

PAUSE. Close Visual Web Developer. We will use it again in the next exercise.

There are two significant advantages to using a separate page for tracing. First, the traced page does not have to be altered, allowing you to see it as the user sees it. Second and more importantly, the entire application can be traced with a single setting; you no longer have to set up each page as you trace your entire site.

Table 6-2 lists the attributes of the <trace> element with a brief description of each.

Table 6-2

The attributes of the <trace> element

ATTRIBUTE	DESCRIPTION
enabled	True or false: False is default. When true, trace.axd is available.
localOnly	True or false: True is default. When false, all users will have access to the trace.
pageOutput	True or false: False is default. When true, trace information will also show on the running Web page as it did in the previous exercise.
requestLimit	Integer: 10 is default. Limits the number of requests to trace.
traceMode	SortByTime or SortByCategory: SortByTime is default. Sorts display information.

■ Handling Web Application Errors

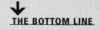
THE BOTTOM LINE

So far, we have handled all the errors using the detailed, generic, or custom error pages. What we will do now is write different custom error pages depending on what kind of error was generated.

Understanding HTTP Status Codes

The *HTTP status codes* are grouped into five classes using the first digit of the code, as shown in Table 6-3.

Table 6-3

The five classes of the HTTP Status Codes

FIRST DIGIT	CLASS DESCRIPTION
1	Information
2	Success
3	Redirection
4	Client Error
5	Server Error

USE HTTP STATUS CODES FOR CUSTOM ERROR PAGES

GET READY. We will be using Microsoft Visual Web Developer 2008 Express for this exercise.

1. Start Visual Web Developer and create a new Web site.
2. Select the ASP.NET Web site template using C# and use the Default name.
3. Double-click the **web.config** file from the Solution Explorer window and find the <customErrors> tag.
4. Uncomment the **<customErrors>** code by moving the comment, **-->,** from just below the </customErrors> tag to just above the <customErrors mode= . . . > tag.
   - A quick way to do this is to select the --> comment and drag it the <customErrors mode= . . . > tag.
5. Change the **<customErrors>** element in the web.config file by setting the mode attribute to **On,** the statusCode attribute numbers to the ones that we need to trap, and the redirect attributes to the names of our new custom error pages as follows:

```
<customErrors mode="On"
defaultRedirect="GenericErrorPage.htm">

    <error statusCode="404" redirect
    ="Default2.aspx"/>

    <error statusCode="500" redirect
    ="Default3.aspx"/>

</customErrors>
```

   - This code will show everyone generic error messages except when the error produces a 404 or 500 status code. We will give these errors their own pages.
6. Place two Standard buttons on the form, place **URL** and **Math** in their text properties, and write the code below for each event procedure:

   Button 1 (URL): Response.Redirect("Invalid URL");

   Button 2 (Math): int x = 0; Response.Write(1 / x);

7. Add two more Web forms (not HTML pages) to your site. Leave their default names and use C#.
8. Place a button on each page and change their text properties to **Bad URL** for **Default2.aspx** and **Divide by Zero** for **Default3.aspx**.
9. For each of these new buttons, set the PostBackUrl property to the original Default.aspx page.
10. From the first page, **Default.aspx,** run the program. Do not allow the web.config file to be modified.
11. Navigate between pages using the buttons.
    - You should now see a different error page depending on the type of error.
12. Close the browser.

PAUSE. Close Visual Web Developer.

Having an understanding of the HTTP Status Codes gives you some flexibility in your handling of Web application errors. Although the exercise only provided two very common errors, many more are available that can improve the Web experience for many users.

SKILL SUMMARY

IN THIS LESSON YOU LEARNED TO:

- Display the appropriate error information to the appropriate user.
- Set the Trace = "true" page directive to turn on page tracing.
- Set the enabled attribute to "true" for the <trace> element to turn on application tracing.
- View the trace.axd page for application tracing.
- Use HTTP Status codes to write custom error pages for specific errors.

■ Knowledge Assessment

Multiple Choice

Circle the letter or letters that correspond to the best answer or answers.

1. What is a rich error page?
   a. A page with too much content
   b. A page that has user interaction
   c. A page with more than one error
   d. A page with lots of error information

2. If the <customErrors> element's mode is set to "On" and the defaultRedirect contains a URL, who will see what?
   a. Everyone sees the generic error page.
   b. Everyone sees the custom error page.
   c. Everyone sees the rich error page.
   d. Only the local computers will see the rich error page.

3. If the <customErrors> element's mode is set to "Off" and the defaultRedirect contains a URL, who will see what?
   a. Everyone sees the generic error page.
   b. Everyone sees the custom error page.
   c. Everyone sees the rich error page.
   d. Only the local computers will see the rich error page.

4. If the <customErrors> element's mode is set to "RemoteOnly" and the defaultRedirect contains a URL, who will see what?
   a. Everyone sees the generic error page.
   b. Everyone sees the custom error page.
   c. Everyone sees the rich error page.
   d. Only the local computers will see the rich error page.

5. How is page tracing turned on?
   a. Set Trace.IsEnabled = true in the code-behind
   b. Set Trace = "true" in the Page directive
   c. Set the Trace property of the form
   d. All of the above

6. Where should the redirect for the error URL to a custom error page be set?
   a. Code-behind
   b. web.config
   c. Asp directive
   d. Properties window of the form

7. What attribute should always be used along with the enabled attribute of the <trace> element?
   a. default
   b. defaultRedirect
   c. requestLimit
   d. none

8. Why do we sometimes opt to turn off debugging when launching a program to debug a page?
   a. Visual Web Developer often catches errors before ASP.NET
   b. ASP.NET often catches errors before Visual Web Developer
   c. Since Visual Web Developer has no debugging capabilities, we have ASP.NET do the debugging
   d. Since ASP.NET has no debugging capabilities, we have Visual Web Developer do the debugging

9. What does setting the enabled attribute to true in the <trace> element do for the Web site?
   a. Lets us see page errors without changing the page
   b. Turns on error tracing at the application level
   c. Allows both local and remote users to see page errors
   d. All of the above

10. Where do we trap HTTP Status Codes for producing different error messages?
    a. Code-behind
    b. web.config
    c. Asp directives
    d. HTTP controls

Fill in the Blank

Complete the following sentences by writing the correct word or words in the blanks provided.

1. The _____ attribute of the <customErrors> element, found in the web.config file is set to the URL of a custom error page.

2. The _____ attribute of the <customErrors> element, found in the web.config file is used to determine who sees the err pages.

3. The _____ element, found in the web.config file has a debug attribute that sets debugging to true or false.

4. To take advantage of the many debugging tools that Visual Web Developer has to offer, the debug attribute must be set to _____.

5. Logical errors will often produce erroneous results and are only caught by _____ an application.

6. The _____ property of the page.trace object is set to true to enable page tracing.

7. Only users of the _____ _____ are privy to trace information.

8. The _____ attribute of the <trace> element, found in the web.config file controls the maximum number of requests for information on the server.

9. _____ is the name of the Web page that is automatically generated when the enabled attribute of the <trace> element is set to true.

10. There are _____ classes of HTTP Status Codes identified by their first digit.

■ Competency Assessment

Scenario 6-1: Watching State Values

The owner of Verbeck's Trucking Co. assigned you the task of creating a Web page that collects the number of loads and the cubic feet of gravel hauled at the end of each day. The data will be used in another page by another Web developer. All you need to do is ensure that the data are stored as state variables somewhere in your page. To prove that the data are actually saved, the owner insists on a printout of the portion of a tracing Web page containing the type of state used, variable names, and the data they contain.

Simulate this task by creating two Web pages. The first page will collect the number of loads and cubic feet. The second page will echo this information. When completed, enter the data into the first page and create a printout of a tracing page containing the type of state you used to send the data. Also, include the variable names and the data they hold.

Scenario 6-2: Displaying Error Information to the User

As you are developing your Web site, you want to have as much detailed information as possible for your errors. Now that you are about to deploy your site, what changes will you make to the web.config file to keep this information from the user?

■ Proficiency Assessment

Scenario 6-3: Displaying Trace Information to the User

As you are developing your Web site, you want to have as much tracing information as possible for your debugging activities. Now that you are about to deploy your site, what changes will you make to the web.config file to keep your debugging information from the user?

Scenario 6-4: Handling Web Application Errors Using HTTP Status Codes

After deploying your Web site, you discover that you have been confusing your users with generic error messages. You now want to provide them with custom Web pages that will improve your communication with your users without revealing sensitive site information. What changes will you make to the web.config file to make this possible?

✳ Workplace Ready

Creating a Manageable Web Site

Suppose you are modifying a Web site that has a lot of user input and the data from this input are shared among many pages throughout the site. Since you have had experience with programming, you place the typical Response.Write statements everywhere you want to see the data coming and going through various pages. Think about all the places that you might miss when deploying the site after you make your changes. What if one of these popped up unexpectedly for a client and it was a message you wrote when you were very frustrated in this part of your debugging process? It could be very embarrassing. With the tools used in this lesson, you can abandon these techniques and have a central location to turn off all your debugging and tracing activities. Even more advantageous is the fact that you can easily turn them back on if something needs to be addressed after deployment.

Now that we are armed with these tools, especially for keeping track of an entire application, the old ways can stay in the past.

Configuring and Deploying Web Applications

LESSON SKILL MATRIX

SKILLS/CONCEPTS	MTA EXAM OBJECTIVE	MTA EXAM OBJECTIVE NUMBER
Configuring Authentication and Authorization	Configure authentication and authorization	5.1
Configuring Projects and Solutions and Referencing Assemblies	Configure projects and solutions and reference assemblies	5.2
Publishing Web Applications	Publish Web applications	5.3
Understanding Application Pools	Understand application pools	5.4

KEY TERMS

<appSettings> element

application pools

authentication

authorization

forms authentication

impersonation

Internet Information Services (IIS)

local assembly

shared assembly(GAC)

updatable site

Web application project

Web solution

Windows authentication

Windows Installer (MSI)

Karen has an application in mind that will just be used for her staff. It does not need to be on the Internet, nor does it need to be a Web application. However, both she and her staff are familiar with the Web interface and would like her local application to have that look and feel. She is also more familiar with Web page development than traditional desktop development.

She found that Microsoft has a product called Web Application Projects that offers the best of both worlds. She can now write an application that looks like a Web site for her staff and deploy it in the same manner as a desktop application.

```
<credentials passwordFormat="Clear">
  <user name="Ken" password="Test1" />
  <user name="Sandra" password="Test2" />
  <user name="Cheryl" password="Test3" />
</credentials>
</forms>
</authentication>
```

5. Run the program to check for errors. Close the browser.
   - At this point, we simply have a blank page.
   - We now move to the authorization settings.
   - Since the `<authorization>` tag is not included in the web.config file by default, we will not be looking for it as we did with the `</authentication>` tag.

6. Place the following code immediately after the `</authentication>` tag:

```
<authorization>
    <deny users="?"/>
</authorization>
```

   - The question mark is used to represent anonymous users, who are now denied access to our Default.aspx page. When we replaced Windows authentication with forms authentication, our identity was converted from a known Windows user to an anonymous user. The bottom line is that we just locked ourselves out of our own Web site!

7. Run the program to view the error we get from being locked out. Then close the browser.
   - Anonymous users trying to access the Default page will be rejected. They will automatically be redirected to a login page if one exists. Otherwise, an error page will be generated.

8. Add a new ASP.NET Web form with C# to our site and name it **login.aspx.**
   - This name, login.aspx, was chosen because it is the default redirect name used by the loginUrl attribute of the `<forms>` tag. If we wanted to use a different name for the login page, we would have to change the loginUrl attribute. An example might be `<forms loginUrl="SomeOtherLoginPageName.aspx">`. However, for this exercise, we will keep the default name login.aspx.

9. Run the program to check for errors. Close the browser.
   - You now have another blank page, which is your login page because you are still locked out of the Default page. You will be redirected to the login page (login.aspx) with any attempt to browse the Default page.

10. Place a **Standard** button on the Default page and place the text **Log Out** on the face of the button.

11. Add the following namespace to the ones in the code-behind of the Default page:

```
using System.Web.Security;
```

12. Use the following code for the Click event procedure of the Log Out button:

```
FormsAuthentication.SignOut();
Response.Redirect("Login.aspx");
```

13. Place the following code into the Page_Load event procedure of the same page (Default.aspx):

```
Response.Write("Hello " + User.Identity.Name);
```

14. Run the program to test for errors, but do not expect to see the Default.aspx page yet. Close the browser.

    • You should see the blank login page whether you click the start button from the Default.aspx tab or the login.aspx tab.

    • At this point, we are still unable to see the Default page because the browser sees us as anonymous.

15. Go to the **Login.aspx** page and include the following namespace in the code-behind:

    using System.Web.Security;

    • The FormsAuthentication object uses this namespace.

16. Go to the **Design** view of the **Login.aspx** page and add two labels, two text boxes, and a button on the form, as shown in Figure 7-1.

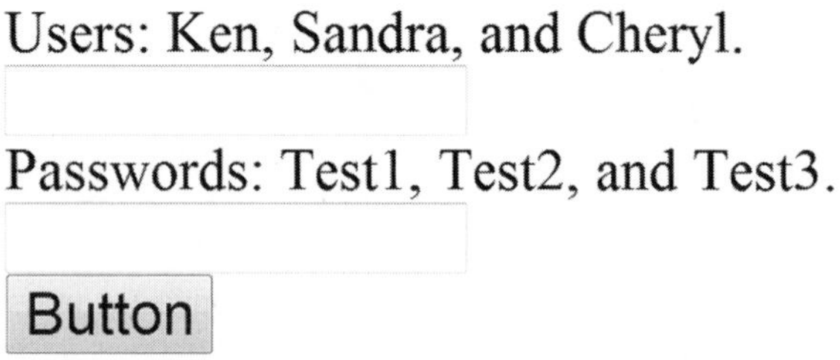

Figure 7-1

The Design view showing the login.aspx form

Users: Ken, Sandra, and Cheryl.

Passwords: Test1, Test2, and Test3.

Button

17. Use the following code for the event procedure for the button in Figure 7-1:

    if (FormsAuthentication.Authenticate
    TextBox1.Text, TextBox2.Text))

    FormsAuthentication.RedirectFromLoginPage
    (TextBox1.Text, false);

    else

    Response.Write("Login Failed");

    • The Authenticate method uses two arguments, username and password, and checks the <user> elements in the web.config file for a match with its name and password attributes.

    • The RedirectFromLoginPage method uses the defaultUrl attribute of the <forms> element to find our Default.aspx page.

    • The first argument of the RedirectFromLoginPage is used for the name of the logged-in user, which we set to read the text property of the first text box that we placed on the form.

    • The second argument of the RedirectFromLoginPage is for cookie handling. Since a cookie is used in the authentication process, you can keep it around for the session (persistent) or let it expire as soon as it is not needed. The latter is recommended to reduce the risk of client-side tampering.

18. Run the program and try different combinations of the username and passwords.

    • You should notice that passwords are case sensitive and usernames are not.

    • All three correctly entered username and password combinations should redirect you to the Default page.

19. Close the browser.

20. Run the program from the **Default.aspx** tab.

- We will still arrive at the login page even when trying to access it directly because we are anonymous and the Default page will not allow anonymous users to access the file.

21. Close the browser.

PAUSE. Close Visual Web Developer. We will use it again for the next exercise.

Using the web.config file for securing your login usernames and passwords is often done for sites having no more than a handful of users. It is very easy to configure and is secure because the data is stored on the server. It also does not require you to create and maintain a database or any other external file besides web.config.

ANOTHER WAY

Creating your own login page is usually limited to sites having requirements beyond the standard login page or sites whose developer wants to be creative. For the standard login pages, ASP.NET provides developers with a convenient generic Login Control. This control is found in the Login category of the Toolbox along with a set of supporting controls.

CERTIFICATION READY
What is the fundamental difference between authentication and authorization and how are they configured in ASP.NET?
5.1

Allowing and denying access to individual files and folders is best controlled by Visual Web Developer's Web Site Administration Tool (WAP) found in the pull-down Web site menu as "ASP.NET Configuration." Manually configuring the web.config file for this level of configuration is much more difficult than using WAP and can easily produce unexpected results.

Understanding Impersonation

Impersonation is put to good use in ASP.NET. When authenticated users need access to resources that require permissions belonging to another user, they can impersonate the other user, or account, and use their access rights to temporarily access these resources. The alternative is to actually give the rights to the user, which can be impractical as well as a security risk.

Impersonation is used when ASP.NET and Internet Information Services (IIS), formerly called Internet Information Server, control the user authorization for a Web site. IIS is a group of network servers, such as Web, HTTP, and FTP, working together to support network applications. We have not been using IIS up to this point because we have been using the built-in Web development server, which is an IIS simulator provided by Visual Web Developer for testing applications.

Since both ASP.NET and IIS control the user rights to resources, they must coordinate their efforts. IIS does the first check on an incoming request to make sure it is a valid IP address for the server. If configured to do so, IIS continues to perform user authentication. By default, it allows anonymous access. If the request remains valid, ASP.NET continues with the authentication. If impersonation is left off (the default), ASP.NET processes the request using its own configured rights. If impersonation has been turned on, ASP.NET processes the request using the authenticated user rights. Between ASP.NET and IIS, there are many possibilities available, depending on configuration settings, for controlling resources.

In the normal course of events, after a user has been authenticated, ASP.NET uses its own identity to access resources. This can be changed with impersonation for all users or for specific users. Either of these configurations can be set manually within the web.config file or automatically using code.

To change impersonation manually in the web.config file, we set the impersonate attribute of the <identity> element. For all users, we would enter <identity impersonate="true" /> and for a specific user we would add the username and password attributes, <identity impersonate="true" userName="SomeAccountName" password="SomePassword" />.

Using code to turn on impersonation for an authenticated user is rather misleading in its simplicity: the Impersonate() function is used to turn it on and the impersonationContext.Undo() function is used to turn it off. However, it takes much more code to apply impersonation to a Web site, and this is beyond the scope of this lesson.

■ Configuring Projects and Solutions and Referencing Assemblies

THE BOTTOM LINE

Both projects and solutions must be configured to work as planned. Even though one is a Web-based application and the other is a Web site, they both use Web technologies and are configured using the web.config file.

Understanding Web Application Projects, Web Solutions, and Assemblies

The differences between the terms *project* and *solution* can be unclear in the English language. It is even more challenging today to get a clear understanding of these terms when they are used to describe the type of software being developed with Microsoft Visual Studio and Web Developer.

In our exercises, we opened Visual Web Developer many times and have been faced with the choice of Web site or project; we have always chosen the Web site option. The project option is what we would have chosen to create an ASP.NET Web application project, as shown in Figure 7-2.

Figure 7-2

Creating a new ASP.NET Web application

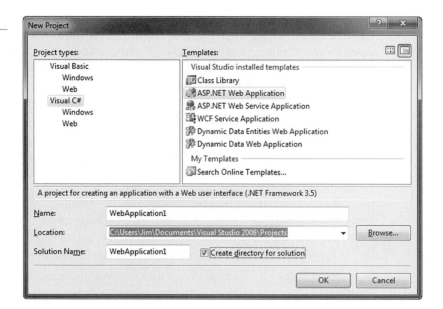

When a new ***Web application project*** is opened, it looks exactly like the Web site template. As the name implies, the Web application project is an application, not a Web site. It is designed to run on the local computer using a Web interface.

Although we have been running the applications in the same way that the Web application project is designed to run, the files used for our Web site, or "***Web solution***," are designed to be deployed on a server using IIS for remote users to run over a network. The files are independent resources to support the site, which means that there is no need to have a project file, as with Web application projects.

The code-behind used for ASP.NET applications must be compiled into Microsoft Intermediate Language (IL or MSIL) before the Common Language Runtime (CLR) is able to execute it. The IL file can be in the form of a Dynamic Link Library (DLL) or an executable (exe).

The web.config settings below show the pre-built assemblies available for ASP.NET projects. These consist of the additional assemblies that are new to .NET 3.5.

```
<compilation debug="true">
    <assemblies>
        <add assembly="System.Core,...
        <add assembly="System.Web.Extensions,...
        <add assembly="System.Data.DataSetExt...
        <add assembly="System.Xml.Linq,...
    </assemblies>
</compilation>
```

Both Web project models use the same default <assemblies> elements. These are the assemblies needed for compiling the project, whether before deployment for applications or after deployment, in real time, for Web sites.

Web sites can create assemblies in real time by compiling code as it is needed, or the developer can precompile the code into assemblies before deployment to save compiling time.

A ***local assembly*** is only referenced by a single application while a ***shared assembly (GAC)*** is referenced by many applications. If a change is made to a local assembly, it only affects a single application, while a change to a shared assembly can cause many applications to change behavior. This means we have to be much more careful about controlling shared assemblies. For example, if the code in the System.Core assembly that is listed in the web.config file changes, it could damage all the applications that we have written in the lessons.

Because local assemblies are named within your environment, there are no naming conflicts. However, a shared assembly must be given a *strong name* that does not conflict with any of their environments. This is done using a utility known as the sn utility. The name includes items such as the version, a public key, and a digital signature. A utility called gacutil is used to install your assembly and place it into a special directory, such as `c:\windows\assembly`. You may want to see which assemblies are available by viewing the files in your equivalent assembly directory.

Once your shared assembly is installed, you can add a reference to it in the web.config file along with the existing entries or place it into the machine.config file for all the applications running on the computer to see.

To reference assemblies outside of the GAC directory, you can use the Add Reference selection from the Web site pull-down menu in the Visual Studio IDE and select it from the .NET tab to use it in your application. Visual Studio does not allow you to use the Add Reference dialog box to reference GAC assemblies.

CONFIGURING <APPSETTINGS> IN WEB.CONFIG

The *<appSettings> element* is a special storage area of the web.config file for holding additional data and for supplementing settings.

The <appSettings> element can be used as a tool for many creative tasks. Its flexibility also makes it prone to abuse. However, when used properly, it can be very beneficial. You can use it to hold global data provided that you are aware that third-party vendors can also use it, potentially causing name conflicts.

The <appSettings> element is also used to allow web.config changes while the page is online without having to perform a restart. This element has a file attribute that embeds the contents of an external file. Changes in the external file affect the page but do not force a restart.

 READ DATA FROM THE WEB.CONFIG FILE

GET READY. We will be using Microsoft Visual Web Developer 2008 Express Edition.

1. Start Visual Web Developer.

2. Create a new ASP.NET Web site using Visual C#.

3. Find the <appSettings /> tag in the web.config file.
   - Notice that it only has an ending tag.

4. Change the web.config file's **<appSettings>** element to add data:

   ```
   <appSettings>
       <add key="TitleOfPage" value
       ="Web.Config Value"/>
   </appSettings>
   ```

5. Place the following namespace near the top of the code-behind:

   ```
   using System.Configuration;
   ```

6. Place the following code into the Page_Load event procedure:

   ```
   Response.Write(ConfigurationManager.
   AppSettings["TitleOfPage"]);
   ```

7. Run the program. Close the browser.
   - The value of the key attribute should have been written to your Web page.
   - Since this is a popular place for connection strings, an element is available just for this purpose.

8. Find the </connectionStrings> tag in the web.config file and change it to the following:

   ```
   <connectionStrings>
     <add name="ConnectionString1"
     connectionString="MyConnectionString"/>
   </connectionStrings>
   ```

9. Add the following code into the Page_Load event procedure:

   ```
   Response.Write(ConfigurationManager.
   ConnectionStrings["ConnectionString1"]);
   ```

10. Run the program. Close the browser.
    - Both values from the web.config file should have been written to your Web page.

PAUSE. Close Visual Web Developer.

Reading and writing to the web.config file can be done using the <appSettings> element. However, it is important to remember that if you need to write to this file using code, the page will have to be taken offline. The technique of using the file attribute to point to an external file allows us to change the external file without bringing the site down.

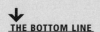 **TAKE NOTE***

It is also possible to move the contents of the web.config in its entirety to an external file, so any configuration change using code can be made while the application is running.

■ Publishing Web Applications

↓
THE BOTTOM LINE

We have come a long way from publishing static content on the Web, where files were simply copied to the server for the viewing pleasure of a site's visitors. Users now expect Web sites to be as interactive as desktop applications, and they expect desktop applications to have the look and feel of Web pages. We now address some of the things we need to consider when publishing Web sites and deploying Web applications.

Understanding IIS Installation and Configuration

Since IIS in an integral part of the Windows operating system, installation and configuration are all done internally by pointing and clicking or running a script.

The first thing you should do is determine whether IIS is already installed on your computer. If your primary hard drive has a directory named inetpub, then IIS is installed. If you do not have this directory, it may still be installed but on another drive. Having the inetpub directory does not mean that IIS is running. To see if it is running, open your browser and type `http://localhost` into the URL and press Enter. If the page says that it cannot display the Web page, then IIS is not running.

Installation is a little different on every operating system. In fact, some operating systems, such as the Home Editions, do not even support IIS. For directions on how to install IIS, go to MSN.com, search "install iis," and choose the site supporting your operating system. If you do not trust unknown Web sites, you can limit your choices to Microsoft sites.

The steps for installing ISS are typically as easy as turning on optional features of the operating system that are set to off by default. Although pointing and clicking your way through the installation is the most common way to install IIS, you are often presented with a script that installs every option without you having to select anything. Of course, you may want to go back and turn off the options that you do not need. Remember to have your operating system software available in case you are asked for information about it.

As with installing IIS, the steps for setting up your site will also vary depending on the operating system. IIS comes with a wizard to help you set up your site. You will have to enter the Internet Protocol (IP) address and the Transmission Control Protocol (TCP) port when asked. You will be designating the drive and directory for the site and setting user access rights to your resources. You can then use the IIS Configuration Manager that comes with the Administration Pack to easily configure your installation.

Choosing the Method to Publish a Web Site Application Based on the Existing or Intended Environment

> The development environment and production environment are usually very different. It is important to understand these differences before attempting to deploy your Web site. You will not be able to make an informed choice without this knowledge.

If your existing environment is based on simple HTML using Notepad, you will be deploying your site by copying your files to a host that may or may not be supported by Microsoft. For comprehensive IDEs like DreamWeaver or Visual Studio, the best choices for deployment are the built-in tools offered by these environments.

If your intended environment is your own server, you will need to address the operating system, network, and database support from the ground up. This requires more expertise than typical Web developers possess. A much easier choice is to use a Web-hosting service, where you pay a fee for the hosting environment.

Some of the items you must research when choosing a Web-hosting service are prices, customer support, reputation, and the software available to run your site. For example, if you are using ASP.NET 3.5 in your development and the hosting site uses version 3.0, you might have a problem. Another important consideration is their support of AJAX technology. You will have to make sure they support all the technologies that you are using to develop your site.

Once IIS is installed and configured, you can use Visual Web Developer's Publish Web Site Utility to publish your site. You simply click the Publish Web Site item on the Build menu in Visual Web Developer. This will bring up a dialog box where you can select the Target Location and click the OK button.

During the Publish Web Site process, you will be presented with the option "Allow this precompiled site to be updatable." To enhance the user experience, keep this box checked so you can offer an *updatable site*. An updateable site only allows changes to layout, not code.

> **TAKE NOTE***
>
> The Express Edition of Visual Web Developer does not support the Publish Web Site Utility.

Understanding MSI Deployment

> *Windows Installer (MSI)*, formerly known as Microsoft Installer, is the preferred method for deploying Web applications.

> **CERTIFICATION READY**
> What applications must be present on your Web server and what applications are used to publish your Web site?
> 5.3

Since Web applications are run on the desktop, they are deployed in a similar manner and MSI is used to create a setup file. Web sites are typically published to a Web server by copying the files. Since there is typically a single installation of the Web site, creating configurations is not normally a problem. For Web applications, however, as many configuration settings as possible need to be created and packaged for multiple installations. Most of these settings can be configured using the Visual Studio Deployment Wizard.

■ Understanding Application Pools

> ↓ **THE BOTTOM LINE**
> *Application pools* is a new security feature of IIS 6.0 that allows you to isolate multiple Web applications that are running on the same computer.

Understanding the Purpose of Application Pools and Their Effects on Web Applications

> Application pools increase the security and reliability of ASP.NET Web applications. These applications are running on a Web server hosting many Web sites.

The application pool feature of IIS is designed to help manage Web servers in which each application must be isolated from the other. Each application is placed into its own pool. Applications running in their own pools will not be affected by errors generated by other applications that are also running in their own application pools on the Web server.

Each application using these pools is configured separately, almost as though they were running on their own computers. IIS has also made it possible to configure these settings without bringing down the applications.

CERTIFICATION READY
What are application pools and how do they improve your Web site?
5.4

SKILL SUMMARY

IN THIS LESSON YOU LEARNED TO:

- Read and write XML dataConfigure authentication, authorization, and impersonation.
- Understand Web application projects, Web solutions, and assemblies.
- Configure <appSettings> in web.config.
- Understand IIS installation and configuration.
- Choose a method to publish a Web site application based on the existing or intended environment.
- Understand MSI deployment.
- Understand the purpose of application pools and their effects on Web applications.

■ Knowledge Assessment

Multiple Choice

Circle the letter or letters that correspond to the best answer or answers.

1. What is the name of the user identification process?
   a. Authorization
   b. Impersonation
   c. Authentication
   d. None of the above

2. What is the name of the process used to prevent an original user from accessing certain resources?
   a. Authorization
   b. Impersonation
   c. Authentication
   d. None of the above

3. What is the name of the process used to give another user's rights to the original user?
   a. Authorization
   b. Impersonation
   c. Authentication
   d. None of the above

4. What is the name of the process used for identifying a user with IIS?
   a. Passport
   b. Windows
   c. Forms
   d. None of the above

5. What is the name of the process used for identifying a user by placing the username and password in web.config?
   a. Passport
   b. Windows
   c. Forms
   d. None of the above

6. What is the name of the process used for identifying a user with Windows Live?
   a. Passport
   b. Windows
   c. Forms
   d. None of the above

7. Which Visual Web Developer project uses a single file for most of its code?
   a. ASP.NET Web application
   b. WCF service application
   c. ASP.NET Web site
   d. ASP.NET Web service

8. Which is NOT something that the <appSettings> element can do?
   a. Configure the application setting for debugger
   b. Place web.config settings into a separate file
   c. Hold miscellaneous string data for use in the application
   d. Hold connections strings

9. What was used to run the Web sites in our exercises?
   a. IIS
   b. Apache
   c. The built-in Web development server
   d. The Web server that was installed in Lesson 1

10. What manages application pools?
    a. IIS
    b. Apache
    c. The built-in Web development server
    d. The Web server that was installed in Lesson 1

Fill in the Blank

Complete the following sentences by writing the correct word or words in the blanks provided.

1. _____ is the process of identifying anonymous users.

2. _____ is the process of assigning the rights that the identified user has for the resources.

3. With Visual Web Developer, we can create either a Web Site or _____ where this second choice provides us with a Web-based desktop application rather than a Web site.

4. The collection of files included in our Web site during development is called a Web _____.

5. The code-behind used for ASP.NET applications is compiled into Intermediate Language (IL), which is executed by the _____.

6. A reference to all the IL supporting ASP.NET applications is stored in the web.config file under the _____ element.

7. A local assembly is only referenced by a single application where a _____ is referenced by many applications.

8. The web.config file uses the _____ element to hold additional data and for supplemental settings for your application.

9. You can easily see if IIS has been installed on your computer by examining your primary hard drive and verifying that it includes the _____ directory.

10. The Visual Studio _____ Wizard can be used to configure most of a Web site's settings before deployment.

11. Placing applications in their own application _____ prevents errors generated by other applications from affecting them.

■ Competency Assessment

Scenario 7-1: Installing IIS

Art's Daycare has grown so much that each work area PC must be connected for sharing important information about each child. A Web site project has been written for the task using Visual Web Developer and needs to be installed on a computer that has access to the local area network. The computer that is to host the site does not have IIS installed. Your job is to choose an operating system and the best version of IIS to support that operating system. Write step-by-step directions for installing the IIS software onto the operating system.

Scenario 7-2: Using IIS

You have just finished your Web application using ASP.NET. You are about ready to deploy it on a computer that you believe already has IIS installed. What steps could you take to first check to see if it is installed and then see if it is running?

■ Proficiency Assessment

Scenario 7-3: Choosing the Appropriate Authentication for Your Site

You have just finished your Web site that is designed for firefighters. It is tied into the National Fire and Reporting System from FEMA. Every fire department that responds to a call must report the details of the call to FEMA. The Web site is strictly limited to this reporting process.

Which authentication system would you use that would best fit this scenario: Windows authentication or Forms authentication? Explain your choice in terms of security and convenience.

Scenario 7-4: Configuring Additional Authorization Security

Although your Web site has been working well, you find yourself being concerned with authorization. You made some changes to the web.config file and find that you locked yourself out of your own Web site. What is the most likely cause of your lockout and what changes will you need to make to get back in? How would you configure the web.config file to increase security and prevent locking yourself out?

 Workplace Ready

Considering a Web Application

Work environments have to tie their computers together more than ever to stay ahead of the competition. Desktop environments have worked in the past, but considering that most of today's needs call for sharing data rather than processing it, Web-based solutions are becoming commonplace. Web-based applications not only provide consistent and familiar interfaces by using the browser, they are designed for sharing data. The next time you're faced with the responsibility of designing a computer solution for your workplace, consider a Web application or Web site rather than a traditional desktop solution.

Exam Objective	Skill Number	Lesson Number
Programming Web Applications		
Customize the layout and appearance of a Web page	1.1	1
Understand ASP.NET intrinsic objects	1.2	1
Understand state information in Web applications	1.3	1
Understand events and control page flow	1.4	2
Understand controls	1.5	2
Understand configuration files	1.6	2
Working with Data and Services		
Read and write XML data	2.1	3
Distinguish between DataSet and DataReader objects	2.2	3
Call a service from a Web page	2.3	3
Understand DataSource controls	2.4	4
Bind controls to data by using data binding syntax	2.5	4
Manage data connections and databases	2.6	4
Troubleshooting and Debugging Web Applications		
Debug a Web application	3.1	6
Handle Web application errors	3.2	6
Working with Client-Side Scripting		
Understand client-side scripting	4.1	5
Understand AJAX concepts	4.2	5
Configuring and Deploying Web Applications		
Configure authentication and authorization	5.1	7
Configure projects and solutions and reference assemblies	5.2	7
Publish Web applications	5.3	7
Understand application pools	5.4	7

Index